— TREASURES OF THE SAN JUANS SERIES —

VOLUME III

SOMEONE ELSE'S JACK

1917-1946

True Stories of Grit, Gumption and Gambles that
Transformed America

BY DON BOOHER

ISBN 979-8-9934766-0-5

Second Edition

Printed in the United States

Cover and Text Design by Laurie Casselberry

Laurie Goralka Design

Cover photo: Lake City's "Stone Bank Block," (circa. 1877), *Courtesy of* Silver World.

booherbookorders@gmail.com

VOLUME THREE

Contents

Dedication

How could it be otherwise. Like Fortress San Juans *and*

Reynolds' Last Best Chance, *this third volume of*

A.E. Reynolds' Henson Canyon treasure hunt owes a king's

ransom to my loving wife Lana. Her inspiration and

encouragement make the telling of this adventure enjoyable.

Acknowledgements

The authenticity of the factual accounts filling the pages of this narrative would not be possible without the Lake City *Silver World* archives and the generous assistance of the *Silver World* editor and local historian, Grant Houston. Thank you, Grant! By the same token, a great debt is owed the librarians and staff of History Colorado who guided me through their archives, most importantly the A.E. Reynolds collection (MSS 1220), and who provided incredibly insightful photographs of the subject matter. I am similarly grateful to P. David and Jan Smith at the Western Reflections Publishing Company who have mentored me throughout the process of writing this book and its two preceding volumes. Not only did they provide invaluable counsel on editorial matters, their knowledge of local mining history contributed greatly to the accuracy of this work. Likewise, Harvey DuChene merits my eternal gratitude for doing his best to ensure that treatment of geology and science in general are as sound as a layman can achieve. Harvey is a member of the Geological Society of America, the Rocky Mountain Association of Geologists, a Fellow of the Explorers Club, and an internationally recognized scientist especially well-versed in the development of San Juans mining and local history.

Whenever possible, this collection relies upon primary sources. The risks of doing so take many forms but are outweighed by their fidelity to their time. Likewise, language and idioms of the times may contain words and descriptions that are offensive to later generations. Understanding the context and consequences of the past requires faithful accounting of words and honest attempts to discern the heart from which they sprang. Admittedly and sadly, sometimes the heart is dark. Journalists, historians and chroniclers along the way probably should have been more sensitive. On the other hand, well deserved more often than not are disparaging remarks by journalists about journalists.

Secondary sources also provided critical insights. Of special note in this regard is Lee Scamehorn's biography, *Albert Eugene Reynolds, Colorado's Mining King*. There is no better example of comprehensive research that explains the character and accomplishments of this giant in Colorado history. Duane Vandenbusche and Walter R. Borneman's *The D&RG Lake City Branch and a Galloping Goose* featured in Colorado Rail Annual No.14 also merits special mention.

Of course credit is due every author or character whose work or words are cited. Particularly descriptive or lengthy quotations are indented and single-spaced for emphasis and a faithful attempt to preserve the language, context, and culture of their day. Paraphrases, author comments, and clarifications embedded in these indented citations are [bracketed] to distinguish them from the direct quote. No effort is made to censor the crude or currently unpopular choice of words, or temper the offensive tones of quotes when that might be the case. As stated above, the objective is to better convey the vernacular and remain true to the circumstances of the experiences in this adventure. Tolerating the use of the term "dago" is a good example of respecting cultural fidelity. "Dago" may be a derogatory term used by some for Italians, but in the early twentieth century it was simply one of many [yes many] common ethnic slangs. It was derived from the Spanish given name "Diego," also a very common name in Italy in the 1800s, and very commonly used in multicultural communities across America. It is found often in historical citations quoted in this work because that was how people talked then and any campaign to excise it would amount to censorship impossible to justify. Likewise, colorful artifacts of earlier times like "going out to see the elephant" are preserved. Similar reasoning accounts for the use of street slang like "jack" instead of "money."

Someone Else's Jack

(**jack** *n.* slang for money)

The boys cheered when I located the vein —
gold assayed poor but native silver served the same.
When reaching pay dirt required calling for more shares,
instead of spare jack all I got back were blank stares.

What good are lads with no money to spare,
rich ore in reach but no mates who care?
Wise men fear veins that pinch out, that's fair,
but why should the risk be all mine to bear?

If only a believer would scratch my back,
someone else's jack is all I lack.
I can hit paydirt with someone else's stash,
maybe a dear spinster or rash gambler with cash?

Oh for the days all veins led to motherlodes,
for the days ore wagons clogged the roads,
for the day my prospect covered my bet,
for someone else's jack instead of deep debt.

— Author —

CHAPTER I

Coxey's Army

No man is an Island, entire of itself…
Never send to know for whom the bell tolls:
it tolls for thee.
— *John Donne* —

In 1916 the wisdom of A.E. Reynolds' investing his proverbial last dollar in his ambitious Henson Canyon haulage tunnel would begin to be decided by the hard scabble characters you are about to meet. Unearthing the Vermont/Ocean Wave treasure was proving difficult, but these survivors of America's mass migrations to the West were up to the task. They were products of America's raucous industrial revolution and its fellow travelers, America's labor movement, modernizing technologies, restless new wealth, and "populism." They were caught up in a societal transformation, helpless if even aware of their perilous journey, but overcomers just the same. America was on the brink of an emerging new order and no one could know where it would end. From coast to coast activists from across the entire spectrum of social thought sought to unravel our young nation's delicate cultural and economic fabric in order to reweave it to their own liking. Henson Canyon miners and mine operators would not escape the effects of this fray they scarcely knew anything about.

Our story begins in 1894 with what came to be known as Coxey's Army. Even in retrospect a century and a half later, we can scarcely appreciate the subtle effects of what it revealed about those times. It also provides a colorful yet profound introduction to Reynolds' hunt not only for treasure but also someone else's jack. A nationwide march to Washington, D.C. [the precedent for countless others to come], and the trains stolen along the way [not so common], illustrated in an unmistakable way the depth of despair overshadowing America's working class. The nation's vaunted melting pot was boiling over. There was need of change. Clear to some, the grassroots rebellion displayed by Coxey's Army would not augur well for mining prospects in the San Juans either. Nor would it augur well for attracting investors, a sea-change A.E. would have to navigate whether he liked it or not.

1894 was the year A.E.'s voyage began, the year his plan to develop the Vermont/Ocean Wave silver properties took shape. In 1894 he was a prosperous capitalist with jack to spare. 1894 also was the year Jacob S. Coxey, a self-styled labor reformer,[1] elbowed his way into public view, concocted a way to ensure news outlets and Congress heard working class grievances, and put a human face on what would become a society-changing grassroots movement. Of course, calling for a nationwide mass march to the steps of Congress was easy compared to marching. Giving second thought to how long that march would be, some "recruits" sought a way to ride.

Other than meddling in mine owner affairs, A.E. would have admired Jacob's entrepreneurial spirit [similar to his own] and his commitment to high-risk gambits [like raising public awareness of the miner's dismal quality of life]. He might even have respected Jacob's ability to inspire unemployed workers from around the country to find a way to join him. In the case of Colorado, miners already assembling in Denver to protest their working conditions, finding a way to join "General" Coxey included rafting down a flood-swollen Platte River. In the case of miners farther south and in the High Country, stealing a Denver & Rio Grande (D&RG) train and steaming east seemed like a good idea.

The last straw for them was an attempt by mine owners to take advantage of a depressed economy's surplus of labor to increase the work day from eight to nine

March to Washington. Despair over dire economic conditions and rampant unemployment struck a chord nationwide. "General" Coxey encountered little difficulty organizing probably the first mass protest march to the capitol. He encountered insurmountable difficulty advancing the social reforms he advocated, but others [famously presidents Wilson and Roosevelt] would master that task in decades to come. (Frank Leslie's Magazine, *Library of Congress*)

hours without an increase in the standard three-dollar wages per day. Hundreds of miners walked off the job. Meanwhile in Ohio, Jacob Coxey, no longer willing to remain idle in the face of a broad range of harsh workplace conditions there, began organizing a protest that soon took on the appearance of a mobilized army. In March of 1894, with probably a hundred unemployed laborers, Jacob began his trek to Washington [Jacob along with wife and youngest son rode in a horse-drawn buggy]. More or less spontaneously, bands-of-brothers as far away as the Pacific Northwest formed up and followed suit.

Coxey's immediate objective was to impress the government with the need to create employment opportunities by funding road projects around the country. His initiative, widely publicized, found a receptive audience in Colorado's Cripple Creek region. Notices appeared everywhere reading "all idle men are requested to meet at the flagpole, Sunday, April 23, 1894…for the purpose of forming a contingent for the Coxey industrial army." [2] Interest in roadbuilding was probably nonexistent, but airing grievances was reason enough to show up. Coxey's so-called army was made up of loosely organized [if organized could even be used] regional contingencies formed spontaneously this way.

Coxey left Massillon, Ohio on March 25, 1894, with one-hundred men enroute to Pittsburgh and points east. In the West a contingent nicknamed Kelley's Army under the leadership of "General" Charles T. Kelley had made its way to the Ohio River, but apparently no farther. Another West Coast band called Fry's Army had marched out of Los Angeles only to be lost to history somewhere before reaching St. Louis. A Pacific Northwest band numbering five-hundred led by William Hogan had commandeered a Union Pacific train and had traveled as far as Forsyth, Montana before being apprehended by federal troops. In every instance, new recruits took the place of faltering brothers falling out along their way.

Counted among Coxey's Army were Colorado's Cripple Creek dissidents. Like their unemployed working-class brethren elsewhere, the "Colorado brigade" also was prepared to take drastic steps to cross the country. Like William Hogan's Pacific Northwest troop, one faction stole a train. Another faction seeking relief in Denver attempted to navigate the Platte River in flood stage. Both factions would have gotten A.E. Reynolds' attention. Apt to sympathize with their plight, he also was apt to be alarmed by their tactics.

John Sherman Sanders, recently arrived from the "Pacific slope," commanded Colorado's Cripple Creek miners. He was elected [and as usual, given the honorary title of "General"] by the angry crowd of unemployed miners. His mandate was to mobilize what ended up by May 3rd being 159 Cripple Creek and 150 Victor, Colorado men ready to besiege their federal government. Their grievances included not only unemployment but a return of silver coinage. Granted free passage from Cripple Creek and Victor to Pueblo, Colorado, by the Florence and Cripple Creek and the D&RGW railroads, the men now numbering 354 were welcomed to Pueblo by the mayor and honored with free meals and a parade. Five days later, free meals and the prospect of free rail travel out of Pueblo ended and another Coxey Army train robbery began.

Recognizing the impossibility of marching to Washington, General Sanders' troops commandeered six coal cars and D&RGW switch engine No.817, loaded their gear, hoped aboard, and proceeded east out of the Pueblo yard. Overcoming a number of attempts to stop them including railroad employees deliberately wrecking trains in their path, nevertheless they were stopped in Scott City, Kansas by a U.S. Marshal and 300 armed deputies. Washington, D.C. was no longer on their itinerary. Detention at Fort Leavenworth was. Even so, they never were held fully accountable for their actions. On June 18, a federal jury found 290 men "collectively guilty of obstructing US mail." That was pretty much it.[3]

Neither General Sanders nor the engineer who drove the train, nor the balance of Sanders' troops, were even subject to this verdict. The engineer, free on bond, failed to appear on his court date and was never seen again. General Sanders, also free on bond, eventually made his way back to Pueblo where he was arrested and charged with seizure of D&RGW property. While free on bond and awaiting trial, the case was dropped when the railroad declined to prosecute. This probably surprised no one — public and private sentiment throughout this period clearly sided with the protesters, witnessed by the thousands of free meals provided them along their way and the lack of interest in punishing the brigands when they finally ran out of steam.

As for Coxey's Denver contingent, sometimes referred to as Coxey's Navy, unlike its Cripple Creek brethren its fate was no laughing matter. In the summer of 1893 a large number of unemployed and homeless men had been housed and fed in "Camp Relief" located along the Platte River in Denver's River Front Park. Thinking better of this practice, the City Fathers ended the program after several weeks and provided the men free train tickets [one-way] out of town. Alas, the following spring many were back, Coxeyites by sentiment if not decree. "Before long, River Front Park had 1,500-1,800 residents, the largest encampment of Coxeyites in the country."[4]

This season there would be no free one-way train tickets out of town. In response, the encampment elected "General" William Grayson who promptly announced he too was prepared to commandeer a train. Attempting and failing to do so, he marched about one hundred of his men as far as Nebraska. It was left to the remaining troops to work out Plan B. In late May, Plan B became "float down the raging Platte River to Kansas City." The Denver Chamber of Commerce, unnerved by the hundreds of hungry and restless Coxeyites in their city, unmoved by the flood condition of the Platte, encouraged their departure by providing enough lumber to build 100 four-by-sixteen foot flat-bottom boats. On June 7, they launched. Five boats sank within the distance of ten city blocks. The rest of them were lost soon thereafter. According to the *Rocky Mountain News*, "Only

God will ever know how many of the Coxeyites were drowned in the Platte last night…" Six bodies were recovered, dozens more were missing. Scores of survivors made their way as far as Julesburg where, imagine this, they tried to hijack another train. Eighty men were arrested and returned to Denver. Tried before a

---

GENERAL JACOB S. COXEY
(April 16, 1854 – May 18, 1951)

Sometimes called Mayor of Massillon, Ohio, more notoriously known as the General of Coxey's Army, Jacob exemplifies yet another class of pilgrims akin to those that account for the pioneering spirit and resilience of our Henson Canyon miners. Neither a pioneer nor a miner, he was a pathfinder, a "social reformer" pathfinder. Of course this was not a life-long ambition of his. No, but it probably was his calling. His life's story tells us a great deal about the making of a populist.

Jacob Coxey was a politician, defeated on numerous occasions at the polls running for Congress until finally being elected Mayor of Massillon, Ohio. Failing to persuade Congress in 1894 that action was needed, he nevertheless was influential in advancing the interests of the early progressive movement that gained further momentum in the early 1900s and during the Great Depression. The Social Security Act of 1935 was a landmark accomplishment enabled in large part by the plight of the working class dramatized by progressives like Coxey.

Jacob Sechler Coxey was born in Selinsgrove, Pennsylvania to Thomas Coxey and Ann Sechler. Thomas worked in a sawmill at the time, but moved the family to Danville to take a job in an iron mill. Son Jacob excelled in school, at age sixteen took a job as water boy alongside his father, and over a period of eight years advanced to the position of "stationary engineer." In 1878, he left the mill to enter into a partnership with his Harrisburg uncle dealing with scrap-iron. On a business trip to Massillon in 1881, he fell in love with the town. Cashing out of his partnership, he bought a large farm and opened a sand quarry. A passionate horse breeder and gambler, twice married, father of six children, and perhaps considered odd by some [he named his youngest son "Legal Tender"], his interests turned to politics with the rise of the People's Party in the 1890s. He became a reformer willing to spend time and money supporting initiatives intended to improve the lot of his fellow man. The severity of the 1893 economic panic moved him to action. The ensuing depression deflated already dismal wages even farther. Lockouts and strikes followed. Coxey's response: assemble unemployed workers and march on the Government.

Often branded a crank for challenging the nation's economic system that had made him wealthy, rarely credited with political influence, he did succeed in living a long, healthy life. Jacob Coxey lived to be 97 years old. When asked his secret to longevity, reportedly he answered, "an array of reasons from elixirs to not resisting temptation." [5]

jury of their peers, five were convicted. They were sentenced to short jail terms, probably quietly released early at that like so many of their brothers elsewhere by sympathetic masters. Not as accommodating, Denver's City Fathers saw to it that their River Front Park was "sealed off for good." [6]

On balance, all of Coxey's Army [and Navy], all of its contingents, ended poorly. By the time the protestors reached the U.S. Capitol the die-hards numbered perhaps an impressive six thousand, but disheartening to most, their ragtag ranks and sweeping complaints were not impressive. Equally disheartening, their own interest in the protest dwindled, the troops melted away, and the first mass march on Washington, D.C. accomplished nothing. Jacob was arrested, fined for walking on the Capital Hill grass, and sent home. Ironically, the march had more of an impact in distant, remote, and sparsely populated Lake City. While his

---

UTE/ULAY AND HIDDEN TREASURE STRIKE [7]

On March 14, 1899, 140 Western Federation of Miners union members blocked the entrances to the Ute/Ulay and Hidden Treasure's underground workings. Eighty of the miners were Italians. All of the miners were protesting the Auric Mining Company policy that single men employed at the mine would have to live in the company's boardinghouse. In addition to the insult of it all, they would have to pay the company for the privilege, further reducing their ability to earn a living wage.

The strikers were well-armed, having bought every gun and box of ammunition available in Lake City beforehand. They also were thought to have stolen fifty Springfield rifles and 1,000 rounds of ammunition from the Lake City Armory. When the sheriff arrested twelve Italians and charged the local union with the theft, the men at the mine took matters into their own hands.

Seriously outgunned, the sheriff appealed to Governor Charles Thomas for reinforcements. Six companies of state militia, four companies of infantry and two companies of Cavalry totaling 326 troops, were promptly dispatched. Accompanying them was Denver's Italian consul, Dr. Joseph Cuerno, hopefully a calming voice in what was shaping up to be a bloody confrontation. According to Historian Wilbur Stone in *History of Colorado*, "wholesale arrests followed." The *Colorado Encyclopedia* reports that Charles Mairo, a Lake City Italian businessman, persuaded the miners that they would not be executed if they laid down their weapons and left the mine. P. David Smith writes that Mairo carried a letter drafted by the militia colonel and Italian consul to the striking men at the mine.

An agreement to end the strike was reached on March 20th without violence. The arrested men were released, the militia returned to Denver, and mining resumed.

reasoning was never stated publicly, A.E. Reynolds shifted his Vermont/Ocean Wave treasure hunt into a "wait and see" mode.

But the populist movement Coxey's Army brought attention to waited for no man. It had profound roots, and as expected its grievances only grew stronger. In 1912, populists elected President Woodrow T. Wilson who would sign progressive legislation and inspire a new generation of progressive activists. In the depths of the Great Depression President Franklin Delano Roosevelt achieved many more of their goals with the passage of his "New Deal" legislation. As promised, he was determined to put a "chicken in every pot."

In retrospect, the opinion of labor historian Carlos Schwantes rings true. The implications of populism were profound. A.E. would have had good reason to consider them greater threats to his last best chance to enhance his fortune

But there were lasting consequences. The Auric Mining Company refused to hire any more Italians, and Hinsdale County officials ordered that all strikers leave the county. The negotiated settlement included a provision that miners could live where they chose, but that single men that had joined the union had five days to leave the county, families had sixty days to do so. Many obeyed the order, but many did not. Many of the local mines also quit hiring Italians, but many continued to do so. A.E. Reynolds continued doing so. The "Italians Must Go" sentiment that had reached a fever-pitch and lingered awhile eventually subsided. More Colorado labor unrest was on the horizon, far more violent than at the Ute/Ulay, but not in Hinsdale County. Does that explain the start-and-stop history of A.E.'s last best chance to make a mine? Maybe so. The popular adage that "all's well that ends well" may be more relevant. Reynolds authorized the beginning of his Vermont/Ocean Wave Tunnel at the height of the Ute/Ulay drama. Stone describes its heartwarming ending that may have encouraged A.E. to proceed.

Half a mile below Henson [site of the Ute/Ulay and Hidden Treasure] a company of six men waited for them [the militia led by the Italian consul in a buggy with a white flag], and after exchanging salutes and bows the men cheered the consul and kissed his gloved hands. The procession went on to the mine and town, where shawled women and their children were, as well as workmen. Although it was bitterly cold the consul then stopped the buggy, got out, took off his hat and unbuttoned his overcoat so as to display the full evening dress underneath complete with a red, white, and green ribbon (the colors of Italy) across his shirt. The crowd cheered and the consul made a speech to the miners and commanded them to salute the militia officers and surrender to the sheriff. The Italians did as told and started walking down the road to Lake City, accompanied by their women and children.[8]

with Vermont/Ocean Wave treasure than any labor strike, of which there was an increasing number. Carlos explains: "In common with the Populist revolt [of which there also was an increasing number], Coxeyism was a democratic movement that called into question the underlying values of the new industrial society....The story of the Coxey movement is ultimately a case study of how ordinary citizens influence—or fail to influence—political and economic issues in modern America."[9]

The debilitating effects on Henson Canyon and nearby Lake City of this populist tsunami were subtle but long-term. They took on the guise of taxes [including the first-ever tax on income], tariffs, rising prices [except metal prices], unemployment, and by 1933 the loss of rail service and a large percentage of the region's population. In 1894, A.E. may have sensed such a trend was developing. His underlying values, capitalism and unfettered individualism, were being threatened. Populism roiled the sea on which he and his kind happily sailed. By 1899 he was more optimistic. To his relief, Coxey's movement seemed doomed to fail. His entrepreneurial instincts kicked in. It was time to resume his Vermont/Ocean Wave haulage tunnel. Then trouble erupted, this time just three miles down the road.

The adjacent Ute/Ulay and Hidden Treasure strike no doubt surprised Reynolds. Labor-management frictions often ran hot in most company-owned mines. Usually strikes could be avoided, but this was different. This pot had been simmering for a long time, but was different in that it was not just about wages and working conditions. It was also about Italians, and from their perspective about their living conditions. It was about populist matters they knew nothing about. Seemingly hopelessly complicated, the emotional intensity of the situation had demanded a quick if not equitable solution. In fact, it ended so quickly and peacefully that A.E. saw no need to stop work on his newly-commissioned tunnel. Nor did he see a need to stop hiring Italian miners. Nor did he outlive the end of raw capitalism and rugged individualism visited on the nation by Coxey's and Wilson's vision of Federal largesse.

But A.E. and son-in-law Bradish Morse who succeeded him did survive most populist reforms longer than most of their contemporaries. They avoided organized labor disputes by increasing wages when necessary or basing compensation on the value of ore produced rather than hours worked, leasing sections of the underground works or profit-sharing by another name. When technology could be deployed to ease their burdens and improve their work environment [notably ventilation, improved power drills, carbide lamps], Reynolds and Morse could be persuaded to invest in it. While these measures minimized labor unrest at the Vermont/Ocean Wave, low-grade ores, transportation costs, and the recurring need to invest in further development work were more troublesome. *Someone Else's Jack* is the rest of that story.

Notes—Chapter One: Coxey's Army

[1] Jacob S. Coxey was an ordinary man who found an extraordinary way to draw attention to his populist views, views that would prove to be harbingers of more society-shaking policies and practices to come. His goal was to pressure Congress to remedy economic hardships and unemployment brought on by the financial crash and ensuing economic depression of 1893. Congress had returned the nation to a gold standard leading to a sharp decline in the value of silver and thus the mining of silver. At the same time, long-standing tensions between mine owners and miners were on the rise. In Colorado the fuse was lit in Cripple Creek when February 1894 witnessed tensions that eventually led to violence.

[2] England, Jim and Sam Bock, "By Rail and River," pg. 21, *Colorado Magazine*, Summer/Fall 2024. Striking miners were not limited to Cripple Creek, nor was violence and the use of military force to deal with them. The "induction" of the Cripple Creek protesters into Jacob Coxey's Army was arranged by no one. Apparently, it just seemed like a good thing to do.

[3] Ibid., pg. 25. Ironically, while the hijacked train drama played out, the Cripple Creek strike took an ugly turn. In late May in response to mines being blown up, more than a thousand "deputies" hired by the mine owners restored order at the expense of a number of miner's lives.

[4] Ibid., pg.26.

[5] "Jacob S. Coxey, Sr.", *Wikipedia*.

[6] England, Jim and Sam Bock, "By Rail and River," pg. 29, *Colorado Magazine*, Summer/Fall 2024.

[7] Smith, P. David, *The Story of Lake City, Colorado*, pgs. 223-226; "Little Rome," *Colorado Encyclopedia*.

[8] Stone, Wilbur, *History of Colorado, Vol. I*, pg. 847.

[9] England, Jim and Sam Bock, pg. 29. According to the authors, the Populist movement peaked in Colorado in 1894. Both incumbent Governor and Congressman failed in their reelection attempts and their People's Party never again succeeded in filling a statewide office.

CHAPTER 2

Treasure Hunt

As we stand and listen to a low and increasing hum, we hear the tramp of thousands that here in the future will come. They will come for the air and sunshine, they will come for scenery grand, they will come for the gold and silver, from every civilized land.

— *The Prospector.* [1]

Here they come by every steamboat, hundreds after hundreds from every place—Hoosiers, Suckers, Corn crackers, Buckeyes, Red-horses, Arabs and Egyptians—some with ox wagons, some with mules, but the greatest number on foot, with their knap-sacks and old-fashioned rifles and shot-guns; some with their long-tailed blues, others in jeans and bob-tailed jockeys; in their roundabouts, slouched hats, caps and sacks. There are a few hand-carts in the crowd... Onward they move, in solemn order, day after day, old and young, tall and slender, short and fat, handsome and ugly, the strong and the weak, the red-faced rum-bruiser and the lean, lank Jonathan, with grimmage sour, striding among saints and sinners, heads up and [stiff] upper lips, march forward as "lords of creation," and seeming "monarchs of all they survey."

— *Missouri Republican*, March 27, 1859. [2]

Someone Else's Jack[3] is the third installment in our three-volume *Reynolds' Last Best Chance* series on what surely is one of the San Juan Mountains' longest and probably most frustrating treasure hunts. Our journey of discovery began in Volume One, *Fortress San Juans*, with gold rushes to California and Colorado's Rocky Mountains that eventually reached deep into the San Juans range. Ultimately these mass migrations introduced us in Volume Two, *Reynolds' Last Best Chance*, to A.E. Reynolds, one of Colorado's most successful mining entrepreneurs. His hunt for treasure settled in on the Vermont/Ocean Wave claims, went underground with his ace-in-the-hole—a daring 1200 ft. haulage tunnel—and by necessity sought silver instead of gold as the prize. In *Someone Else's Jack* the Vermont/Ocean Wave, hampered by seemingly endless setbacks and continuing shortages of funds, nevertheless remained Reynolds' last best chance to redeem his fortune and his reputation.

The 1858-1860 Colorado gold rush, hot on the heels of California's 1848-1849 gold rush and America's "annexation" of what became the nation's southwest, was the indisputable beginning of the end of the ability of the fortress-like San Juan Mountains and their Ute landlord to fend off development of the region's mineral resources. Still, a civil war and another fifteen years of preparation would pass before the San Juans gold rush could begin. Each volume in our adventure stands on its own, but viewing them as a continuum and digesting them in chronological order will help

Albert Eugene Reynolds (1840-1921). Once known and respected as a highly successful mining entrepreneur, as the turbulent 1890s wound down he invested what little remained of his vast assets in his Vermont/Ocean Wave claims. Risky as that was, he considered them his last best chance to redeem his fortune and his reputation. *(A.E. Reynolds, ca. 1915, History Colorado)*

the reader grasp the profound transformation of America they exemplify. In less than a century the nation would transition from a struggling agrarian society clinging to the Atlantic seaboard into a two-ocean global superpower capable of having its way with the colonial empires of that day. Innovation and industry, and immigrants and mass migrations, under the firm direction of visionary leaders faithful to what they believed was America's manifest destiny, accounted for most all of it. Buffeted by most all of it, treasure hunts abounded. A.E. Reynolds' hunt for the Vermont/Ocean Wave treasure is our tale here.

Whenever possible, our story unfolds as though seen through the eyes of the men and women who lived it, and through the eyes of those who came alongside them and filled newspaper columns about them. Both classes of society are populated often by colorful characters but always authentic examples of the fiercely self-reliant generations that define the nineteenth century social mosaic. Sometimes crude or unsavory by current standards, sometimes living on the fringe of social norms, still their experiences represented a distinguishing facet of the American experience. They have earned a place among America's nation-builders whose qualities and courage give "American exceptionalism" its name. [4]

When America's westering legacy was reborn by the San Juans hullabaloo, A.E. Reynolds was a prospering merchant and rancher reborn into a mining entrepreneur. He would become the owner of hundreds of mines and earn the

A.E. REYNOLDS

Albert Eugene Reynolds, often referred to as A.E., was born in Newfane, New York, on February 13, 1840. He grew up in Lockport where the family relocated when he was an infant. Parents Henry A. Reynolds and Caroline Van Horn Reynolds owned and operated a Lockport general store and a nearby farm, both pursuits no doubt providing young Albert with valuable grounding for his own adventurous life. As the eldest male among nine siblings, biographer Scamehorn reports that:

> Albert was the natural leader, the achiever, and he invariably succeeded at any task to which he devoted attention and effort. This characteristic not only set him apart from his siblings but also prompted them to look to him for their well-being. Albert was ambitious, self-confident, aggressive, tenacious, and competitive, qualities that his brothers and sisters lacked in varying degrees. He was uneasy when dependent upon people but willingly encouraged others to become dependent upon him. He readily accepted responsibility for the actions of his siblings and supported and looked after them in numerous ways throughout his adult years.[5]
>
> For reasons one can only imagine, the call of the West surely among them, in 1866 A.E. took flight with eighty dollars to his name and landed in Junction, Kansas on the outskirts of Leavenworth, future site of Fort Riley and home to the U.S. Army's 1st Infantry Division. Employed a short while in a local general store, then a mercantile of his own in Richmond, Missouri, then in Fort Lyon, Colorado Territory, as an agent of a Leavenworth merchant responsible for a trading post where his western legacy began.

Fifteen years hence—several partnerships and business ventures including a general store, freighting and ranching later—A.E. rooted himself in Lake City, Colorado. Married in Columbus, Wisconsin on April 25, 1883, to Dora (Eudora) Earll, the Reynolds's lived in Lake City until the birth of their only child, Anna Earll on January 26, 1884. That year, A.E., disgusted with Lake City shenanigans, and Dora, uncomfortable on the frontier, moved to Denver where they lived for the balance of their lives. For A.E., that balance ended March 21, 1921, while tending to business in Nashville, Tennessee.

right to be called Colorado's Mining King. While Denver became "Queen of the Plains," mining camps like Lake City became mountain towns, and Colorado became a mining mecca, Reynolds became convinced that the Vermont/Ocean Wave lodes were worth investing his last dollar, and anyone else's dollar he could attract. Still remote by modern standards, the San Juans and Lake City dream-chasers did not struggle in a vacuum. Overshadowing their idyllic, isolated world was a world at war and on the brink of seeming extinction at the whim of a horrific global pandemic. Subtle at first, both would take their toll on Reynolds' last best chance. If they were not burdensome enough, America's worst economic depression was close behind.

The roots of our story run deep, at least a half-century deep. The significance of the 1848-49 discovery of gold in California cannot be overemphasized. It would change the course of history, American and San Juans history for sure. It drew adventurers from around the world to American shores, and it drew Americans from shore to shore. For centuries the vast American heartland and mountain west had resisted intruders—the San Juan range most convincingly—but that would begin to change in 1848-49. Ordinary people with exceptional courage, unfulfilled by their daily lives or simply intrigued by the treasures and opportunities in the West, willingly embraced the hardships of trail and camp in search of a better life. Fearless or foolish, romantic or real, their mass migration and subsequent accomplishments would define the human fabric of expansionist America. The acquisition of California (indeed the entire southwest), and the stunning wealth California gold fed into America's (as opposed to Mexico's) coffers fed the nation's economy for a decade to come. When its effects began to ebb, Colorado gold and soon silver would come to the rescue. In both cases it is the men and women on the frontlines that merit our attention, men and women who weather the inevitable reversal of fortunes that garner our highest praise.

The motivation underpinning this three volume series began with a look into the tired eyes of adventurers and emigrants that risked everything to pursue dreams and fantasies always west of wherever they were at the time. They

---

THE MERCANTILIST

— Lake City *Mining Register*, August 8, 1884 —

A.E. Reynolds, Dealer in General Merchandise, Lake City, Colorado: our stock consists of Dry Goods, Clothing, Boots & Shoes, Miners' Goods, Hats and Caps. Ladies' Cloaks and Furs, and Gents' Fine Overcoats, which will be sold at exceedingly low prices. We carry Heavily all Lines of staple Groceries, and in Canned Goods and Relishes. We have a Full and Complete Stock of All Grades.

Death on the Trail. Early caravans originating in the relative safety of settlements east of the Mississippi River were not always rushing for gold but many were. Homesteads and a fresh start on life motivated several generations of immigrants, mass emigrations to be sure, to risk health and survival crossing the Great Plains and interior Rockies. *(Public Domain.)*

populated social clans that represented generations and eras spanning centuries and half a continent. Listening to their faint voice helped personify the faceless crowds that transformed the land. Of course today we can only see and hear them through writings. And of course accounts of them are few among millions and volumes of first-hand observations and scholarly histories only skim the surface. Nevertheless, the experiences of the few adventurers ring common and true. Despite the passage of time, despite being lost in the flood of information deemed more important, despite being long forgotten in archives or attic boxes inherited from kinfolk long dead, they still pulsate with life and meaning. They still inspire appreciation for the benefits we enjoy thanks to the sacrifices and character of those who have gone before us. Under the weight of daily privations, threatened by global wars and economic perils they had neither control over nor understanding of, still they marched on.

Why did they do what they did? Some were simply divine appointments, some were epic political or cultural transformations that produced irreversible societal change, and some were visions of entrepreneurs like A.E. Reynolds and his faithful servants like Cousin Harry and John E. York and those that picked up where they left off. These men and the pilgrims and camp followers portrayed alongside them can teach us a great deal about geology and mines, but more intriguing they can teach us about the nature of the society that molded them and now us.

In the final analysis, what seem like amazing feats to the modernist, in the nineteenth and early twentieth centuries were simply expected. These men and women filed no claim for uniqueness or reward despite being worthy of both. On the following pages greet the few that exemplify the many who helped transform the San Juans and America's southwest into the western United States of America. In so doing, they not only made Reynolds' last best chance a chance at all, they did so both in good times and bad, both with and without someone else's jack (money, that is).

The Vermont and Ocean Wave lodes interested A.E. for a number of reasons. First, they tapped the same proven mineralized vein system that enriched the nearby and highly productive Ute/Ulay and Hidden Treasure lodes. Second, their development history correlated well with his understanding of geoscientific and mining criteria governing the likely presence of silver-rich ores. Reynolds was a farmer by birth and a shop-keeper by trade, but he was gifted as a mining magnate blessed with an ability and willingness to tailor lessons-learned by others to his own circumstances. Third, the physical proximity of the Vermont and the Ocean Wave to each other, and the short distance between the Vermont and the county wagon road five hundred feet below it, were ideal for construction of a cost-saving haulage tunnel leading from the deep lower workings of each mine to heavy-duty freight wagons plying the county road. Costly hoisting of ore buckets up five-hundred feet of shafts and winzes to the surface only to be packed on burros back down a steep five-hundred vertical-foot trail to the county road and transferred to wagons could be avoided. Finally, while Reynolds bided his time, he was content in the knowledge that an impressive amount of development work at an impressive expense was being funded and performed by someone else. When the time was right—"right" in Reynolds' mind meant bargain basement prices—and "everything else was equal" (meaning the price of silver was at the bottom of its market cycle), he would act.

In 1899 he acted. He secured all necessary rights to the Vermont and Ocean Wave lodes and commissioned the construction of what became the 1,500 ft. Reynolds Tunnel. As risky a venture as any he had undertaken, its redeeming feature was this "ace-in-the hole" patterned after his hugely successful Virginius/Revenue haulage tunnel above nearby Ouray, Colorado.

Progress was slow and more expensive than expected. The tunnel crew worked without the aid of power tools and soon learned that the rock they pounded drills into was the hardest they had ever faced. The local *Lake City Times* editor, ever ready to boost one's spirit on local matters, saw it this way:

(Lake City Times, March 9, 1899) Two men have been at work this week on the Vermont property excavating for the blacksmith shop, powerhouse, etc. The contract for cutting and supplying the timbers for the Vermont tunnel and houses has been awarded to C.A. Wiers. The largest contract ever let in this county was awarded to George Staples and Dan McLeod today by J.J. Abbott, A.E. Reynolds representative in this county. The contract is for the driving of a tunnel from Henson creek level to cut the Ocean Wave and Vermont veins, the estimated distance being 1,200 feet. Messrs. Staples and McLeod are miners

of great ability and many years of experience and, although the contract is a large one, they will prove equal to the occasion. [The height and width of the tunnel, eight feet by five feet, are considered large by contemporary standards. The length would have been challenging for any small-town contractor.]

Staples and McLeod did not "prove equal to the occasion." Nor did others who took their place. Progress was made, the introduction of powered drills accounting for much of it, but at an unacceptable pace and thus an unacceptable cost. Work was suspended in 1902 for a long rest. The haulage tunnel was in over 1,200 ft., tunneling on the Vermont/Ocean Wave mineralized vein was underway, but ventilation was life-threatening and money was gone. For all practical purposes, so was the global silver market and so was peace on earth. Wars and

Hammer & Drill. Even when circumstances afforded the construction of a surface plant (e.g. boiler, compressor) to power drills and ventilation fans in the underground workings, often budgets precluded their use. In the case of the Vermont/Ocean Wave upper workings, access precluded their use. *(P. David Smith)*

the threat of war came hand-in-hand with the birth of the twentieth century. A.E. Reynolds faced a bleak future and so did his last best chance to redeem his fortune. Redemption did not materialize until 1914. Ironically, World War I also materialized. For reasons never adequately revealed, with the dawning of 1914 came A.E.'s renewed interest in the Vermont/Ocean Wave and the haulage tunnel he believed would make them profitable. If the war had anything to do with this epiphany, it would be its inflationary effect on the value of metals, notably lead more than silver and gold.

Of the likely reasons that were unstated, the most persuasive include Reynolds' lasting belief in the still elusive treasure near where work had ceased, the costly surface plant and underground workings that he believed were still serviceable [they were not], his faith in his own abilities to attract investors as he was no longer able to self-finance his visions, and his expectation that what quickly became World War I would improve the demand for silver [it also increased the demand for lead, zinc and copper, present in abundance in the Vermont/Ocean Wave] and thus its price. All that he lacked was a mining engineer and superintendent of the same caliber as those he had relied on a quarter of a century earlier at the Virginius/Revenue Tunnel and his other bonanza mines. Oh, yes, he also lacked someone else's money.

Meet Cousin Harry. Harry Van Horn filled both needs. Like most others in his day, he was a self-taught mining "engineer." Unlike most others, he had $25,000 to invest. He also was available, bored, and best of all, a trusted and close relative—his mother and A.E.'s mother were sisters. And, not only were Harry and A.E. cousins, Harry was a proven employee who had served Reynolds as superintendent at his highly profitable Commodore Mine in Creede. His compensation at the Vermont/Ocean Wave would be a combination of "mill returns" from shipped ore and $25,000 worth of company stock.

In April 1914 Cousin Harry visited the Vermont/Ocean Wave and assessed the status of the surface plant and underground workings. With the exception of the high-pressure compressor, the balance of equipment looked serviceable. Returning to Creede, he recruited five trusted employees, John E. York among them. You will know York better soon.

After two years at the helm, Reynolds and his last best chance mine were not played out, but Harry was. His reward at that point amounted to $759 on an out-of-pocket investment of $25,000 that had ballooned to $34,000. Interesting, is it not, how the lure of treasure as yet only hinted at can stretch one's tolerance for risk and financial loss. Acknowledging Harry's disheartening turn of events but without apologies, Reynolds proposed changes in his operating contract. On November 13th with winter upon them, A.E. wrote to his "partners" [meaning Harry and his "boys"]. Addressed "To the Subscribers to the Funds for Opening the Ocean Wave Mine," A.E. penned a "new deal" grounded in his earlier six page assessment that they were looking at ten years of marketable ore but needed more capital and a mill. Further development of the Vermont was nowhere in his thinking at the moment, still believing that geology favored developing the Ocean Wave end of the vein. Of course the case for this conclusion was not iron-clad, witnessed by subsequent actions that kept the Vermont a viable option. To parrot G. Thomas Ingham's thinking [Ingham was the self-educated "mining engineer" who had Reynolds confidence and is discussed in Volume II], the Vermont and Ocean Wave drifts were equally encouraging or discouraging. In other words, "No one actually knows—keep digging dirt until you find out for yourself."

Reynolds presented his new deal artfully and without exaggeration. He explained that funds to date yielded eighteen months effort without paydirt. The project was nearly out of cash. There were clues pointing to marketable ore just a few hundred feet ahead, but more capital was needed to recover it. He advised that subscribers had the option to purchase the mine, continue with the current agreement, or he would help them structure a new arrangement. His advice was:

1) build a fifty tons/day mill [most likely he was envisioning a basic "mine-mouth mill"] next summer costing probably $15,000; 2) continue developing the vein this winter; 3) given that ore was heavy, what went into the dump was worth one half to fully as much as that shipped to a smelter. An on-site mill would solve this problem; and 4) the vein was about one thousand feet overhead. Probably at the point where they were now, that meant that it was one thousand feet to daylight, five-hundred feet to get under the old workings, something over five hundred feet with more or less ore the entire distance up to the surface.[6]

Mine-Mouth Mill. Most likely the on-site mill recommended by A.E. looked like this. It was not a budget-buster to purchase and operate unless the operator had no jack, that is money, to spare. *(Library of Congress)*

Without saying so exactly, Reynolds was hedging his bet. He was but one pace ahead of bankruptcy and clearly looking to lessen his financial exposure. In plain street parlance of the day, "he was up against it." He needed someone else's jack. For the "subscribers," most of whom were also working the mine, their investment was emotional—as was Reynolds'—as much as financial. Along with superintendent Van Horn, also still somewhat tempted to carry on under a new deal with Reynolds, they continued driving the Ocean Wave drift while they mulled over his proposition. Yes, they knew they were working at risk, but they had been miners long enough to know three things: 1) the Christmas season was always downtime in the best of times; 2) mining law ensured they would be paid the day they were sent home; and 3) mining law was no substitute for hard cash that thus far there had been little to none. There were two other unstated but obvious factors influencing their practical considerations. They were unaccustomed to failing in their obligations and were loath to accept defeat. And, as smitten as any treasure-seeker could be, they began each day eager to decipher the last clue and uncover the next one. Their options were clear. They could quit or work for pay—getting paid in either case was not certain—or they could work for a share of future ore sales, also not certain. They had at least to the New Year to decide.

Marginally better, nevertheless Harry ultimately declined the new deal. Taking no offense, Reynolds was content with Harry facilitating a contract with the balance of his crew. Apparently he could tolerate the loss of Harry provided his crew led by York stayed onboard. John York was fully capable of developing a profitable mine, both in terms of mining experience and character, but like his predecessors and his owner, the mountain before him and the scarcity of money backing him challenged his confidence but not his commitment. York and a skeleton crew worked without a signed contract through December save for a one-day Christmas break. We rejoin Reynolds' treasure hunt with the dawn of 1917. Underground work resumes in earnest. So does the deadliest year of World War I, and America's belated march into the thick of it.

Notes – Chapter Two: Treasure Hunt

1 Darley, George M., *Pioneering in the San Juan*, pg. 15.

2 *Cited in Colorado Gold Rush*, Vol. X, LeRoy R. Hafen, ed., pg. 285.

3 "Jack," cockney slang for "money", was a common 19th century term that is often heard to this day. The first two volumes are *Fortress San Juans* and *Reynolds' Last Best Chance*.

4 Many take offense to the term "American exceptionalism." It is rarely if ever intended to devalue the collective experiences of other cultures, societies, or nations. That is certainly not the intent here—American exceptionalism does not preclude exceptionalism of others. That said, the significance of the term cannot be diminished in the *Fortress San Juans* series. The American experience, the forming of America's collective values, was rare if not unique—exceptional—and to a large measure remains so despite being under assault.

5 Scamehorn, Lee, *Albert Eugene Reynolds, Colorado's Mining King*, pg. 7.

6 November 13,1915, Reynolds Collection, History Colorado Library, MSS 1220, Box 17, FF1255.

CHAPTER 3

Jack-of-All Trades

I think we will make a hundred feet or possibly a little better this month…
There is a pay mine here if we can hold out long enough to develop it. [1]
— John E. York, Reynolds Tunnel, 1916 —

The road to Reynolds' ace-in-the-hole—the "ace" being the Reynolds Haulage Tunnel, the "hole" being the Vermont and Ocean Wave mines—had been round-about and hard-trodden by treasure hunters from many lands. Of course, they had no idea where they were going or what they would find when they got there. Early adventurers responded to excited claims of gold in Colorado, in the San Juans, eventually in the upper Lake Fork of the Gunnison watershed. The Golden Fleece and Golden Wonder claims testified to its presence, but they were difficult, sporadic producers, and rare. Soon disappointed by the upper Lake Fork prospects, our treasure-seekers turned to nearby Henson Canyon where they were more often rewarded. The San Juan gold rush that spawned fledgling Lake City would yield treasure after all. Gold would not be the prize, but silver would do.

The treasure hunt had legs. There were just enough claims producing just enough paydirt to fuel ongoing searches and feed Lake City merchants three decades later. In the case of the Vermont and Ocean Wave lodes, in the winter of 1916-17 the responsibility for ferreting out their prize landed in the capable hands of John E. York. Responsibility for standing with him during the worst of times rested with friend Rowland Ewart.

A.E. Reynolds' 1899 vision for these properties had changed little over the intervening decades. Despite being idled from time to time, despite having an erratic production history for a variety of reasons common to hard rock mines in general, his plan for a haulage tunnel should surely put both mines on a smooth path to immense success. That was his belief, that was probably his nightly prayer. Of all the hundreds of mining properties in his elephant corral, the Vermont/Ocean Wave was best suited to become his next bonanza. Given the volume of dirt to move, it also was the project in greatest need of a fresh infusion of jack.

Less appreciated but obvious, given his shortage of funds, Reynolds also would need a jack-of-all-trades, a single, trustworthy, hourly wage earner with multiple skills. When it came to mines, a jack-of-all-trades was someone skilled at timbering, blacksmithing, drilling, and blasting. He was someone capable of operating and repairing boilers and compressors. He was an electrician, a welder, a plumber, and an underground gandy-dancer artful at laying and aligning track. And he was someone gifted in underground prospecting. That's right, prospecting. A jack-of-all-trades miner knew how to read the dirt that surrounded him—where the vein could no longer be seen—and deduce where to place his next round of charges in hopes of recovering the lead. The worst case was not that the vein "pinched out," the worst case was that it had ended. In circumstances like these the differences between a miner and a prospector were reduced to one who worked in the daylight and one who worked in the dark.

Not only was John York a trusted replacement for Cousin Harry, he was that jack-of-all-trades. Skills acquired in his youth on his family's Iowa farm—an aptitude born out of a love for machinery that was perfected in Colorado mines—his toolkit of abilities fit nicely into Reynolds' tight-fisted budget. As did his disposition. In response to the death of his young wife, he became stoic and he became disenchanted with Iowa and maybe with life. The end product of both, John York was perfectly suited to the operational needs of the Vermont and Ocean Wave, the irregular Reynolds paychecks he would have to cope with in the years to come, and the solitude. Reynolds grand 1899 plan had come down to a remnant of faithful workers and a few thousand dollars budget. While the San Juans fortress and its castle-keep had yielded to determined interlopers, the Vermont and Ocean Wave properties remained loath to yield treasure to anyone. That said, "York the prospector" was convinced there was treasure, and he would follow the clues until he found paydirt. Reynolds believed. York believed. York's crew was not so sure.

Jack-of-All-Trades. Low-budget mines needed a variety of skilled craftsmen they could not afford. A common workaround was hiring a single jack-of-all-trades [master of none]. Chief among them was Vermont/Ocean Wave's John York. *(William Darton – Public Domain)*

On November 12, 1916, superintendent York sent A.E. his first of many Reynolds Tunnel reports. As usual, it was rich in soul and mining details missing in textbooks or rattling around in lecture halls.

Johnson and I arrived here and went to work 26th of last month taking up the small pipe and rails that we put in for the last hundred feet, and replaced them with the three inch pipe and heavy rails.

We put in one round last month making the breast of the tunnel 1,275 feet to the beginning of the contract. We have driven 36 feet since the first of the month; everything is in good shape and I think we will be able to make good progress.

The breast is getting wet and shows a little quartz but no mineral has shown up so far. In regard to the night shift Van Horn was talking about I am of the opinion that the extra powder the other shift would burn would make so much gas that we would not be able to stand it as the one round of shooting is about all we can stand. [2]

Immigrant Rowland Ewart. Young Rowland perhaps dressed for church would soon board a ship for America and don the course threads of a hard rock miner. *(Courtesy of the Ewart Family)*

York added that they were out of coal, needed one case of "Renown Engine Oil," 3-inch flanges for the steam pipe running into the drift, and ¾ inch gaskets for water glasses on the boiler. On a positive note, York reported that Fred Anders would take stock but not until December, and friend Rowland Ewart had decided to take five-hundred shares of company stock but needed his November pay first in order to settle some debts he owed. Rowland also was a jack-of-all-trades, or nearly so. He also brought a highly praised gift to the party. He could cook.

On November 16, 1916, York wrote a heart-felt letter to friend Harry thanking him for checks. The scope of Harry's involvement at this time is unclear. He was no longer on-site or responsible for day-to-day operations, but apparently he continued partially bankrolling operations either with his own money or on behalf of unnamed others. It is possible he simply felt some obligation to help his former employees through a dry spell.

York also reported that they drove fifty feet since the first of the month when they shut down due to no coal despite borrowing two loads from the railroad. [Not only were Lake City merchants willing to "grubstake" the project—they had their limits—so was the D&RG Railroad despite struggling with its own problems. A.E. had been informed and coal was supposedly on the way.] York continued: "I had a hard time getting anyone to take Fred [their one and only draft animal — horse, burro, or mule was never stated] to winter on account of his age; but finally got Mr. Dan Baker to come up and take him. He will charge six dollars per month and said he would put him in the barn every night." [There is no record of Fred returning to the mine. If not Fred or a fit replacement, one of the crew had to push the one-ton ore carts out of the tunnel with muck destined for the waste dump or promising ore transferred to freight wagons destined for distant mills.]

York concluded his report with ever-important good news. The Ocean Wave drift was in 1,325 ft. from its junction with Reynolds Tunnel, 2,600 ft. from daylight. But there also was bad news. The drift broke into ground requiring stulls and lagging. ["Stulls" are timbers positioned against the "walls" or "ceiling" of a tunnel to support lagging. Lagging is a series of planks forming a retaining wall behind the stulls to prevent unstable dirt from collapsing into the drift.] "Hardy put in 24 stulls at $1.00 each and 62 lagging at $0.50 each." Stulls and lagging not only meant additional expenses, they meant that the crew was no longer in hard rock but into dangerous ground. Unstated but probably understood by Reynolds, adequate ventilation was again becoming a serious concern. Neither development was encouraging.

Learning early in life that it was best to report progress—sixteen and a half feet was the best progress he could point to—ahead of problems, on November 19, 1916, York wrote to Reynolds that

we made 16½ feet last week. Out of coal two days; first load came up yesterday. There is no material change in the breast from last report; still stays a little wet. No snow on the ground and weather fine. Yours very truly, J.E. York.

York also was of the view that "respectfully short" was wiser than "tediously long" when it came to reporting to men like A.E. Reynolds, and it was counterproductive to make excuses for marginal performance. "Sixteen and a half feet" for a week's worth of effort was considered "marginal performance." With regard to coal, Reynolds was responsible for ordering it. York also thought it best to let his owner make the connection between no coal and just sixteen and a half feet progress.[3]

On November 26, 1916, York reported making twenty-nine feet for the week, 81½ feet since the first of the month. The Ocean Wave drift was in 1,371 feet.

> *I think we will make a hundred feet or possibly a little better this month. Water still drips from the back and the hanging wall has straightened up and has about the same dip now that the vein has in the old mine, about 71 degrees. No mineral showing in the breast; the soft gouge streak remains about the same, a kind of brown rock ground up mixed with talc.* [4]

On December 3, 1916, York included in his weekly report another request for coal and the number of feet driven the prior week: sixteen and a half feet. The total number of feet driven for the month of November was 101. He added, "while there is no ore in the breast there is quite a change in the formation. The full face of the breast is a decomposed mass. There are streaks of a brown-colored, I would call it mud, all over the breast and getting more water each round of shots." [5]

Changing tunnel conditions sounded ominous, but neither Reynolds nor York seemed to care or were ready to say so. Maybe they were clueless, but probably not. On December 10th at the 1,418 foot mark, York reported that the number of feet driven during the week was twenty-one, an accomplishment he was not proud of given the condition of the ground they were in.

> *The boys on the [drilling] machine fell down last week, I think for the reason they did not keep the drift as large as they should. I told them they would have to make it larger so I think we will be able to make better progress.*
>
> *Last night's round opened up a body of water that flooded the track. It boiled up along the hanger with considerable force; came up from the bottom of the drift. The breast is not as wet as it was but has tightened up considerable in the last few rounds.*
>
> *The soft gange matter that was in the breast a few days ago has pinched out but it may be all over the breast again in the next round or two. It is in and out every few days and gets very hard in a round or two then softens up again as suddenly. There has been little particles of lead and zinc scattered over the breast for the last twenty feet.* [6]

As end-of-year reconciliation of accounts drew near, York was quick to respond. In keeping with Reynolds' Denver office penchant for detail, York's December 13th reply to the "front-office" request for November expenses was indeed detailed. November was the first month of Reynolds' latest "new deal" and York's new responsibilities. York may have overreacted, but the precedent was set. All subsequent reports would be equally detailed. Perhaps tedious in retrospect, they nevertheless reveal interesting insights into broader matters. For example, note the use of candles despite the availability of admittedly more expensive lamps. For Reynolds, knowing that his superintendent was frugal was important to him. For York and the boys, spending money responsibly meant less criticism from A.E. and hopefully more days on the job.

> *Number of feet driven: 101 @ $11/ft. = **$1,111 earned** by crew.*
> *Less following expenses:*
> *Coal: 15 tons @ $8.50/ton = $127.50*
> *Powder: 450 lbs. @ 24¢/lb. = $108.00*
> *Fuse: 1400 ft. @ 50¢/100 ft. = $7.00*
> *Caps [blasting]: 150 @ $2.00/100 = $3.00*
> *Oil: 5 gallon @ 37½ ¢/gallon = $1.90*
> *Telephone Service: $6.65*
> *Candles: 1 box @ $5.25/box = $5.25*
> *Telephone Call to Denver = $1.45*
> ***TOTAL EXPENSES: $260.75***
> *Payment due York and "the boys": **$850.25*** [7]

On December 17th York dutifully filed his weekly report, lackluster compared to the week before, but overshadowed with a building sense of anxiety. He included a request for more powder and a case of fuse to run through January. There was twenty inches of snow on the ground. The mine drift was in 1,435 feet. Feet driven during the week: seventeen. He wrote,

> *the breast has tightened up and is very hard now but I think [the crew] will be able to make fairly good headway now since they have made the drift larger. Yesterday's round opened up a small gouge streak next to the hanger but showed no mineral. The flow of water that they encountered last week has dried up but a little water was running from the gouge streak in the breast.* [8]

In 1,452 feet, York sent A.E. his Christmas Eve update. Seventeen feet was driven for the week. "No mineral in the breast which is just hard rock with no gouge streak at all." Coal is being delivered, "better than two feet of snow on the ground and still stormy." [9]

York filed his final 1916 weekly report on December 31st, no rest for the weary. As Vermont/Ocean Wave years went, 1916 was neither encouraging nor discouraging. Considerable underground development work had been performed, but no new treasure had been uncovered in the Vermont/Ocean Wave vein. There had been the customary clues, but no bonanza. A.E. had signed off on a new deal for York and the boys, but York and the boys were not being paid. Again, York began his report with the best news he could conjure up.

We haven't been able to get in a round since my last report. We have been sewed up by cold weather; thermometer stood from sixteen to thirty below nearly all week. Our water supply pipe froze up solid one night and we had to take it all up and thaw it out. We had a lot of bursted (sic) pipes and the heater bursted, that is a crack on one side that allows it to leak some but not bad.

Then came his itemized December earnings and expenses…

> *Number of feet driven: 63 @ $11/ft. = **$693.00 earned** by crew.*
> *Less following expenses:*
> *Coal: 12 tons @ $8.50/ton = $102.00*
> *Powder: 450 lbs. @ 24c/lb. = $108.00*
> *Fuse: 2000 ft. @ 50c/100 ft. = $10.00*
> *Caps: 200 @ $2.00/100 = $4.00*
> *Oil: 3 gallon @ 37½ c/gallon = $1.15*
> ***TOTAL EXPENSES: $224.15***
> *Payment due York and "the boys": **$468.85**.*

… followed by a mournfully desperate plea: "When can we expect some money? We are all broke and the merchants refuse to carry us any longer. Very truly, J.E. York."[10]

The new year dawned with no news of money in the mail, but like most everything else in life after the death of his wife, York was unmoved. No money in the mail did move one of the boys. Anders quit. Loss of a worker did not bother York, either. In fact, he advised A.E. that Ander's departure was a good

---

CARBIDE LAMPS

Carbide lamps burn acetylene gas produced by calcium carbide reacting with water. Acetylene burns with a clean, bright white flame. First discovered in 1836 by Edmund Davy, Frederick Baldwin is credited with patenting the first mining lamp in 1900. Commercialization of a variety of designs commenced soon thereafter. They were much improved relative to oil-wick lamps or candles in non-gaseous environments which was generally the case in hard rock silver and gold mines. Carbide lamps produced no carbon monoxide, consumed less oxygen, and yielded four to six times the light of a candle. Their popularity was mixed. Many miners preferred traditional candles. By 1918 electric battery powered lamps were competitors, largely replacing carbide lamps by the 1930s.

— Smithsonian Institution, National Museum of American History —

thing. His attitude had been disrup-
tive. But he also was owed $250 which
York asked A.E. to send. On January
7th, York filed his first 1917 weekly
report. The Ocean Wave drift was in
1,464 feet, but only twelve feet farther
than at the start of the year.

> *We have about an inch of ore in
> the breast which has been running
> along for three or four shifts. It is
> lead, zinc and yellow copper; it looks
> as though we might encounter anoth-
> er body of ore at any time. The breast
> is dry and very hard, no gouge mat-*

Let There Be More Light. Far brighter
than candles, still many miners resisted
using carbide lamps long after they were
available. Even better battery-powered
lamps available in the 1930s also were
slow to gain acceptance. No wonder
critical indicators of pay dirt could be
overlooked. (*"Carbide Lamps," Wikipedia*)

> *ter in the vein. We have been making
> very poor progress for the past month
> as you have noticed by my reports.
> The cause has been almost wholly due
> to one thing, this man Anders that
> came down from Denver has been
> the cause. [York reminds A.E. that he
> needs the money to pay Anders what
> he is owed before he can be sent to the house – Reynolds knows well that min-
> ing law requires payment of earned wages the day a miner is terminated.]* [11]

On January 14th York reported twenty-eight feet of new Ocean Wave drift
for a total distance of 1,492 feet. Funds had arrived and Anders was on the proverbial "porch with the dog."

> *During the week the ground softened up very materially showing small
> particles of lead, zinc, and yellow copper through the rock and occasionally
> small strata's of ore running off into the foot wall. There is a small talc streak
> next to the hanger and the breast is getting a little wet again. [With a bit of
> attitude of his own, he reminded A.E. to order powder.] The powder we are
> using is "The Red Cross Gelatine."* [12]

One week and twenty-one feet farther down the Vermont/Ocean Wave vein
York reported that the going had been rough but Anders' departure had helped.
As helpful would be additional funds. He reminded A.E. that the merchants
would not carry them any longer. Perhaps more meaningful to Reynolds, they
also would be out of powder and fuses at the end of the month, and their candles

"will barely run us a week longer." Almost as an afterthought, with an element of bitterness barely concealed, York added, "As I have received only $150 on last year's wages I am up against it proper." Stating the obvious, York added that work will stop if grocery bills cannot be paid. As for the mine:

> *We still see small pieces of ore in the muck and still continues wet. The hanging wall is very rotten and sloughs out necessitating considerable work mucking. We have not had to timber any so far. Almost half the breast is that brown rotten ground up rock.* [13]

January 1917 ended with unwelcome news from every quarter. The Ocean Wave drift was only advanced fourteen feet during the previous week, 1,527 feet from the starting point at its junction with the Reynolds Tunnel. The ground was challenging. Equipment was failing, jack was not forthcoming. When serious expenses appeared on the near horizon, York and the boys rightly concluded their days were numbered if they failed to break into paydirt. York's report was not encouraging. The hanging wall continued broken up with "rotten brown matter with a little quartz mixed with it." Their air-line, after connecting a length of pipe and getting up to pressure, burst at the butt weld [at the joint of two sections welded end to end]. The result was lost time making repairs outside resulting in only 4 rounds that week. Ironically, York reported an abundance of coal, but too much to properly store on-site. Not ironically, he also reported he only had four rounds of powder left.[14]

On February 2nd, in a rare expression of frustration, York turned to friend Harry. He needed more jack to pay wages and debts, chief among them probably Lake City grocers, otherwise two more of the boys, Foster and Johnson, would quit. He also believed they were being shorted coal delivered by F.S. Williams. He further reported they only made eighty-six feet in January, "half the contract" newly signed with Reynolds.

York wrapped up his sad report with a sad conclusion:

> *The breast is all that brown rotten matter that is so plentiful in the old mine [Ocean Wave]. We see little pieces of ore every day or two. We are in now 1,525 feet from the cross cut [Reynolds Tunnel].* [15]

Three days later York sent A.E. his January expense and payment report and braced himself for the response. There was no response. Knowing A.E. as he did, no response was no reason to be cheered.

*Number of feet driven: 86 @ $11/ft. = **$946.00 earned** by crew.*
Less following expenses:
Coal: 18 tons @ $8.50/ton = $153.00

Powder: 600 lbs. @ 24c/lb. = $144.00
Fuse: 1500 ft. @ 50c/100 ft. = $7.50
Caps: 150 @ $2.00/100 = $3.00
Oil: 3 gallon @ 37½ c/gallon = $1.15
TOTAL EXPENSES: $308.65
Payment due York and "the boys": $637.35 [16]

On February 8th York again reached out to Van Horn:

> *Friend Harry – we are down and will be down till the powder gets here.*
> *We could not get but just a little from Foster, I think they had it but did not*
> *want to let us have it. [Foster not only worked for York at the mine, he owned*
> *a General Store in Lake City.] The vein is now six feet wide or better and is*
> *beginning to be mineralized all through and looks very favorable. Very truly,*
> *J.E. York.* [17]

On February 18th York filed his first report to A.E. since his January summary. The Ocean Wave drift was in 1,555 feet from the Reynolds Tunnel crosscut. The report covered the first of February up to the present date. Feet driven was twenty-eight. Powder did not get there until Wednesday, the 14th, but they were able to go five feet with powder borrowed from town. "It is six feet between walls and the vein is filled up with that brown rotten material, mixed with quartz but no ore except now and then we see a small piece. It is getting wet again." [18]

Three days later York sent A.E. the rest of the story, even worse bad news. He desperately needed money or they could not go on. He would not have a crew after the first. Then, as if having come to his senses, he switched to a positive note such as was possible. As of February 25, 1917, they were in 1,575 feet. For a change in style if not attitude, York also introduced his weekly update with contrition—"Dear Sir"—and a mystery—a question mark. "Dear Sir?" Yes, the question mark was really there. Was it an overlooked mistake or a subconscious thought? Maybe he struck the "question mark" instead of the "colon" key on his typewriter and did not care. Yes, he had a typewriter and usually used it. The report that followed the intriguing greeting was anemic:

> *There is no material change in the breast and we still encounter small*
> *strata of ore. They aught (sic) to lead to a body of ore pretty soon. The vein con-*
> *tinues about the same width and the formation is about the same. Very truly,*
> *J.E. York.* [19]

Back to his normal self on March 4th, faithful York accounted for February earnings and expenses in customary fashion. He also expressed his gratitude for a $250 check sent by A.E. It was much smaller than what was needed or owed, but it was enough to keep them working. In all likelihood, it was all A.E. could scrape together at the time. There were no new subscribers much less lessors anywhere in sight. In a bare bones manner—no chit-chat or weather forecast this time— York ripped off his February report and hoped for the best:

> *Number of feet driven: 56½ @ $11/ft. = **$621.50 earned** by crew.*
> *Less following expenses:*
> *Coal: 12 tons @ $8.50/ton = $102.00*
> *Powder: 300 lbs. @ 24c/lb. = $72.00*
> *Fuse: 200 ft. @ 50c/100 ft. = $1.00*
> *Caps: 100 @ $2.00/100 = $2.00*
> *Oil: 2 gallon @ 37½ c/gallon = $0.75*
> ***TOTAL EXPENSES: $177.75***
> *Payment due York and "the boys": **$443.75*** [20]

York also reported that they were having "hard ground" but it was loosening up. He pointed out that they lacked powder, fuses, and rails – they needed at least 125 feet more to finish their contracted five-hundred feet. He ended with: "Received the check for $250. Many thanks for same." [21]

On March 11th York's weekly report began by describing changes in the geology. They had only advanced twenty feet and geology rather than weather must have seemed to him the best way to help the bitter medicine go down. York wrote: "Dear Sir," [with a comma]:

> *The whole width of the drift is a kind of red quartz and about as hard as rock grows. There is a little ore scattered through it and there seems to be a change coming of some kind. We are in now a little over 1600 feet from the cross-cut and we must be getting pretty close to being under the old mine.* [22]

On March 18th York reached out to both A.E. and Van Horn. To A.E. he reported they advanced thirteen and a half feet with no change in the breast; he would send him a sample per Harry's request; a piece of ore that showed yellow copper laid against the hanger; he needed 18# rails soon. To Van Horn he wrote:

> *If you will look at this sample with a glass you will see very fine lead through it. These black thread streaks is mostly lead, however I do not believe you can make pay dirt of it. Before we go much farther I think we had better determine whether we are on the right vein. [He also reminded Harry that he could not pay for food and supplies.] The store is throwing the harpoon into us good and plenty on the prices. [He informed Harry that rather than distribute the last check according to each man's shares, he gave $100 to Rowland – one of his daughters had broken both arms.]* [23]

John York was more than a mine superintendent or a jack-of-all-trades. He was a widower and a compassionate leader. Earning loyalty and inspiring diligence in his workforce was the new love in his life. He also knew where his duty lay, and the importance of sharing his guarded optimism that the clues they were encountering pointed more certainly than ever to the treasure they sought. On March 25, 1917 York wrote A.E. that the Ocean Wave drift was in 1,628 feet, fourteen feet driven during the past week, and that persistence would reap long sought-after rewards. At the same time, the trail of enticing clues had only led to another enticing clue, not the high-grade ore they had teased. Treasure-seekers that they were, the crew still awoke each morning eager for the hunt. A.E. awoke each morning weary for lack of a "paying mine."

> *The breast of the drift is changing very materially, and I (sic) for the better. The gang (sic) rock is about two feet wide in the breast and has strata's of ore, yellow copper and lead, all through it, from the thickness of a knife blade to three inches thick. I think within a few more rounds we will see a considerable change. There is a pay mine here if we can hold out long enough to develop it. We need more rails as we have left only two short lengths, and we should have those three inch "T"s that I ordered some time ago. Very truly, J.E. York.* [24]

On April 1st York again combined his weekly update with his monthly expense and earnings report, none of which would be welcomed by A.E. Total feet in from the Reynolds Tunnel crosscut: 1,646. Feet driven for the week ending March 31st: eighteen and a half. As for the condition of the Ocean Wave drift itself, "we have had a complete change of formation in the breast, still we have no ore yet, any more than very small streaks and the seams running through the rock is plastered over with lead and yellow copper about as thin as it can be spread on." York added that rails were in town, but as was often the case in early spring and late fall, the county road was impassable due to snow and mud.

March Expenses and Earnings:
*Number of feet driven: 66 @ $11/ft. = **$726.00 earned** by crew.*
Less following expenses:
Coal: 18 tons @ $8.50/ton = $153.00
Powder: 700 lbs. @ 24c/lb. = $168.00
Fuse: 2250 ft. @ 50c/100 ft. = $11.25
Caps: 200 @ $2.00/100 = $4.00
Candles: 1 box @ $4.45/box = $4.45
Oil: 3 gallon @ 41c /gallon = $1.25
TOTAL EXPENSES: $341.95
*Payment due York and "the boys": **$384.05*** [25]

Two days later York was joyful as well as business-like and said as much to A.E. He thanked him for a $300 check. He also asked for more coal. They only had enough to last until mid-April. Not inclined to end on a sour note, York offered up an early April progress report and a tried-and-true weather bulletin:

> *The vein is now nearly seven feet between walls and getting wet and looks very encouraging, however it has looked encouraging for a long time without ore. If the ore is not ahead of us it must be above us for every indication shows that we are near an ore body. About a foot of snow fell last night and today but tonight is clear and cold. Very truly, J.E. York.* [26]

On April 8, 1917, the Ocean Wave drift was in 1,666 feet, nearly 3,000 feet from the Reynolds Tunnel adit and daylight. York and the boys contributed nineteenth and a half feet of this during the first week of April. York reported no change in the breast, a little more water dripping, and spots of lead, zinc and yellow copper. The long-awaited rails arrived, but without fishplates or bolts to tie them together which rendered them useless. In a handwritten note at the bottom of his typed report, York could not resist noting the irony that the rails came with "plenty of track spikes." [27]

On the 15th York reported that the boys only made seventeen feet. On the 22nd they only added eleven feet. York explained, "we ran out of coal Tuesday…. There was about two feet of snow fell (sic)." On the 29th he reported that they had accomplished no mine work for the week. Problems were wide ranging. Also, "a slide came down into the road a little ways below the mine and filled the road about forty or fifty feet deep and is about three hundred feet long. County Commissioners sent five men who after a week 'did not hardly scratch it.' Not going to spend any more money on it." York offered to pay half the cost, but to no avail. Adding to his problems, Rowland the trammer, mucker, and cook went to town to care for his sick wife.[28]

York's April Report was devoted exclusively to dollars and cents, probably a prudent move. Other matters would have been seen for what they would have been, attempts to divert attention to less dramatic albeit equally disappointing news.

April Expenses and Earnings:
*Number of feet driven: 47½ @ $11/ft. = **$522.50 earned** by crew.*
Less following expenses:
Coal: 10 tons @ $8.50/ton = $85.00
Powder: 300 lbs. @ 24c/lb. = $72.00
Fuse: 550 ft. @ 50c/100 ft. = $2.75
Caps: 100 @ $2.00/100 = $2.00
Candles: ½ box @ $4.45/box = $2.25

Oil: 1 ½ gallon @ 41c /gallon = $0.65
TOTAL EXPENSES: $164.65
Payment due York and "the boys": $357.85 [29]

Overall, April had not shaped up to be a good month for Reynolds' last best chance, but it was no doubt overshadowed by even worse national news. After two and a half years of domestic political wrangling, isolationist America was finally sucked into Europe's war to end all wars. On April 2, 1917, President Woodrow Wilson presented his case for declaring war on Germany to the U.S. House of Representatives where it was accepted by an overwhelming majority of Congressmen. The resolution calling for a declaration of war passed 373 to 50 with most of the dissent coming from the West and Midwest. The U.S. Senate vote on April 6th followed a similar trajectory: eighty-two Senators in favor of war, six opposed. The measure was approved in a Joint Session of Congress and sent to the President. The following afternoon President Wilson signed the declaration and the United States stepped into an international activist role that persists to this day.

War with Germany and its allies was not a popular proposition with A.E. Reynolds or among the public in general. War with neighboring Mexico, which was a recurring possibility, or even Spain, was one thing. War with powerful, determined, and distant Germany quite another. Nevertheless, the die was cast and in keeping with national values, Americans rallied to the call to arms. The common man in remote San Juan mining camps, scarcely aware of the matter and preoccupied with their own daily battles to fight, were slower to respond.

War clouds barely appreciated for the hardships about to be rained down on the nation did not make a noticeable impression on John York and his crew. They resumed their routine underground work on May 16, 1917. In addition to what had become routine shortages of funding and labor, they had been shut down a month due to the incredible difficulty of removing ice, snow, and debris from the April avalanche. The county road leading off the mountain to town had been totally blocked which totally prevented delivery of critical supplies. Nevertheless, on the 20th of May, York was able to report that progress in the Ocean Wave crosscut amounted to thirteen feet for the week and 1,707 feet overall since the beginning of the crew's new deal. He also reported that there were little bunches of black ore [paydirt] scattered over the breast. "I saw a little gray copper [often paydirt] today the first I have seen for a long time. We will have barely enough powder to finish the contract as we have 66 ft. to drive yet." [30]

A week later York was more talkative. The boys had driven twenty-four feet, a respectable accomplishment all things considered. The breast showed a little more ore. "Every seam is filled with mineral, then there are small spots of lead through the rock." He reported that the vein was wider than the drift which was five and a half feet wide. The first ore shoot *we encountered is 735 feet from the crosscut. We have in a chute at 800 feet where we started a raise a little more than a year ago and this is the place where we got the largest bunch of gray copper. The ore in the back of this raise is about four feet wide…the back of this raise is about fifteen feet from the track. [York suggests another raise 300 feet farther in where they took out about four tons of ore as they "drifted through it." Without saying so, York was getting excited.]* [31]

York's June 3rd expense and earnings report for May was only marginally better than April's report which was of minor comfort to the boys and no comfort to A.E.

York to A.E.: May Expenses and Earnings:
Number of feet driven: 51½ @ $11/ft. = **$566.50 earned** *by crew.*
Less following expenses:
Coal: 8 tons @ $8.50/ton = $69.00
Powder: 450 lbs. @ 24c/lb. = $108.00
Fuse: 1000 ft. @ 50c/100 ft. = $5.00
Caps: 200 @ $2.00/100 = $4.00
Candles: ½ box @ $4.45/box = $2.25
Oil: 1 ½ gallon @ 41c /gallon = $0.65
TOTAL EXPENSES: $188.90
Payment due York and "the boys": $377.60 [32]

In a separate letter also dated June 3rd, York reminded A.E. that they were 1,749½ feet into the Ocean Wave drift, only twenty-three and a half feet short of fulfilling A.E.'s New Deal. This should be accomplished within the week. They had no powder but expected to get enough in town [meaning another merchant grubstake]. Alas, yet again the plans of mice and men often went astray. On July 1st, York reported no mine work since the last report, again for a variety of operational reasons no one could have foreseen. Fifty feet of track leading to the waste rock dump had settled and had to be repaired. High water washed out the county road, thus blocking their coal delivery. The water line feeding their boiler filled with sand and had to be taken up, cleaned out, and reinstalled. John York must have wondered what else could possibly go wrong. [33]

Notes — Chapter Three: Jack-of-All-Trades
[1] This mantra summarizes the thread of hope that fueled Reynolds Tunnel efforts for decades.
[2] November 12, 1916, Reynolds Collection, History Colorado Library, MSS 1220, Box 18, FF 1301.
[3] November 12-19, 1916, MSS 1220, Box 18, FF 1301-1302.
[4] November 26, 1916. MSS 1220, Box 18, FF 1303.
[5] December 3, 1916, MSS 1220, Box 18, FF 1304.

6 December 10, 1916, MSS 1220, Box 18, FF 1305.

7 December 13, 1916, MSS 1220, Box 18, FF 1305.

8 December 17, 1916, MSS 1220, Box 18, FF 1306. ["Gouge" refers to a layer of soft material along the wall of a vein favoring the miner by enabling him after gouging it out with a pick to attack the solid vein from the side; a layer of soft material between the true lode and the enclosing host rock.]

9 December 24, 1916, MSS 1220, Box 18, FF 1307.

10 December 31, 1916, MSS 1220, Box 18, FF 1307. [The Colorado Bureau of Mines report for 1916 shows 1,000 feet of drift at a cost of $10,000.]

11 January 7, 1917, MSS 1220, Box 18, FF 1309.

12 January 14, 1917, MSS 1220, Box 18, FF 1309.

13 January 21, 1917, MSS 1220, Box 18, FF 1311. [Note that candles are still preferred to carbide lamps, available long beforehand.]

14 January 28, 1917, MSS 1220, Box 18, FF 1311. ["Hanging Wall" is the upper side of an inclined fault, fracture or mineral vein or deposit; also called the roof. The surface on the opposite side of a fault, fracture or vein is the footwall. A miner stands on the footwall. He might bump his head on the headwall.]

15 February 2, 1917, MSS 1220, Box 18, FF 1312.

16 February 5, 1917, MSS 1220, Box 18, FF 1312.

17 February 8, 1917, MSS 1220, Box 18, FF 1312.

18 February 18, 1917, MSS 1220, Box 18, FF 1314.

19 February 21-25, 1917, MSS 1220, Box 18, FF 1314-1315.

20 March 4, 1917, MSS 1220, Box 18, FF 1316.

21 Ibid.

22 March 11, 1917, MSS 1220, Box 18, FF 1317.

23 March 18, 1917, MSS 1220, Box 18, FF 1318.

24 March 25, 1917, MSS 1220, Box 18, FF 1319.

25 April 1, 1917, MSS 1220, Box 18, FF 1320.

26 April 3, 1917, MSS 1220, Box 18, FF 1320.

27 April 8,1917, MSS 1220, Box 18, FF 1320.

28 April 8-29, 1917, MSS 1220, Box 18, FF 1320-1322. [This snow slide is better described as an avalanche which probably ran down a well-established Copper Gulch chute.]

29 April 29,1917, MSS 1220, Box 18, FF 1322.

30 May 20, 1917, MSS 1220, Box 18, FF 1324.

31 May 27, 1917, MSS 1220, Box 18, FF 1325.

32 June 3, 1917, MSS 1220, Box 18, FF 1326.

33 June 3-July 1, 1917, MSS 1220, Box18, FF1326-1329.

CHAPTER 4

Bug-Holes

"Things ain't what they used to be and never were."
— Will Rogers —

June 1917 was a transition month for the Reynolds Tunnel and a relatively successful one at that. A.E.'s "new deal" created 500 feet of additional drifts, but no paying ore and thousands of dollars of unpaid merchant invoices and crew wages. Yet work continued. Details are lacking, but based on subsequent mine reports, York traveled to Denver in mid-June to meet with Reynolds and Van Horn where they negotiated another new deal, one that was supposed to eventually settle all prior claims as well as compensate York and his crew going forward. July was its first month. Wages based on dollars per linear foot of tunnel was replaced with dollars per shift, paid monthly. That was a long time between pay days, but better than no pay at all. Belief in long sought-after treasure surely near at-hand remained strong in the hearts if not minds of all parties concerned.

On July 22, 1917, York could report that his earlier contract with Reynolds had been fulfilled. Assuming his boys had broken into the cross vein that interested them at the 1,749½ foot mark, they continued past it in the Ocean Wave drift another nine feet to 1,758½ , then "on the cross vein" they drove twelve feet north and six feet south. They did not stop there. A switch was installed, corners were rounded at the intersection, and tunneling in all three directions continued. Total distances as of July 22nd exceeded 500 feet. Without missing a beat, York and the boys began counting dollars per shift.

A great deal of dirt work [incredibly hard rock in this case] was accomplished in July, but from Reynolds vantage point it may not have seemed to be the case. Contractually, superintendent York and the boys settled on an IOU from Reynolds for unpaid wages under Reynolds first new deal, and accepted Reynolds' offer to convert all July wages to dollars per shift, also "paid" with an IOU. The accounting for July was detailed in York's August 25th report to A.E. [Apparently York filed his original report August 1st, but it never reached A.E.] Most of the boys who were owed back wages no longer worked for Reynolds and York, but they were included in the settlement. Friend Rowland remained on site and in the settlement. Cousin Harry, also included in the settlement, returned to lend a helping hand, but did not report his time. The result: July earned wages for J.E. York was thirty shifts at $5.00/day totaling $150.00; Rowland Ewart, thirty shifts at $4.00/day, $120.00. York could not have been comfortable with such a skeleton crew. Little did he know matters would worsen.[1]

As for the dirt work governed by A.E.'s second new deal, it gained momentum late in July. There was reason to believe they were within a few feet of striking the Ocean Wave vein or one like it containing high-grade silver ore. Was this the treasure trove they have been hunting?

They were literally at a crossroads, at the junction of what they thought was the east-west Ocean Wave vein and a promising north-south crosscut vein. The prize was farther ahead, to the east, or it was behind, to the west. Or possibly it was south, or it was north. Or maybe It was overhead, or deeper still. G. Thomas Ingham[2] was right — the only way to know was to keep digging. York was perplexed—maybe A.E. could help solve the riddle. If not A.E., then Cousin Harry. Most of July and half of August focused on it. Beginning on July 8 through August 12, 1917, York, Van Horn, and A.E. exchanged a series of letters describing the drift in both hopeful and haunting terms.[3]

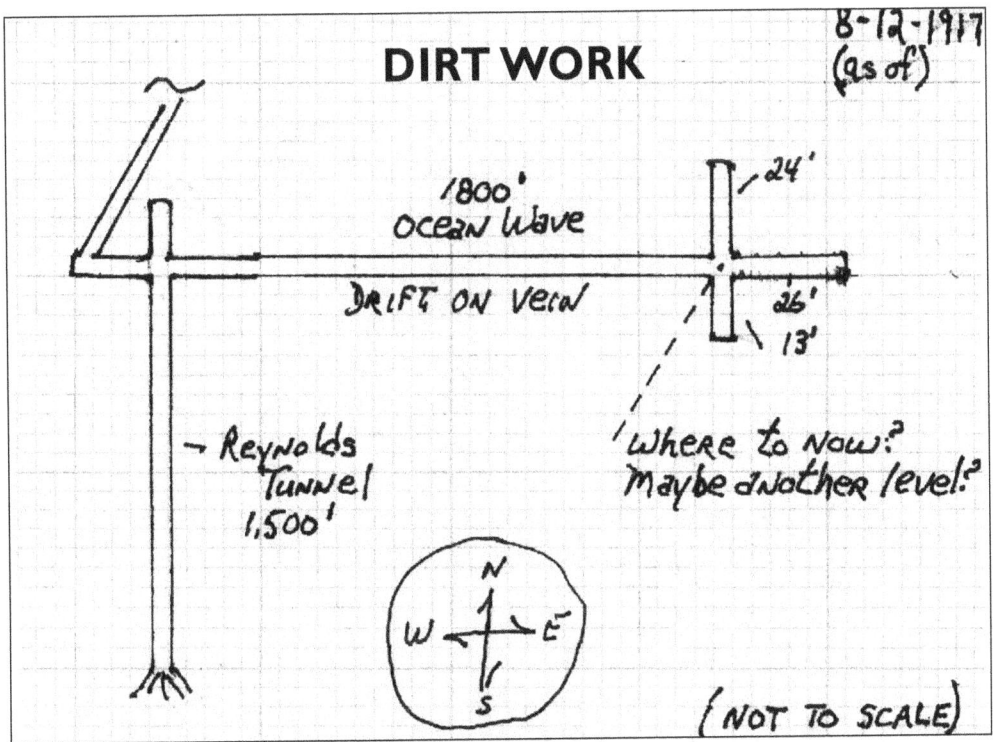

Now Which Way. Clues to pay dirt pointed in all directions, not only horizonal but overhead and underfoot. *(Author's Collection)*

[July 8, 1917] This cross vein goes through our vein and is wider than on the face of the wall where it went through our vein and has a streak of ore on both walls but not pay ore. It looks as though it had reversed its dip and changed its course but we cannot be sure until we get farther in on the vein. On the foot wall [opposite the hanging wall] side the quartz streak is some wider and shows some lead but does not show quite so much copper.

[July 22, 1917] We have driven on the Ocean Wave vein 9 feet from the cross vein with no ore in sight yet more than small particles shot through the rock. On the cross vein we have driven 12 feet north or into the foot of the main vein. There is five or six inches of quartz on the foot of this vein with a little copper and lead and on the hanger about ten inches of quartz which shows a little copper and lead. The balance of the vein is gang rock and blue talc with a little mineral through it all.

We are in on this vein to the South or into the hanger of the main vein, six feet. There is a small streak of lead on either wall with a very little copper and the balance of the vein is hard rock. [York reported a lot of mucking as the "ground is very rotten at the junction of the two veins and every round of shots loosens up a lot of the back and we have to pick it down and it is getting too high now so we will have to timber it."]

[July 29, 1917] Harry states that it is hard to estimate number of feet of work since they [York and Ewart] were taking out corners to be able to turn cars in the cross veins; [they did drift ahead on the] Ocean Wave vein about fifteen feet, four feet on the cross vein in a southerly direction, and twenty-two feet on the cross vein in a northerly direction. [Harry wrote that the only good showing was in the breast of the northern cross vein. It improved with each shot, opening up "considerable yellow copper and lead."]

The streak itself I [Harry] believe is pay ore, and we are saving what we can of it. [He thought "the ore chute" was 100 feet ahead on the Ocean Wave vein; he wanted to develop the cross cut vein to demonstrate its course that looked strong, four foot wide.]

In rare fashion, perhaps knowing A.E. all too well, Harry wrapped up his July 29 report with a whine. There are only three of us here, he said, so progress is necessarily not very rapid, and

it is thirty-three hundred feet to tram from the breast to the end of the dump. I operate the power plant while they [York and Ewart] are drilling, then help do the mucking after they shoot. [Most likely, the boys lament the absence of draft animal Fred—pushing a loaded one-ton ore car over a half-mile was painful and slow.]

Also on July 29 York reported no tunneling on the Ocean Wave main vein since his last report. Instead the crew installed a switch and track in the cross-vein going north where a streak showed more lead. The cross-vein was now thirty-five feet from breast to breast, "so far is running straight as a line and the dip is almost perpendicular." The vein was five and one half feet between walls and looked very promising for ore. York advised that "Harry wants to drive on this vein far enough for a survey while we are at it."

On August 12, 1917, Harry reported that the Ocean Wave drift was in twenty-six feet beyond the cross-vein, 1,800 feet in from its origin at the Reynolds Tunnel. The ground was very hard and tight, no moisture, no mineralization "at present." All efforts, he wrote, "are focused on this northerly drift." It was in twenty-four feet, showed considerable mineralization all the way in with the same appearance on the breast. The crew "shot off the corner, made a switch and laid (sic) track into this drift." The southerly drift of the cross-vein was in thirteen feet with a very good showing in the breast, an eight inch wide streak of quartz, lead and some yellow copper. Harry continued:

> *This cross-vein is apparently a later fill than the Ocean Wave vein, and had nothing to do with cutting the ore off from coming west, and as none of the workings above ever cut this cross-vein, it shows that there is a barren zone between this cross-vein and the ore-chute they had in the workings above. This cross-vein dips to the east as it goes down, so the breast of our drift is now getting pretty close to being under the old workings. [Van Horn added that A.E. ordered the wrong "powder" — it is "Red Cross EXTRA instead of Red Cross GELATIN, not as powerful, more smoke, boys getting sick/headaches nearly every day."]*

It is unclear exactly who in mid-1917 remained an active part of the Ocean Wave Mining & Reduction Company other than Reynolds, York, Ewart, and Van Horn. Regular reports continued to go to Reynolds, as did requests for supplies like coal and pleas for money. Reynolds' latest new deal did not change much. Nor had setbacks run their course. In the wake of the August setbacks, York made a strategic decision. He persuaded Cousin Harry that he should be the one to update Reynolds weekly. Sunday, September 2, 1917, was Van Horn's first day in this role. Like York, he had learned a long time ago that it was best to begin with whatever good news he could truthfully drum up. In this case, good news was limited to reporting that a seventeen ton shipment of coal had finally arrived. Then the shocking news:

> *Upon entering the tunnel, after having done nothing in the mine since the 24th of last month, we found one of the sets about fifty feet from the entrance, had broken and let in about thirty tons of dirt, so we spent all day to-day (sic)*

and will part of tomorrow in repairing that, then I hope we will be able to go ahead in the breast again. [A broken "set" sounded ominous, a harbinger of weakening timbers in every decades-old set, but this possibility did not seem to bother anyone. While waiting for coal, they worked outside covering the water line from the creek to the boiler. Freezing winter nights—yes, in September—were upon them.]

[They also worked at fixing] our waste track on the dump, putting in a ventilator in the compressor room, and in addition at the request of Mr. Morse, we opened up the [adjacent] upper Lellie tunnel enough so we could get in to the breast, and after wading through about a foot of water until we got into the vein, we found we could not go ten feet either way on account of caves, so we abandoned the job. [As for the required update on tunneling, Cousin Harry reported that the breast of the Ocean Wave was in thirty-nine more feet and] is as tight and hard as it is possible for anything to be. [He ended his August report with a request that A.E. try and pay York and Ewart, he could get by. They worked without weekends off, 30 days in July, 27 days in August, then have been waiting for coal.] [4]

There was no response from A.E. There was a curt note from an uncommon source. On September 14th A.E. was reminded that the project had creditors other than the boys at the mine or merchants in town, a Mrs. Wm. Hardy, an especially annoying one at that. Mrs. Hardy was the local telephone company "Exchange Manager." Her handwritten note to the Ocean Wave Mining and Reduction Company did not mince words: "As you are three months behind for your Telephone Bill, I had order from Grand Junction to disconnect it if not paid up by Sept 25th. Yours very truly, Mrs. Wm Hardy, Exchange Mgr., Lake City." Probably not the first embarrassing notice ever received, but attention-getting just the same. Apparently Mrs. Hardy was no one to trifle with. Like most utility company representatives, there were no acceptable excuses for unpaid bills. Failure to remedy the matter immediately was akin to a capital offense, service termination for sure. [5]

On the 16th of September Van Horn piled on, but not before he reacted to A.E.'s suggestion that he should "drive a total of 80 to 100 feet into the hill on the cross-vein." Van Horn thought Reynolds' suggestion unwise and said so. "I believe we are on the right streak now." He explained that the breast had loosened up considerably during the last few rounds, and that "gouge matter on the hanging [wall was] nearly two feet wide today." Harry proposed that another complete survey be done including the Lellie Tunnel. The Lellie was an idle adjacent property with extensive underground workings. Bradish Morse agreed, but wanted to wait for A.E.'s return from New York where he was in search of investors. They were now sixty feet into the north cross-vein, twenty-one feet in the last fourteen days. They needed coal, and Harry again asked for cash "for the boys who are getting pretty well down in the mouth…" [6]

On the 17th of September, John York was back in the catbird's seat. His two weeks absence was never explained, attitude-wise or otherwise. Cousin Harry never protested giving up his recently delegated reporting duties. Quite likely, John's life-long sense of duty and Cousin Harry's sense of knowing when to call a matter quits kicked in again albeit just for a time. York wrote A.E.:

> *We have not received our salary for either July or August. It was my understanding that we would get our money each month when I was in Denver last June. If we keep going we will have to have our money as we cannot pay our bills. Very truly, J.E. York.* [7]

Again there was no response from Reynolds, nor any paper trail that money was sent. Nor were there any more reports written by York, not one, until March 1918. Yet he continued to work—we know this from later reports documenting the length of the tunneling—but apparently he was over maintaining civil communications with Reynolds. Van Horn was again the de facto spokesman for the boys who nevertheless still considered York their superintendent and brother-in-arms throughout his quiet time. Two weeks after York's last plea, clearly aware of his friends' frame of mind, Van Horn took another run at A.E. In a hand-written note he reported exciting news: "Mr. Reynolds," he began rather formally given he was writing to his cousin and longtime employer. He described two samples he had just taken in the cross-vein, one of which he thought was "pure gray copper" with gold, silver, lead and copper, which he reported were on their way to Denver. "The streak [where the samples were collected was] about six inches wide in the bottom and not quite so wide in the top." A six-inch "streak" was nothing to shout about, but it was respectable and often an indication of more to come. On a separate matter, no doubt with counseling from son-in-law Morse, A.E. had agreed to commission a survey of the underground workings to accurately locate exactly where their tunneling had taken them. As an afterthought, Harry added that Mr. Miller, the surveyor, was already on the job. [8]

In fact the samples did prove high in silver—192 oz. and 629 oz. respectively—high enough to dislodge Reynolds from his Denver office perch. After a quick visit to the mine, many questions remained, but his commitment to continue the work seemed unshaken. Was this promising streak and these handsome samples just tempting clues that would lead nowhere? Was this crosscut vein the portal to the treasure trove he had been seeking since 1899? Upon inspection of the mine, the king was impressed with what he observed. He authorized vendors to deliver supplies and the boys to continue the work, presumably being paid at least some portion of a living wage. Van Horn reported on October 21, 1917:

> *Nothing new in the way of ore since you were here. We are now in 56 feet, and it has been comparatively soft all the way until today, and now it seems*

very hard again. [He informs A.E. he needs more coal, also that he will visit his sister in Denver the following week who he has not seen in 19 years. He thinks better of trying to explain much else.] [9]

For the balance of 1917, Van Horn reported typical progress and setbacks. According to the Colorado Bureau of Mines, from November 1916 to November 1917, four-hundred feet of tunnel at a cost of $11,000 with no production was all this skeleton crew had to show for their efforts. Van Horn faithfully reported the details, our only insight into the crews' attitudes, demeanors, and working conditions.

On November 18, 1917, Harry reported that the breast of the cross-cut was in 84½ feet. There was little ore his last two rounds, but some yellow copper, no gray. He mournfully added, "hope it will amount to something this time." A week later it seems that it had. On November 25, 1917, Harry wrote that the breast of the cross-cut was in ninety-five feet, ten and a half feet for the week. In his words, there was a "quite strong vein with us now, although the ore streak is about the same as last week." The streak was still six inches wide, yellow, no gray copper. He added that he was running low on coal — he was convinced slow delivery to the mine was due to failure to pay bills.

On December 1, 1917, Harry confessed that the breast of the cross-cut was only in 103 feet, making eight feet for the previous six days. They planned to put in another round that Sunday. The slow progress was due to a frozen pipe-burst. The ore looked good, better all the time. They had put nearly two tons "in the ore house of very good looking stuff." [This is the first mention of an ore house. For the first time, Harry also mentioned meals and the practice of paying for them— dinner at the mine cost forty cents. Most likely Rowland Ewart was the cook.]

December 2, 1917, Harry advised A.E. that he had sent a few samples from the cross-vein by parcel post. "Some of the rock contains little specks of what some of us think is Ruby Silver. If you have any of it sampled, would be glad to know the result." A week later, on December 9, 1917, Harry reported that the breast was in 111 feet. A little ore continued, "although the porphyry coming in has nearly cut it out." No doubt reluctantly, he added that they should be six feet farther in but they ran out of coal. They would not make the vein by Christmas. [10]

Either coal never arrived or York and Ewart were forced to find something else—dead work—to do. In any event, the customary Christmas break was upon them. In some cases that break could be limited to a single day, in some cases it could be weeks. The 1917 Vermont/Ocean Wave Christmas break would be lon-ger still. Van Horn went to Denver. The *Silver World* editor reported on December 27th that "Rowland Ewart and John York of the Ocean Wave mine came down Monday to spend Christmas, the former with his family and the latter with friends." On balance, 1917 was a disappointing and stressful year from just about every perspective imaginable despite an occasion or two that looked like the hunt for treasure was coming to a fruitful end. The crew had been reduced to three die-hards, at times just two if Cousin Harry left for Creede or Denver, or Rowland had to tend to family matters in Lake City, which was not uncommon. Fred the tram-horse [or tram-mule] was not back.

January 1918 would be better, it had to be. There was no particular reason to think so, but typically miners were optimists. Gamblers, on the other hand, were all about "the odds." No accomplished gambler would have bet on Van Horn returning from Denver, but return he eventually did. The same gambler would have bet his last dollar on the return of York and Ewart, and as odds would have it, that gambler would have won. York continued to prefer the role of jack-of-all-trades [with the exception of taking on Fred's role which was really demanding work] rather than superintendent. Communicating with A.E. would remain Harry's lot, at least until it was not. Reported progress was insightful.

On January 7, 1918, the cross-vein breast was in 143 feet; the face of the drift was sprinkled all over with "little seams of lead and yellow copper" and more mineralized with each round of shots. In Harry's words, "we must be getting quite near the Ocean Wave vein, although we have scarcely any moisture; it is snowing to beat the band here to-day." Harry signed in pencil, explaining, "Excuse pencil, have no ink." On January 13, 1918, Harry reported that the cross-vein was in 151 feet. There was no sign of the Ocean Wave vein yet. The face looked the same: knife blade seams of lead and yellow copper. He ended with "we are about out of supplies," specifically "DuPont 1-1/8th inch x 8-inch Red Cross Gelatin, caps, fuse, pipe fittings, 2 inch pipe, 400-600 feet 16# rails with fishplates,100# drum of ¼ inch carbide, parts for rock drill, and a 30# Waugh drifter." He reported that coal for several weeks was delivered before roads got bad—a lot of snow. York and Ewart worked twenty-nine and a half shifts each in December. The request for carbide suggested that they were finally using carbide lamps instead of candles.

On January 20, 1918, the breast of the cross-vein was in 162 feet. There was no change in the face, no vein cut, or any "slip of any kind." Harry reminded Reynolds of his order for supplies, and included a weather report: thirty inches of snow, minus eighteen degrees. The only travel on the road was the mail carrier on a saddle horse. At risk of receiving a "stop-work" order, Harry dared to ask A.E. what he was thinking since no vein had been cut. Again, there is no indication A.E. answered Harry's question.

On January 30, 1918, Harry sent rock samples of what they had been going through for seventy-five feet. [Sample #1] "shows ore streak going right through the porphyry; this streak has been continuous all the way, and has been from one inch to three inches wide." [Sample #2] "shows a knife-blade seam of ore in the porphyry; these little seams have been in and out and at times have been scattered all over the breast, sometimes on one side, then on the other, and entirely independent of the main ore streak." [Samples #3 & #4] "show little bunches of lead that come in here and there in the solid porphyry, but are scattered and not continuous." Harry added that the drift is bone dry all the way in until the previous Sunday when on the left side 170 feet in, "right out of the solid porphyry, there is now flowing a good stream of water, and has been since Sunday."

Harry continued, "we are drilling again today, and from the appearance of things there is a change coming. In examining what we call the Vermont vein in the main [Reynolds] Tunnel, I find it stands nearly straight up and down; the Ocean Wave vein may straighten up and be several feet ahead of us yet. I believe if we ever get through this porphyry we will find the vein; by golly it must be there for there is no other place for it." A week later Harry was not so sure. On February 6th he reported that "there is not much new." The breast was in 185 feet. Van Horn and York went in that night and "found the face of the drift nearly clean across in hard solid rock, the same as in the hanging wall of the Vermont vein." Whether it was the wall of the vein they were looking for or not could be determined after a couple more rounds. Harry wrote that "this round broke well and it will take us all day tomorrow to muck out."

On February 13, 1918, the breast of the cross-vein was in 193 feet. Harry reported that there was little if any change, but that "the water is still running out of the wall back at the 170 foot mark, and we had a little moisture in one of the lifters in our last round." He ended with the bad news: the four-inch flue on the boiler was leaking and getting worse. York and Ewart each worked thirty-one shifts in January — they "need a pay day very badly."

On February 18, 1918, the breast was in 198 feet. Harry wrote, "Just a few lines to say that during the last five feet quite a change has taken place in the breast of our cross-vein; the vein matter is two feet wide between solid hard walls, and consists of the hardest kind of quartz, and contains yellow copper, lead, iron, and a little gray copper can be seen in places. Heretofore, it has been practically all porphyry. The whole two feet looks as though it would be pay ore, and if it continues after another round, we will shoot it by itself and save it." Always the optimist, Harry reported that they needed more coal—they used sixteen tons in January. "It is possible, and I rather think it probable, that this enrichment in our cross-vein, comes from the Ocean Wave vein ahead, and it may be we are getting close to it." [11]

Not known to exaggerate, Harry's reporting generated excitement in the camp. Even so, whether Harry prodded A.E. once too often on pay for the boys and lack of supplies, or the oft-repeated but never realized forecast was wearing thin that the long sought after Ocean Wave vein and presumably final clue to the whereabouts of the treasure "was just ahead," or simply that Harry needed a break is unstated. What is clear is for the next four weeks John York was back in the crosshairs updating Reynolds on progress and needs. Probably uncomfortable with this assignment, York fulfilled his duty, short and sweet, beginning with a March 3, 1918, report. The ore streak was now three feet between walls. There was one foot or possibly a little better of good ore on the left hand wall. He reported that the rest of the vein had some ore all through it but "not pay" so he would take that with waste and leave good ore "on the wall. Very truly, J.E. York." On March 10, 1918, he was somewhat more talkative:

Shot down the ore yesterday and trammed it out and sorted most of it and when it is all sorted we will have close to twelve tons. The ore streak shows now in the breast about like it did when Harry and I took the sample. I think this ore shoot is practically all above our level as there has not been much ore in the bottom of the drift. [He added that coal has been delivered except for 4 wagon loads.]

Four days later, on March 14, 1918, still in a talkative mood, York reported that the last round he shot:

rather spoiled the looks of our ore streak. While there is a good streak of ore in the back of the drift going ahead it narrows down to nothing about half way down the drift. The vein in the back is about three feet wide and narrows to about one foot in the bottom. Twenty-three feet back from the breast the ore first showed up and I am inclined to think that the ore will come in again." [Almost always, York typed his reports. Along with a telephone, seldom used it seems, how unusual was it for a rustic miner's cabin in a remote location to shelter a miner fond of using a typewriter to prepare weekly reports? To this report York appended a handwritten P.S.: "The ore in the back is about ten inches wide."]

Three days later, on March 17, 1918, perhaps responding to an A.E. inquiry, York reported that he could only see the breast halfway down to the bottom of the drift due to mucking to be done. That said,

the vein looks better than it did and is getting wider again. [It] *"shows ore and is quite wet. The whole vein was more or less wet and showed moisture out in the wall rock. There is quite a stream of water running out from under the muck pile."* [In general, water was not a good thing.]

On March 20, 1918, most likely with considerable hesitation, York sought to minimize a new water problem in reporting that there was no vein that they had been hoping to find,

although we have quite a flow of water out of the vein we are following. The whole vein is wet but the heavy flow is from the bottom; I should say it was making fifteen gallons per minute. The vein is two and one half feet wide and mineral more or less all through it. The vein is mostly black and white quartz. One streak shows black and gray copper — about six inches wide. Will measure up Sunday.[12]

Van Horn was back on site on March 24th. Back from where—Denver, Creede—is unknown. Possibly he spent time in Denver with his sister, more likely he spent time with Cousin Reynolds. Frustration over the elusive Ocean Wave vein remained high but was not pointing to signs of another shutdown. To the contrary, equipment was upgraded, supplies ordered, and wages paid albeit partially and late. Someone else's money, never specified but likely Harry's or Bradish's, no doubt proved helpful. Typed on yellow paper [signed by Harry, but dictated to and typed by York?], Van Horn resumed his correspondent duties with a flurry of reports. At the same time, scarcely noticed and never commented on, the nation continued its hesitant march into the fury of WWI.

On March 24, 1918, Harry reported that the breast of the cross-vein was in 222½ feet, and that it was making considerable water. The vein was about three feet wide with streaks of ore scattered all through it, but "practically impossible to save much…." The vein changed with every round and he could not tell how it would look three feet ahead. [Three feet was the average distance advanced by a round of charges when rock fractured according to plan.]

On March 27, 1918, Harry reported that they needed more coal; there was no change in the breast, and that they had to let the fire go out under the boiler to fix the leaking flue. Four days later Harry wrote that the breast of the cross-vein was in 232 feet, the vein was over four feet wide, and practically the full width of the drift, and that it was mostly quartz with streaks of waste with a little mineral scattered through it. Water continued about the same as it had been for the past two weeks, definitely an unhelpful condition. On April 8, 1918, in no hurry to report, Van Horn reported that only two rounds of holes had been drilled in the breast since his last report, and that there was not enough ore in the vein to save. Worse yet, there was more water coming in from the face of the drift. They tried drilling and blasting the roof back where the last ore was collected, but they "hardly got a 'hatfull' (sic) out of what we shot down." Harry concluded his dark assessment with a simple statement that they were out of coal. A week later and clearly out of patience, Harry wrote A.E.:

> *Just a line to advise you that we are still without coal, this Sunday being the eighth day since the coal arrived in Lake City, so of course have done nothing in the mine during the past week; however, we have been busy all the week shooting out big boulders and throwing out the rocks from the creek so it will be safe when the high water comes [typically in June]. In two or three more days we will have that in good shape. [Use of sparse funds on this activity was not likely to impress Reynolds.] We think we have about fifteen tons of ore in the bin, and it was our idea to have it hauled down and shipped when*

*they commence hauling the coal, whenever that is. [That information would
be more to A.E.'s liking.]*

On April 16, 1918, surely in a better mood, Harry acknowledged that they
had received a $500 check from A.E. Not so encouraging, Harry reported that
the crew had to help shovel snow off the county road in order to get F.S. Williams,
the local freighter, to deliver a couple of tons of coal to the boiler. With steam
restored, they were able to restart the compressor. With the compressor running,
they could drill and put in a round the next day if it were not for the fact that the
powder was still in town. Harry was not sure where the caps were. Also, almost
as an aside, he reminded A.E. that York and Ewart each were owed for working
thirty-one shifts in March.

A week later, on April 23, 1918, without a great deal of conviction Harry
wrote that "we have managed to get in two rounds in the breast." They are 242
feet into the cross-cut. Unfortunately, the rock is "as hard as it is possible for
rock to be." Worst still, there was very little mineral showing, "but over three
feet of hard quartz full of bug-holes, which makes the drilling extremely difficult." Harry's grievances continued. They needed more coal and there was no
sign of Williams since he delivered the two tons of coal on April 15th. "This
makes nearly two weeks of this month that we have been waiting on him...
If the trials and tribulations of this job aren't enough to make a Saint curse,
then I don't want a cent."Harry used $200 of the $500 check from A.E. to pay
Williams—he charged six dollars per ton for hauling coal—who Harry suspected
was slow-walking his orders until he saw some jack. Harry concluded his report
with a reminder that there were other debts begging to be paid: Closest to his
heart were crew wages, Rowland Ewart was owed $116 for wages dating back
to November. John York's September back-wages were seventy-five dollars. The
Vermont/Ocean Wave was into C.P. Foster for $46.85, probably for their food
and powder. We already mentioned Mrs. Hardy over at the telephone company
anxiously looking for her $35.85.

BUG HOLES

Bug holes are small cavities caused by gas bubbles that were trapped in quartz
veins as they cooled. Bug-hole quartz was hard to drill. The drill tended to bind up,
deflect, or get in a hole and follow it instead of adhering to its intended path. When
this happened it caused the hole to "fitchure," and could cause the shots not to go
off in rotation. When that happened the ground did not break properly and had to
be shot over again. Maintaining the course of the drift could be more challenging
and a day's labor and the budget would be compromised.

Rock Drill Hammer Machine. Reynolds' Vermont/Ocean Wave progress was no longer a question of current technology. The questions yet to be answered: "Was there any treasure there in the first place, and how long could they afford to search for it?" *(Rand Illustrated Catalog)*

On April 29, 1918, clearly frustrated, Harry reported that Williams still had not delivered the coal they desperately needed, and that "all efforts to find out by telephone [maybe Mrs. Hardy was not so ridged after all] when we might expect some have proved fruitless. This makes nineteen days this month that we have been down on his (Williams) account." Harry added that in the meantime they had been trying to repair leaks in the air pipe and other odd jobs. Faithful Ewart had gone down to Lake City to visit the family until they were ready to restart. He had worked twenty-four shifts in April. Jack-of-all-trades York had worked twenty-eight.[13]

On May 2, 1918, Reynolds sent Van Horn another $500 payment along with a letter stating that "any expenditure you make in hastening the work is satisfactory." The boys must have been shocked senseless—they were accustomed to opening an A.E. letter only to find a stop-work order. [Turnabout being fair play, Reynolds was accustomed to opening a York or Cousin Harry letter only to find bad news.] On May 9th Cousin Harry did not disappoint, He sheepishly wrote, "and now I come with another tale of woe." He needed a new drilling machine. The machine they had was completely worn out after four years use. He wanted a Denver Rock Drill Company Clipper Model 50 hammer machine with hollow steel for water, It would pay for itself in short order, he assured A.E. On May 19th he was not sheepish, he was jubilant. A.E. had meant what he said. He had agreed to the purchase of a new, expensive hammer machine. They also had enough supplies until the 4th of July. Harry wrote, "When York heard it was coming, he had a smile on his face all day." York also was happy to receive back-pay for the balance of September and part of October 1917 [eight months late].

Ewart was brought current through December 1917 [still five months short]. On June 5th the Clipper Model 50 arrived. Van Horn reported that Ewart worked twenty-four and a half shifts, York and Van Horn [without wages] worked thirty shifts in May. The north cross-vein off the Ocean Wave drift was in 270 feet. All was good and about to get better. Why did he think so? Maybe the most recent assay report of samples had something to do with it. On that same June day the Clipper Model 50 and smelter report presumably arrived, Van Horn also presumably with joy in his heart wrote to Reynolds:

> *Received the smelter sheet for our little dab of ore, and am very much gratified with the returns; it is even better than I expected; this was gathered up and saved in candle boxes from little streaks as we went along, and was a mixed-up lot, but I am looking for better things when we cut the vein, and it must be we are getting close to it now.*[14]

Two weeks later, on June 19, 1918, Van Horn's mood was still joyful and improving. He had received a rare letter [and a rare $1000] from A.E. who had asked rare questions about the Vermont. Work on the Vermont crosscut had ended June 13, 1915, in favor of working the Ocean Wave crosscut. At that time the Vermont crosscut was in 139 feet from Reynolds Tunnel to the raise connecting it to the historic upper workings [and natural ventilation] and thirty-two feet farther west to the breast. Believed to still contain large quantities of valuable ore, apparently it was considered a treasure trove reserved for a later day. Three years later was looking like that day had arrived. Reynolds was returning to the Vermont. His June 19th letter was filled with promise but uncertainty as well.

> *Now that you have the new drill I am anxiously watching for you to make better progress with the work; 285 feet apparently puts you vertically under the lower level in the Ocean Wave and somewhere about 375 feet, apparently puts you under the apex. There may be a possibility that the apex that Miller [surveyor] has been figuring on may be something else. I feel very much that this vein will be found to be practically vertical, and there may be a possibility also that the dip has changed at some point and is going away from you and you will have to go farther to reach it. I feel like going 100 feet from where you now are before absolutely throwing up the sponge and saying that I am defeated.*
>
> *It is a matter of great interest to me, because the burden is falling at this time on me, and I wish to see a termination of it as quickly as possible; whether we have to go 20 feet or 100 feet, so that I can make my plans to take care of my liabilities in case of a failure, which I am not yet ready to concede will happen. As you are so close to definite results in this work, I have had a talk with Mr. Hendrie and have readied an agreement with him that I can have an option*

on the Vermont property for $15,000 ($5,000 payable in one year, $10,000 payable in two years.[15]

Doesn't Reynolds' description of where he believed they stood relative to the Ocean Wave, and where to go next, read like clues written on a treasure map, or the feeble words of a proverbial buccaneer on his deathbed? Once again, despite a long list of frustrating missteps, A.E. had not lost faith in his ace-in-the-hole and the role his darling elephant played in his vision. At the same time, shrewd as always, A.E. did not want to settle up on the Vermont until he had more evidence that Ocean Wave paydirt was also within easy reach. As a hedge, in the same June 19th letter, he offered the boys an "opportunity" to share in the booty [and the risk]. In the absence of concrete results soon, A.E. seemed inclined to cut his losses "unless you people think that you would like to take the gamble even if you fail with the Ocean Wave." [At the very least, attracting someone else's jack was an essential component of his plan.] Very truly, A.E. Reynolds [16]

In 1915 when Reynolds directed that development work on the Vermont cease and all efforts should be focused on locating the Ocean Wave vein, he did so without explaining his thinking. His vision of opening the tunnel through the old Vermont workings to the surface with natural ventilation as a consequence had been achieved, but why not exploit the Vermont's likely ore as well? In 1918 Reynolds provided the answer. He was saving the proven Vermont reserves for a rainy day in favor of a slightly more inviting treasure waiting beneath the historic workings of the Ocean Wave. Apparently that rainy day had dawned.

Van Horn also knew how to hedge. Regarding Reynolds' invitation to join his gamble, he responded on June 23rd. He was in 289 feet on the north cross-vein of the Ocean Wave and still not seeing what he was searching for. As for the Vermont proposition, he advised Reynolds that "in case we make good on the Ocean Wave, I think your agreement for an option on the Vermont is a good one." Not exactly a direct answer, certainly not clear, but it was good enough.[17]

As for Reynolds' anxiety concerning making better progress, Van Horn crafted a more thoughtful, if not always encouraging, assessment that he threaded throughout his June 27th, July, and early August progress reports. On June 27, 1918, Harry wrote that there was little change in the breast. The face of the drift was still half "that hard bug-hole quartz, with a little mineral scattered through it." Not surprisingly, he needed more coal. On July 3, 1918, he reported that they were now in 300 feet, but there was no sign of the Ocean Wave vein. The last ten to twelve feet were hard bug-hole quartz. He predicted improved conditions were coming [sound familiar?] He ended on the best news he could muster: "Tomorrow being the Fourth, the boys will lay off and go to town, returning Friday evening, so we will be idle for two days."

On July 15, 1918, Harry reported ominous news. They had run out of rails and went down to the Lellie [adjacent idled mine] and "got some and had the stage man haul them up for us." Now in 311 feet, he confessed that there had been no change for the past month, except harder ground and "one of the lifters in our last round flowed so freely with water that it was difficult to load it, as the water kept pushing the powder [dynamite stick] out. The quartz streak has been so hard and difficult to drill that we have gradually turned our drift [bug-hole effect], and will now go along by the side of it for a ways and see if we cannot make better headway."

On July 17, 1918, they were in 315 feet. There was no change except more water running out of all drill holes now. They had continued to drive alongside the quartz streak. Harry invited A.E. to come down and spend a week to help size up the situation. He advised A.E. that his wife and daughter were there: "We will try and make it comfortable for you, and the weather here now is just perfect." [The frequency of Cousin Harry's reporting is significant. There is an air of expectancy—urgency really. But A.E. is more difficult to "read" than usual. On the one hand, he is funding new equipment and paying wages, on the other hand he seems prepared to end the hunt for Ocean Wave paydirt and pivot back to the Vermont vein, or even end the project all together. Also significant is Cousin Harry's invitation for A.E. and family to visit him in Lake City, a family dynamic not often seen.]

On July 21, 1918, the breast of the drift was in 320 feet, quite wet, with a little more water with each round. Harry wrote that the last round "showed quite a change in the formation."

> I mean by that, in the way it stands: it is more blocky, and has the character of rock that has been broken up at some time or other, and the seams are standing about in the right position to form the hanging wall of the vein we are driving for and the water should indicate that there is open ground ahead or that we are nearing the vein.

> [Uncharacteristically, Harry apologized for not making more progress. He again reminded A.E. that] there are only three of us, and we have to do everything there is to do. We work early and late, and often have to go back at night to shoot some missed hole, so it will not interfere with work next day. We have been having quite a lot of trouble with having shots miss fire since it has been wet, and I think it is on account of the fuse, as the last case they sent was 'BEAR' fuse instead of 'MONARCH' the kind we had formerly been using. Today we mucked and trammed eight cars, sharpened the steel, laid some track, and are already (sic) to drill again tomorrow.

> [July 25, 1918] They are in approximately 325 feet with no change, less water but quite damp. Harry reports that it is "hard to tell which way the seams are dipping, as some dip one way and some another." He wonders "aloud" if they missed crossing the vein. There was one "seam or crack, tight, back 150 feet from breast or 175 feet from main drift."

[July 29, 1918] On the premise they did miss the vein and maybe it was the seam or tight crack reported last time, they went up to the old Ocean Wave workings and into one of the lower tunnels [Dago Tunnel]. Based on "taking the dip of the vein there," Harry writes, "it seemed quite probable, at least not impossible, that the little seam I spoke of might be the vein."

They put in one round in the breast and one in this seam. The first round in this streak broke (sic) down 17 cars of muck — a lot of work — but they continued on in. Harry proposes continuing one round in the seam, one in the breast to be sure. The breast of the drift is in 330 feet, "only 45 feet from being vertically under the apex, and some distance past being vertically under the lower workings [of the Ocean Wave's Dago Tunnel], and unless it has reversed the dip, we should have had it before this."

[Harry changes subjects and addresses the "tight crack" they by-passed.] "The cross-vein we have been following is practically all in the porphyry at the point where we discovered this little seam, which is 175 feet in from the main drift, and it could be possible that it has cut the vein off, which we will determine, if you think it advisable to drive a ways on this, providing the indication should warrant, after we have put in two or three rounds. I am almost persuaded now, and if we do not get the vein ahead soon, I will feel quite certain that the vein must cross at this point."

On August 2, 1918, in the process of trying to manage his increasing confidence they were nearing their goal, Harry reported that they put one round into the breast and one into the "crack," whatever and wherever that was. There was no change in the breast, but one more charge would probably put them back into an ore streak. A little steak in the crack was still going in, one or two inches wide, and showed quartz and talc. Harry added that they had "not got away from the porphyry in the cross-vein yet." Not to overlook the troublesome matter of wages, Harry ended with "York and Ewart put in 29 shifts for July." So did Van Horn, but he was not counting and he was not being paid. On August 6th Harry reported that they started drilling in the breast of the north cross-vein but the "boys came out sick at noon from the gas; also shot over into ore streak—named it the "New Place"—and found some hard quartz and a little ore.[18]

The "New Place." Take note of this. Van Horn sent A.E. a sample of ore from there that could confirm their treasure hunt was on the right track or could condemn their entire project to the dustbin of history. Clearly the array of clues, clearly pointing in no decisive direction, clearly befuddling the crew, nevertheless held great promise. The boys were encouraged that there was treasure ahead, but which clue should they follow now? They sensed they were on the cusp of victory. They also sensed A.E. had to be running short on patience. There was no sensing about A.E. running short of cash.

Not all clues were created equal much less fruitful. And remember, Cousin Harry was a Reynolds, too. Like his uncle, he could be conflicted by conflicting clues and was increasingly so, now. After one more round Harry stopped and did not plan on continuing unless A.E. told him to do so. If told to go on, he would shoot off corners and install a switch and track. Confident A.E.'s curiosity had been sufficiently aroused, he ordered more coal and went home for the night.

"New" of course was relative. Pike Snowden had located the vein now referred to as the New Place in 1876. He could have told John York or Rowland Ewart or Harry Van Horn a long time ago where to look for it and a great deal more if they had cared to ask and he had cared to answer. Now, in the middle of 1918, it was too late to ask and it did not matter anyway. York, Ewart, and Van Horn had clumsily tumbled to it despite themselves. Why they had tunneled past it earlier without giving it proper attention was never explained, or at least documented. Tunneling in bad air by candle-light and eventually with carbide headlamps was probably reason enough to bypass a critical clue. In any event, numerous other inviting leads had distracted them to no satisfactory outcome. Considering this one with the same skepticism was a legitimate excuse, too.

With expenses mounting and still no assurances the New Place was indeed the Ocean Wave vein, Reynolds did grow more and more anxious about the prospect of more development work with no pay dirt to show for it. Sensing Reynolds' mood in faraway Denver, Harry's anxiety heightened as well. He knew his cousin's temperament. At moments like this, A.E. was apt to order a shut-down, even abandon the project entirely. His commitment to his vision of another Virginius' Revenue Tunnel had weathered nearly three decades of encouraging breakthroughs and frustrating setbacks, but the thrills of the hunt surely had limits even for A.E. Reynolds. And in Denver, far from the mines of Hinsdale County in more than distance, the effects of world war and the home front consequences of President Wilson's belated shuffle into it were beginning to take their toll.

John York also was anxious, anxious about pulling up short of the treasure he too believed in, but even more about the ever increasing amount of back pay he was owed. In this matter, Rowland Ewart stood with York. A rapid series of reports to A.E. could have mimicked their pulse rates as much as conveying what was on their minds. Having no better plan, on August 11, 1918, Van Horn reported that another shot into the New Place showed that the *"penal mark"* (sic) was becoming a vein with "quite a little quartz showing over the breast."

> *I had Ewart fire the shots while York and I went up to the old workings [Dago Tunnel] and listened to ascertain if we could locate where we were at; we got into an old stope next to the lower level, where we had a good opportunity to hear the sound from the shots; we could distinctly hear every one, and they sounded exactly in the vein below.*[19]

Imagine their excitement. The next day they shot in the breast of the north cross-cut, listened from the Ocean Wave stope, and concluded the breast was beyond the Ocean Wave vein and the New Place was where they should continue. Van Horn wrote, "I am completely discouraged about getting ore ahead in the [north] cross-vein, and unless otherwise directed, will confine our efforts for the next two weeks in driving ahead in the New Place, when I expect to come down to Denver." Feeling especially bold, he added, "Hope you have not overlooked ordering the coal." [20]

Van Horn was not "otherwise directed," and A.E. did order more coal. Work continued probably energized inflated expectations. On August 19, 1918, Van Horn reported:

> During the last week we have been working entirely in the "New Place"; had to shoot off the corners and make a switch and put it in, which of course delayed our progress in the breast, however we have gone about 24 feet altogether; the little seam continues on in, and there is some quartz, but have seen no mineral as yet; the breast is dry and tight. [Coal arrived. Van Horn was going to Denver the following week to confer with A.E. York would "take up the slack."] [21]

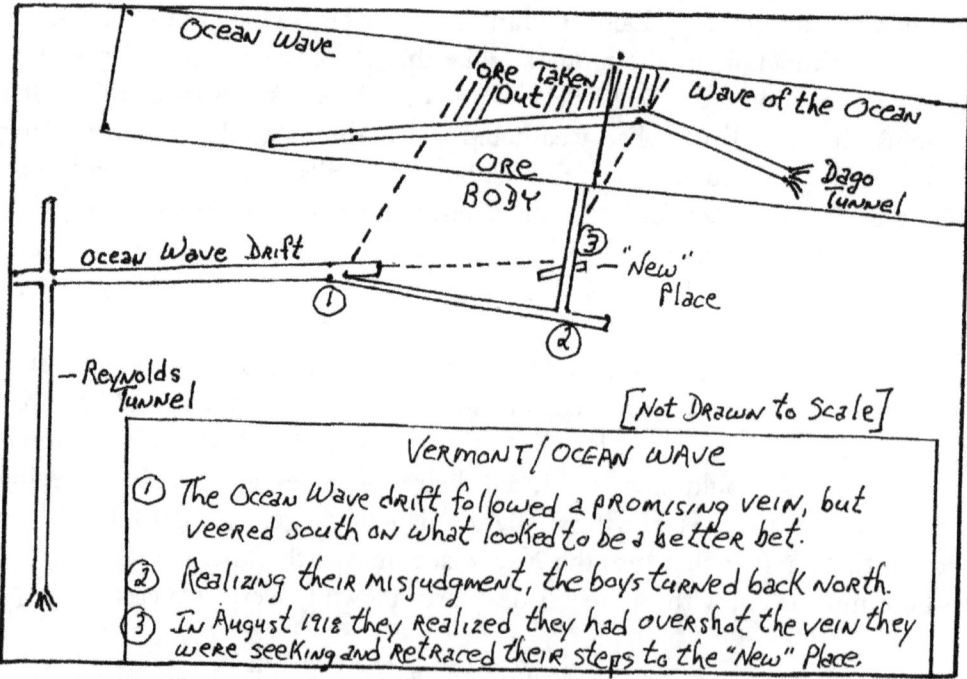

The New Place. More than one crosscut and a raise or two later and the "boys" [with A.E. Reynolds' funding and advice] returned to a vein they had bypassed. This was the same vein Pike Snowden located and Sam Jack mined in the Dago Tunnel at a higher elevation decades earlier. (Author's Collection)

On September 2, 1918, secure but uncomfortable in his familiar catbird seat, John York reported to A.E. that the New Place "looked as though the vein had split and one prong running to the left." He continued,

> *Since Harry left we have pushed this place in 13 feet. There is a quartz streak in the breast about 18 inches wide that has considerable mineral in it. I brought out this morning about a powder box full that I think would run pay. There was considerable gray copper all through it, yellow copper and lead. This place is in from the cross-cut that Mr. Abbott drove approximately 1,235 feet. According to the needle of the compass it is running 45 degrees east of north. I will put in one more round and that will be all we can do in this place without putting a track. Will start in the other place unless advised differently after I put in another round in this place. [Apparently he had been "advised differently" — he continued work on the New Place.]* [22]

In unusual fashion—at best a weekly accounting of progress could be expected—just three days later on September 5, 1918, York reported that he set off another round the day before, that the quartz streak still went ahead about the same width, and it was not yet paydirt but had quite a little lead along with yellow and gray copper.

SELECTIVE SERVICE ACT OF 1917

Abandoning neutrality—favored by a large majority of the American public—and entering into the largest and most deadly war in modern history, did not result in a rush of volunteers for military service. This was a change from prior calls to arms. One explanation was that the "Gilded Age" had introduced a mind-numbing array of technologies that included the means to graphically communicate the horrors of trench warfare along the Western Front. No wonder American enlistments were down. The National Defense Act of 1916 authorized a 165,000 man army augmented by a National Guard [state militias] of 450,000. The count in early 1917 was nowhere near these levels: 121,000 army, 181,000 national guard. Six weeks later only 73,000 had volunteered for service. The Selective Service Act of 1917 was the answer. Enacted May 18, 1917, it was designed to raise a million-man army and did so. By the end of the war two million men had volunteered and an additional 2.8 million had been drafted. Indicative of its unpopularity, the Act was promptly cancelled on November 11, 1918, the very day the war ended.

Initially, all men aged 21 to 30 were required to register for military service. In August 1918 Congress amended the law to raise the age to forty-five. When John E. York took a day off without pay to register he was fifty.

The lifters make water and a little moisture shows higher up in the breast; outside of the quartz streak the formation is stratified and is almost perpendicular. We have neither wall yet. As we can put in another round very nicely I think it best to do it while we have the tools and machine there. [Almost as a footnote, York added that he needed to go into town September 12th to register for the draft under the new "military Draft Law" — he wanted paid before he goes.] [23]

York missed having Van Horn run interference for him with A.E. during Harry's stay in Denver. Despite the distraction of the promising New Place, a tense working relationship surfaced again. Reynolds was his normal self, York was not. Rather than communicating with A.E directly, on September 7, 1918, York resorted to reporting to Friend Harry.

Friend Harry. Sending a sample of high grade ore, albeit small amount; encouraged, on the right track at last; more gray copper shows up each round; have two days of mucking and getting bottom taken up so that we can get the track on a grade. August shifts: York 31; Van Horn 27; Ewart 29½. [24]

Apparently in a better mood, at least a patriotic mood, and probably in response to an A.E. inquiry directed at him, early on September 12, 1918, York wrote to A.E. that twenty-one feet of track was in the New Place. There were still small streaks of lead. He expected yellow and gray copper in stratified formations for a few more rounds, then a change for the better. Almost as an afterthought, he reminded Reynolds he had an appointment with the Selective Service: "I have to go to town today and register my kick against the Kaiser so will lose today." [25]

Remembering the Lusitania. The military draft was incredibly unpopular when introduced to isolationist America. A concerted public relations campaign reaching back to the Lusitania appealed to patriotism and moral justice. It resulted in a United States military establishment befitting an emerging world power.[26] *(Casey MacLean, National Oceanic and Atmospheric Administration)*

Notes — Chapter Four: Bug-Holes

1 August 25, 1917, MSS 1220, Box 18, FF 1334.
2 G. Thomas Ingham was a self-taught mining engineer, geologist before there was a geology discipline, and author of *Digging Gold Among the Rockies*, a 19th century historical and scientific "textbook" filled with explanations that remain valid to this day.
3 July 8-August 12, 1917, MSS 1220, Box 18, FF 1329-1333.
4 September 2, 1917, MSS 1220, Box 18, FF 1335.
5 September 14-17, 1917, MSS 1220, Box 18, FF 1336.
6 September 16, 1917, MSS 1220, Box 18, FF 1336.
7 September 17, 1917, MSS 1220, Box 18, FF 1336.
8 October 2, 1917, MSS 1220, Box 18, FF 1338.
9 October 21, 1917, MSS 1220, Box 18, FF 1340.
10 November 18-December 9, 1917, MSS 1220, Box 18, FF 1342-1344,
11 January 7-February 18, 1918, MSS 1220, Box 18, FF 1347-1351.
12 March 3-March 20, 1918, MSS 1220, Box 18, FF 1353-1354.
13 March 24-April 29, 1918, MSS 1220, Box 18, FF 1355-1358.
14 June 5, 1918, MSS 1220, Box 19, FF 1362.
15 June 19, 1918, MSS 1220, Box 19, FF 1363.
16 Ibid.
17 June 23, 1918, MSS 1220, Box 19, FF 1364.
18 June 27-August 6, 1918, MSS 1220, Box 19, FF 1364-1368.
19 August 11, 1918, MSS 1220, Box 19, FF 1369.
20 Ibid.
21 August 19, 1918, MSS 1220, Box 19, FF 1369.
22 September 2, 1918, MSS 1220, Box 19, FF 1371.
23 September 5, 1918, MSS 1220, Box 19, FF 1371.
24 September 7, 1918, MSS 1220, Box 19, FF 1371.
25 September 12, 1918, MSS 1220, Box 19, FF 1372.
26 Early in 1915 German U-boats sank three American merchant ships. Wilson, still wanting to believe neutrality was possible and wise, considered these incidents to be "accidents" whose "claims" could be settled later. Imagine, "accidents" and "claims." In May 1915, the British passenger liner *RMS Lusitania* was torpedoed resulting in the deaths of 1,198 civilians including 128 Americans. Wilson's confidence in the sanctity of his concept of neutrality was shaken but not shattered. Germany managed to promise to be more careful. In March 1916, a German submarine sank the *SS Sussex*, a French ferry with four Americans aboard, in the English Channel. Wilson complained. Germany, not quite ready to deal with a hostile America, pledged to limit attacks to warships and did so for the better part of that year. Anglophiles and fellow hawks of all persuasions still called for retribution. There was none. Afterall, it was a French ferry in the English Channel with only four Americans aboard. "The poor souls should have known better in the first place," would have been a common response.

CHAPTER 5

Wilson's War

I have a rendezvous with Death
At some disputed barricade,
When Spring comes back with rustling shade
And apple-blossoms fill the air—
I have a rendezvous with Death
When Spring brings back blue days and fair.

It may be he shall take my hand
And lead me into his dark land
And close my eyes and quench my breath—
It may be I shall pass him still.
I have a rendezvous with Death
On some scarred slope of battered hill,
When Spring comes round again this year
And the first meadow-flowers appear.

God knows 'twere better to be deep
Pillowed in silk and scented down,
Where Love throbs out in blissful sleep,
Pulse nigh to pulse, and breath to breath,
Where hushed awakenings are dear…
But I've a rendezvous with Death
At midnight in some flaming town,
When Spring trips north again this year,
And I to my pledged word am true,
I shall not fail that rendezvous.

— Alan Seeger —

Pausing our treasure tale to address the state of world affairs suddenly imposed on it cannot be avoided. Even in retrospect, even with a century to reflect, it is difficult to appreciate otherwise how profound were the impacts of World War I (WWI), the Spanish flu pandemic, and the Great Depression, on the values and expectations of our Lake City and Henson Canyon pilgrims. Poems like Alan Seeger's *I Have a Rendezvous With Death* help, but you will have to take my word for it. Sadly, the spiritual darkness that relentlessly assaulted young America's frontier independence and dogged this generation's once confident steps rarely found expression in their words. The transformation of the nation lurched forward with WWI, a war unlike any other war America had witnessed. By the time it ended it would restructure the nation's economy and how the government intervened in the affairs of its people.

The dawn of the twentieth-century introduced an age of wars and threats of wars, unprecedented inflation, disease, and depression that were armed with the means to threaten civilization wherever civilization could be found. Isolated mining villages with their dank hard rock mines were no exceptions. European and Asian empires on collision courses for centuries finally erupted in mortal combat over matters large and small. The consequences were unimaginable, consequences amplified by innovative technologies and an intensity of nationalism that would roil the earth to its core for decades to come. Hardship and sacrifice reached far beyond battlefields, landing hard on a working class accustomed to three-dollar wages for a twelve hour day. All of it landed with emotional effects held quietly within the hearts of every soul, evident only in the troubled stares and willing sacrifices of every household.

America's first industrial-age wakeup call took the form of protest marches and strikes. Some of them were violent, but all of them had limited effect. Not until WWI did the cumulative weight of social imbalances close ranks with global grievances to shake the nation to its core. Previous wars with Mexico and Spain were no match for the scope of destruction or the emergence of a military-industrial complex[1] to contend with it. The familiar American experience, the San Juans' and Lake City's way of life, would never be the same. A wartime economy required a bigger and more intrusive federal government that by its very nature required a bigger and bigger share of the nation's and the individual's resources. By its very nature—unprecedented federal largesse, progressive welfare by another name—ensured that the economy and thus society could not return to its former self once war was ended. It also ensured that the value of silver would never exceed the cost of mining it. Understandable in hindsight, this harsh reality did not land until the end of a second and even worse world war.

A dark and deadly world, indeed. Woodrow Wilson was not born into such a place. He did not grow up in a society accustomed to intrigue and war like most of the rest of the world had always known. He was an isolationist and a pacificist long before he was an American politician and wartime president in a conflict

President Woodrow Wilson. Reluctant as he was, America's entry into World War I redefined the nation's international role. Failing to persuade Congress to authorize America's entry into the League of Nations redefined the nation's international role yet again. *(Public Domain)*

that truly circled the globe. He did not start WWI, but from the vantage point of a nation divided on the matter, he soon owned it and the new balance of global power that it would spawn.

Not afflicted with an abundance of humility, once shamed into action Woodrow Wilson rose to the occasion in stark ways culminating in 1917 with formal entry into the war. Once shamed into action, he embraced the opportunity to reshape the geopolitical world into a caricature to his liking. More relevant to our treasure tale, his national and international practices and policies could not help but shape the future of Colorado's San Juans mining heritage. Make no mistake about it, they did. In his wake Wilson left the rest of us with the federal income tax, the Federal Reserve [central banking system based on Federal Reserve Notes in lieu of silver or gold certificates], the Federal Trade Commission, the Internal Revenue Service, and two constitutional amendments making "Prohibition" [later repealed] and "Women's Suffrage" the law of the land. None of these "social reforms" sat well with the San Juans "immigrant class."

Early Twentieth-Century America was a simmering melting pot of millions of newly-arrived immigrants from around the globe and millions of native-born Americans who still cherished their immigrant roots. The pot simmered in the midst of a society that included the San Juans struggling to keep up with radical changes—agrarian to industrial, rural to urban—propelled by the rapid and seemingly endless introduction of amazing new technologies. Motorized vehicles spooked horses off byways, flying machines soared with the eagles, and radio broadcasts competed with old-school newsprint to be the first to herald the glories and the gore of the preceding day.

Seasoning the melting pot was a vibrant culture of American patriotism largely the product of several generations of westering and several episodes of military conflict on the southwestern frontier. European powers infringing on American hegemony in the Western Hemisphere had provoked the young nation into enforcing its Monroe Doctrine, further evidence of the popular belief in America's God-given manifest destiny. Only when conflicts arose between expansionist America and Old World powers-at-large was American single-ness of purpose questioned. This was the WWI geopolitical world Woodrow T. Wilson had to navigate. He was leader of a population with heritages nurtured in countries at war with one another—Lake City and Henson Canyon mines experienced the same cultural tensions. In 1917, on the 6th of April, President Wilson took sides and entered the nation into their suffering. With approval of an overwhelming majority of the Congress—he did not have even a simple

THOMAS WOODROW WILSON

(December 28, 1856 – February 3, 1924)

Thomas Woodrow Wilson, rarely called Thomas, never called Woody, was the third (first son) of four children born to Joseph Ruggles Wilson and Jessie Janet Woodrow. His paternal grandfather migrated in 1807 from County Tyrone, Ireland, and published a pro-tariff and anti-slavery newspaper, *The Western Herald and Gazette*, in Steubenville, Ohio. His maternal grandfather, the Reverend Thomas Woodrow, migrated in the late 1830s from Scotland to Chillicothe, Ohio. Joseph and Jesse met and married in Steubenville. Soon thereafter Joseph was ordained a Presbyterian minister. Two years later the family moved to Augusta, Georgia, then to Columbia, South Carolina in 1870.

The Wilsons were loyal supporters of the Confederate States of America. After the war, Joseph became a theology professor at the Columbia Theological Seminary and Woodrow went off to Davidson College and then to Princeton University where he studied political philosophy and history. He attended the University of Virginia law school, dropped out due to health issues, and eventually abandoned law as a career in favor of higher education. He earned his Ph.D. at Johns Hopkins University and taught at a number of colleges and universities before entering the political arena. His academic writings and his progressive reforms including Princeton University policies and practices elevated him to nationwide attention.

Bolstered by the University's prestige, Wilson attracted a nationwide audience for his progressive views on higher education. Active in Democrat Party politics, ten years later he was governor of New Jersey where he attracted an even broader audience for progressive reforms. Never burdened by a paucity of ambition, he successfully cobbled together a coalition of progressives and Southerners to win the 1912 presidential election, narrowly won re-election in 1916, and was awarded the Nobel Peace Prize in 1919 for his role in ending WWI. (*"Woodrow Wilson," Wikipedia*) majority of support from a divided American public—President Wilson committed America to the fortunes of Britain, France, and their allies.[2]

Most American's had taken great comfort in remaining neutral, comfort in avoiding what could justifiably be seen as another European war among proud, power-hungry monarchs and dictators. United States national interests would not be served by an American dog in their fight. A strong voice to the contrary were those of British descent, also a large percentage of the population who long ago had gotten over their own battles with the British crown. On the opposite end of the public opinion seesaw, as one might expect, were those of Irish descent, Ireland which had a long and current history of its own problems with British rule. German Americans had even greater conflicts of conscience, nevertheless heritage was mitigated by a growing sense that the Kaiser's excesses, notably unrestricted submarine warfare and alleged battlefield atrocities, did not reflect their values.[3]

The national debate was complex, hotly executed, and indecisive in the end. Local newspapers, usually stingy when it came to allocating column inches to national much less global affairs, dutifully reported the ebbs and flows of Europe's war and the nation's debate. Some of the loudest voices were staunch isolationists, non-interventionists, pacificists for moral or nationalistic reasons. Not only had their European forebearers warred against each other for centuries and the current conflict was just a continuation of their corrupt and colonizing nature, those

Unrestricted Submarine Warfare. Despite persistent calls for maintaining neutrality, moral if not materialistic outrage over German sinking of trans-Atlantic merchant and passenger vessels began tipping the scale of American public and political opinion in favor of declaring war on Germany. *(Willy Stower, Library of Congress)*

very features of their native lands were precisely what they fled to America to avoid. In short, they sought new beginnings where independence and individualism could thrive, where socialism and historic hatreds had not taken root much less bloomed. They were not inclined to return to Old World ways.

Long frustrated Anglophiles rejoiced upon learning the nation was entering the war. First-generation Germans, their new American families, and their forebearers, quietly sympathized with their former homeland's battles on the Eastern Front against Tzarist Russia but remained more passive regarding the Western Front.[4] In light of German submarine atrocities, even the Irish, typically hostile to British interests, were largely content to leave their grievances with the British in the hands of their European cousins. Italy was allied with the Western Powers, likewise Lake City's Italians had no complaints. Gradually the horrors of trench warfare and the loss of life at sea would overcome any lingering ambiguities and divided loyalties, first among the political class, then among most citizens at-large. A final nudge into war if it was needed came in the form of a German telegram.[5]

"The German Telegram," Zimmermann's telegram, surfaced in February 1917, just weeks before America's April 6th declaration of war. Whether or not Germany's decision to resume unrestricted submarine warfare would have been enough to persuade President Wilson and Congress to declare war is not clear. Discovery of Germany's plan to entice Mexico to invade the United States—spelled

Pancho Villa. General Francisco Villa, larger-than-life Mexican patriot or bandit depending upon the year in question or who was asked, brought a heightened sense of danger to the state of U.S.- German affairs on the brink of America's entry into WWI. His 1916 raid on Columbus, New Mexico heightened a sense of danger throughout the Southwest. *(Wikipedia)*

out in Zimmermann's telegram—put the matter in a far clearer light. In fact, the German initiative was so well-conceived and cunning that even the most committed isolationist could not continue arguing that neutrality was a sustainable policy. A Mexican invasion, after all, was plausible, and its intended objectives if achieved would be catastrophic. Was there not a century of territorial grievances. Wasn't California and the Southwest part of Mexico just a few short decades ago? Did not Pancho Villa's raiders just months earlier terrorize American border communities and evade America's year-long "Punitive Expeditionary Force?" Should not San Juans and Lake City militias be alarmed? America's southwestern border was clearly porous, and America's military was poorly equipped to do anything about it. In 1916 Pancho Villa demonstrated Mexico posed a credible threat to the homeland.[6] In 1917 Germany's "Zimmerman Telegram" demonstrated that where there was a will, there was a way Germany could help.

The Zimmerman Telegram was an encrypted instruction from the German Foreign Office in Berlin sent in January 1917 to the German Ambassador in Mexico. It directed the Ambassador to propose an alliance between Germany

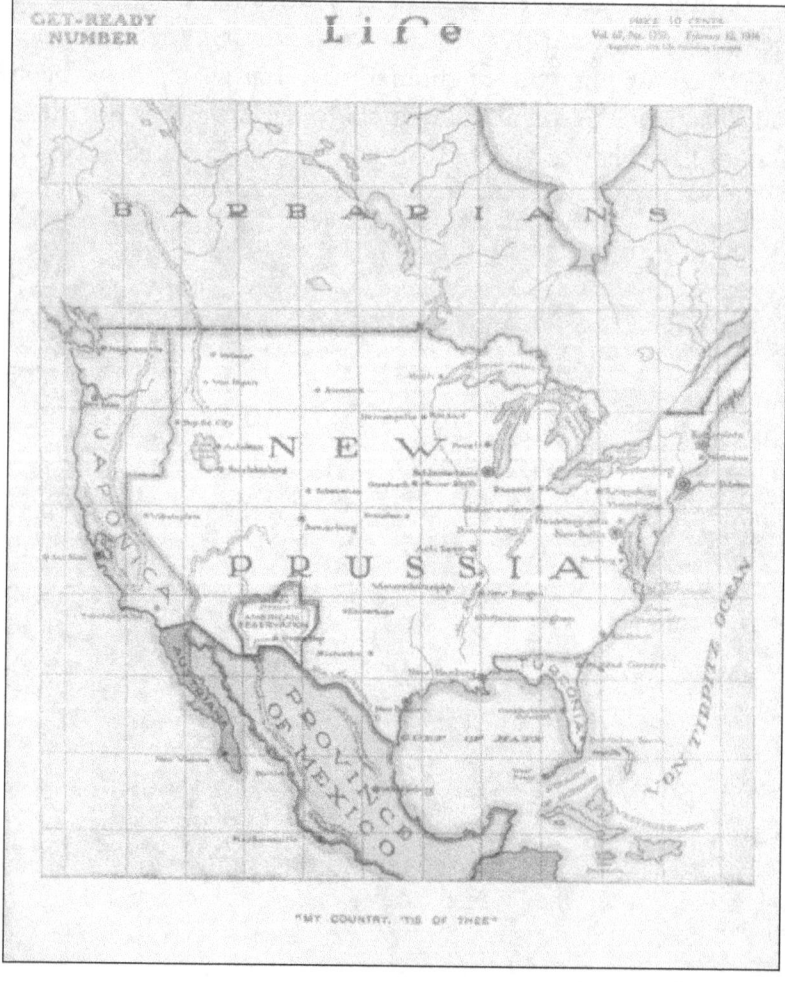

Imperial Germany's Plan for the Americas. German global ambitions knew no bounds. *Life Magazine* captured this sentiment in a satirical rendering of North America on its February 10, 1916, cover. German ambitions were no secret to Americans at-large. *("American Entry Into WWI," Wikipedia)*

Zimmermann's Telegram Backfires.
Germany understood their national survival was at stake. Bringing Mexico into WWI on their side could be decisive. Attempting to exploit lingering Mexican resentments over the loss of their northern territories [California and America's Southwest] in the 1848-49 Mexican-American War, this German initiative demonstrated the extent they were willing to go to keep America off European battlefields. Discovery of the plot had the opposite effect. *(Kirby in the New York World,)*

and Mexico that would result in Mexico recovering Texas, Arizona, and New Mexico. Enlisting "Old Mexico" in Germany's cause was not a piper's dream.

Zimmermann's Telegram was intercepted and decrypted by British intelligence. Thought by some to be a clever British attempt to draw the United States into the war, in the end it was deemed authentic [inexplicably it also was acknowledged publicly to be genuine by Arthur Zimmerman, its German author]. The die was cast. It accomplished what the 1915 sinking of the RMS Lusitania and scores of ships thereafter had not accomplished. It united the United States behind a delayed but vigorous mobilization of immense industrial resources and the recruitment of a million-man army. It united the country and Lake City in support of rationing, war bonds, and registering for a first-ever military draft.

Unappreciated at the time, what would become recognized as a president's right to exercise extraordinary "war powers" would be at the expense of everyone else's civil rights. Also unappreciated at the time, there would be no retreat from this realignment of rights after the war ended. "Big government" had come calling. So had sovereign debt and inflation, so much so that silver and gold-backed currency would become an artifact of times past. Promising silver mining opportunities in Hinsdale County would become artifacts, too. [7]

There were more unwelcome consequences. Recognizing inflation would soar, the Wilson Administration further raised taxes. This would do nothing to dampen the rate of increase—in fact it would fuel it—but it would service the nation's immediate need. It would provide increased revenues needed to offset the rising costs of funding the new government programs. The War Revenue Act of 1917 and the Revenue Act of 1918 established a top income tax rate of seventy-seven percent, increased the number of citizens subject to income tax, and taxed "excess profits" of businesses. Not enough, the Treasury Department issued low-interest, tax-free bonds. These were so attractive—they were deemed totally secure and their tax-free feature more than compensated for their low interest rate—that their purchase volume also increased the nation's inflation even more. Lake City patriots and businesses were not likely to be affected by higher tax rates and excess profits—most probably did not pay any taxes—but tax-free bonds were another matter. Buying bonds was a way everyone could contribute to the war effort.

To counter the conflicted public discontent, conflicted both by the battlefield carnage with no seeming end and by Wilson's newfound belief America needed to join it, in 1917 the President created the Committee on Public Information, ostensibly a public service organization, but in the minds of some a propaganda

INFLATION

Not totally unknown, along with World War I came unprecedented inflation. European rivalries seemed of little consequence to Henson Canyon cousin-jacks and mossbacks trying to get by on four to five dollars a day if anything—but they were far from immune to the corrosive effects of inflation on their quality of life and ultimately it contributed to their inability to remain in Hinsdale County. In 1900 the county population was 1,609. In 1920 it was 538.

In addition to the classical driver of inflation—too many dollars chasing too few goods—the influx of European gold to pay for massive munitions imports and the simultaneous U.S. transition to a wartime economy introduced rationing of essential commodities and the transitioning of industrial production from civilian to military outputs. The transition was economy-wide, but perhaps most dramatic in heavy industry. Increasingly popular motorized cars and trucks were sidelined by newly popular battlefield half-tracks and tanks. For Colorado miners, evolving priorities replaced interest in gold and silver with interest in lead, copper, zinc, and molybdenum. Suppliers struggled to keep up with increased demand. The two-edged sword of inflating prices, at the same time a cause and a cure, did their best to impose an unpopular equilibrium clearly seen on the shelves of every country store.

Federal spending surged as America prepared for combat. Outlays for troops, weapons, and munitions increased fifteen-fold from 1916 to 1920. According to the U.S. Bureau of Labor Statistics, food prices between 1911 and 1920 more than doubled. A steep increase in the rate of inflation began in 1916. The 12-month change rose from 3.3 percent in January to double-digits by October. "Prices rose at an 18.5 percent annualized rate from December 1916 to June 1920, increasing more than 80 percent during that period." [8]

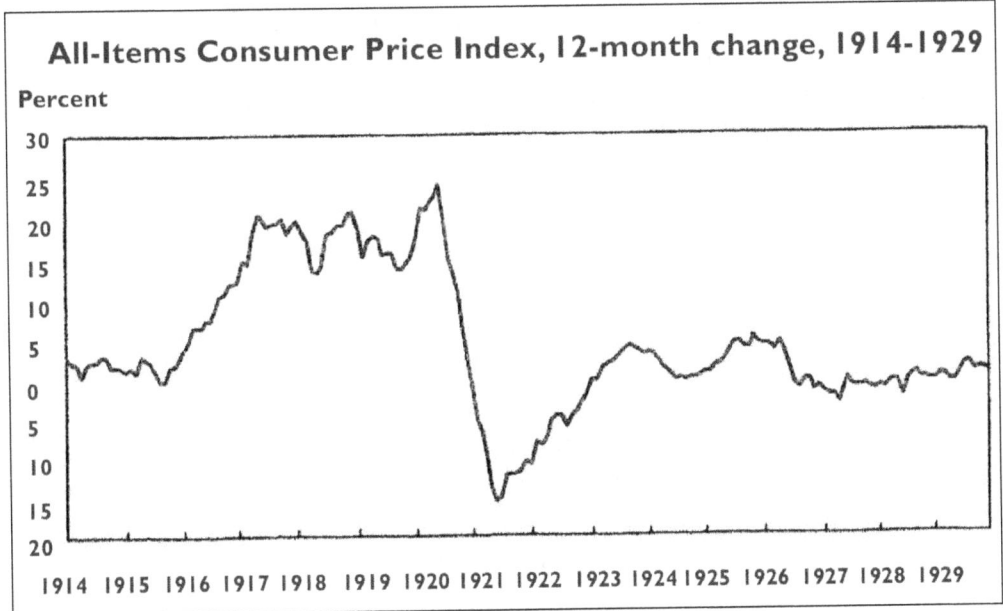

All-Items Consumer Price Index, 12-month change, 1914-1929

Percent

Inflation and Deflation Rock The Nation. WWI inflation followed by deep and persistent deflation set the stage for America's Great Depression. Remote Hinsdale County, comfortably protected by Fortress San Juans, would not escape the wrath of the war, its pandemic, and the global depression that followed. *(Stephen B. Reed, U.S. Bureau of Labor Statistics)*

service empowered to censor and label as disinformation any opinion that challenged the government's point of view. For those now committed to subjecting the nation to war on behalf of the Allies, it was sorely needed. America had to be protected from demoralizing enemy propaganda, some of which could come from ethnic sources within the country. To the contrary, America needed to be informed of Allied accomplishments. For those of a libertarian persuasion, the Committee on Public Information—even the title reeked of totalitarian control—was a dangerous tool and a threat to free speech, indeed a threat to a free and informed citizenry. In prior wars demoralizing discourse was more likely to enter the public square, during WWI there would be little of it tolerated in Lake City.[9]

Colorado throughout WWI was a microcosm of the Midwest and the mountain mining West. Emotions and loyalties were mixed and predictable. Based on 1910 federal census data, 16% of the state's population of 799,024 residents were foreign-born. Those of German and Austrian heritage numbered 28,000. English and Scottish accounted for 17,000, Italians 14,000. Most Americans of German lineage did not identify with Wilson's lofty ideals. Nor were Scandinavian or Irish-Catholic communities with British grievances of their own inclined to sign on. Neither were Protestant denominations prepared to abandon their pacificist principles—likewise the women's suffrage movement. The labor movement saw themselves as likely cannon-fodder.

In crass economic terms, WWI would prosper Colorado's agriculture and mineral interests. Some predicted a rebound in silver values. This did not happen. Some abhorred the thought of profiting from the carnage unfolding before them. This did happen. Two prominent Denver personalities in this camp were Ben Lindsey, nationally known for promoting "juvenile justice," and Helen Ring Robinson, the first woman elected to Colorado's State Senate. They sailed with Ford to Europe on Henry's failed peace mission. Ben Salmon, another Colorado anti-war activist, stayed home and passed out leaflets reminding Denverites of Wilson's pledge to keep the nation out of the war. When Wilson reversed course, so did Ben Linsey and Helen. Patriotism trumped pacificism. Helen toured the Front Range and the Western Slope promoting war bonds—Colorado patriots invested $150 million in them—and Ben toured the Western Front encouraging the troops. [10]

Naturally in a nation of immigrants, America's war decision was agonizing and far from unanimous. Three hundred seventy four Congressmen voted for it. Two of Colorado's four Congressmen—Benjamin Hilliard of Denver and Edward Keating of Pueblo—with 48 other mostly midwestern and southern representatives voted against it. Neither predictable nor surprising, Hilliard and Keating were defeated in their next election. Equally unpredictable but no doubt surprising, the cost in Colorado lives was high—1,009 according to historian LeRoy Hafen. Poet Alan Seeger honored their sacrifice with his prophetic *I have a rendezvous with Death*. LeRoy Hafen honored their sacrifice with this insightful praise.[11] The sentiment of both was not lost on our Lake Fork pioneers.

Never before had the people at home taken such a part in a war and never had they accomplished so much. Without raising invidious distinctions, the soldiers from Colorado [Lake City included] were the finest product of the great West. They had the boldness of the great mountains governed by the spirit of initiative and enterprise. They incorporated the character of the country which they represented. One who saw the soldiers from all parts of the country said, "They were of unsurpassed physique, hardy and enduring." The men of the mines and the ranches, the forests and the factories, the shop, the office and the store and the college seemed to have assimilated from this wonderful climate and the stimulating air, power and resolution and the spirit to conquer.

On the average our men [General Pershing's American Expeditionary Forces] received six months training in this country, two months in camps in Europe, and remained one month in a quiet sector before entering the battle line. A few weeks after we entered the war, at the urgent request of our allies, we began to ship troops overseas. The first contingent of troops arrived in France, June 26, 1917. The second a month later, on July 27th. The Forty-Second (Rainbow) Division containing National Guardsmen from every state including Colorado landed in France, November 30, 1917. During the year 1918 the troop movement reached enormous proportions. But the miracle of transporting 2,000,000 soldiers to Europe in a few months reaching a maximum in July 1918, when more than 10,000 a day embarked from our ports, has been so often and so well told by so many others that it does not need to be repeated here.

On October 21, 1917, Americans first entered the battle line in the quiet Toul sector, and at first here and elsewhere they were attached to the forces of the allies. It was not till May 28, 1918, that they made their first attack in force when they took Cantigny. Germany had been contemptuous of our military prowess, and ridiculed us as a money-seeking and luxury-loving nation. The Germans did not believe we would be able to create an army, and transport it to Europe before they had won the decision.

Our Allies hoped we would stand the test of battle-but they did not know till they could see us in action. But after our men had been tried and not found wanting Germany had a sudden and disappointing reversal of judgment. Our Allies, who had nearly reached the breaking point, were greatly cheered. and elated and our people at home were proud, and the judgment of our optimists was fully justified. [12]

WWI hostilities ended November 11, 1918 with an Armistice,[13] but the specter of mass worldwide casualties did not end. The new enemy was not a foreign army, it was a plague. Emotionally, America was conditioned to celebrate the end of a horrific decade with optimism and goodwill. Standing in the way of what would become the Roaring Twenties—a decade of indulgences and renewed confidence in the wisdom of speculative investments in Henson Canyon mines—was a pandemic that came to be known as the Spanish flu.

The horror began in Spain, or maybe China or Camp Funston in Kansas, no one could be certain.[14] What is certain is the alleged origin of the flu was pinned on Spain because Spanish authorities, unlike wartime leaders everywhere else, did not censor early newspaper accounts of the deadly outbreak spreading throughout their country. Before the flu ran its course, some five-hundred million people around the world—one-third of the world's total population—would be infected. Fifty million including 675,000 Americans would die. And protesting Spain would don the mantle of scapegoat. For those who valued certainties, comfort was only found in knowing that what became known as the deadliest plague in world history [up to that time] was the unquestioned handmaiden of what became known as history's deadliest war [up to that time]. There was one more certainty. The flu gave no quarter. No corner of the populated earth would be spared its wrath, not even the remote San Juans.

The speed and ferociousness of the flu's advance was part of the terror. According to author John Barry:

Although the influenza pandemic stretched over two years, perhaps two-thirds of the deaths occurred in a period of twenty-four weeks, and more than half of those deaths occurred in even less time, from mid-September to early December 1918. Influenza killed more people in a year than the Black Death of the Middle Ages killed in a century; it killed more people in twenty-four weeks than AIDS has killed in twenty-four years.[15]

Of the 675,000 American's who succumbed to the flu, Colorado contributed more than its fair share. Eric Twitty in *Basins of Silver* explains. Remote communities would fare better than congested cities, but isolation did not ensure safety. It did improve the odds. Towns in the San Juans, some blessed with bold leaders, a doctor or two who believed distance was a remedy, and time to react, yielded early positive results. But even for the duller class, the seriousness of the disease was unmistakable by September/October 1918.

Responses varied state to state. There was no nationwide authority to standardize public health—that day was coming—not to mention from jurisdiction to jurisdiction within each state. Record-keeping was spotty, but some contrasts can be deduced. The common success factors seemed to be population density and the extent to which a community was willing to sacrifice personal liberties. Lake City with a population of five-hundred or so residents posted armed guards, sealing off the town and quarantining anyone who dared challenge their authority. According to Barry, no flu deaths were reported in Lake City. On the other hand, Twitty continues, neighboring Silverton with perhaps two-thousand residents and numerous active mines nearby—forty or so miles from Lake City by way of a treacherous mountain road—instead only ordered businesses closed.

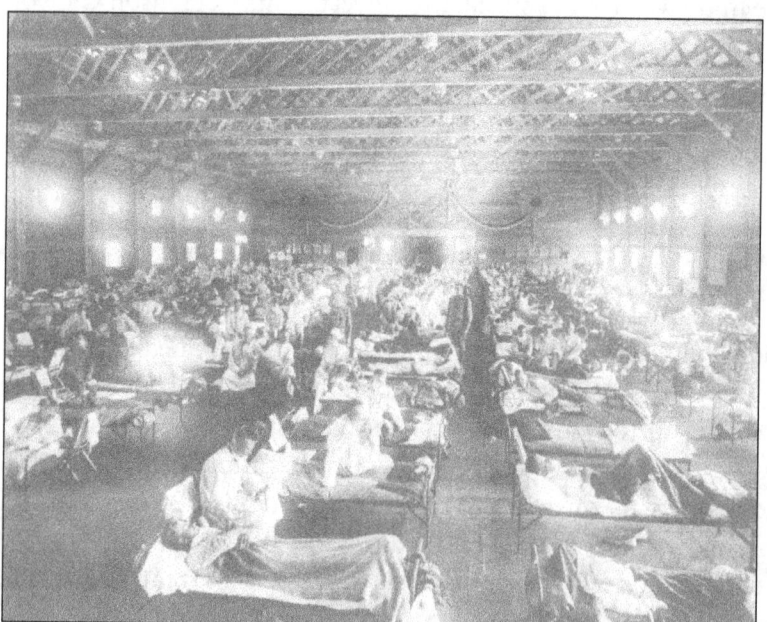

Camp Funston. Taken circa 1918, this emergency hospital like others attempting to cope with the widespread outbreak of the deadliest influenza in centuries could do little but ease terminal suffering. *(National Museum of Health and Medicine)*

In one week the flu killed 125 there.[16] A short distance away, Ouray "set up a 'shot gun quarantine,' hiring guards to keep miners from Silverton and Telluride out. But the virus reached Ouray as well [number of deaths unknown]." [17]

Gunnison, fifty miles north of Lake City, defied even steeper odds. Far from being tiny and isolated, Gunnison was a San Juans regional supply hub, railroad town, and home of Western State Teachers College. Faced with daunting vulnerabilities, the City Fathers took aggressive actions. In early October Gunnison along with smaller nearby communities banned all public gatherings, followed by a quarantine of the entire town.

> *Gunnison lawmen blocked all through roads. Train conductors warned all passengers that if they stepped foot on the platform in Gunnison to stretch their legs, they would be arrested and quarantined for five days. Two Nebraskans trying simply to drive through to a town in the next county ran the blockade and were thrown into jail. Meanwhile, the nearby town of Sargents suffered six deaths in a single day—out of a total population of 130.[18]*

To its credit, contrary to nationwide newspaper efforts to avert panic, the *Gunnison News-Chronicle*, minced no words: "This disease is no joke, to be made light of, but a terrible calamity." [19]

Gunnison recorded no flu fatalities. Farther afield, Monument and Ignacio, Colorado not only banned all public gatherings, they banned customers from entering stores. Stores could remain open, but orders were shouted from the streets and set outside by the shopkeepers.[20]

The public at large was fair game for the plague, but miners were the prize. Vulnerable to infection from conditions affecting most everyone else, they were especially vulnerable in close quarters, high altitude, extreme cold, unheated buildings, and foul air in their underground workings. Twitty writes:

> *From the moment a miner entered the workplace, he was exposed to a raft of biological and mineralogical respiratory offenses that put his whole system on the defensive. In addition, the underground environment was cold and damp, the work hard, and the commute from the tunnel portal to the safety of the boardinghouse frigid, especially when the miner was saturated with water and sweat. Physically taxed by a combination of these conditions, the miner was predisposed to pathogenic illnesses that were easily transmitted in crowded boardinghouses.[21]*

The curse did not lift in October. It would rebound in November with even greater vengeance, and not retreat decisively for another season or more. In addition to the loss of human life the toll included the loss of the economic health of the entire region.

Women packed their families, miners left, and mining companies closed wither out of sanitary reasons or because attrition reduced their workforces to skeleton crews. The situation grew so severe that the conservative Engineering & Mining Journal *was moved to state, "Spanish influenza caused more than 130 deaths in Silverton district in the last three weeks. Mines shut down will have difficulty in resuming normal operations owing to labor shortage, many miners having left camp. Epidemic appears under control."* [22]

In keeping with the somber epitaph that it was, Twitty adds that "most of the public halls and buildings became infirmaries and morgues. As the dead accumulated, the plain coffins were exhausted, forcing flu committees to bury the bodies in wooden boxes and even blankets. In January and March of 1919, two more waves of contagion swept through the region, leaving Silverton as an epicenter of despair."[23] Lake City and Henson Canyon escaped the worst of it, but the Vermont/Ocean Wave crew did not.

The November issue of the *Engineering & Mining Journal* had been premature regarding the end of the nation's flu season, but Wilson's war did in fact end in November. With the Armistice signed on the 11th, the world's great powers set aside their weapons but could still not breathe easier. The flu pandemic would not release its death-grip for a while longer. Both had managed to touch the San Juans in horrifying ways. Neither had spared John York's best efforts to make Reynolds' last best chance a bonanza mine.

Notes — Chapter Five: Wilson's War

[1] America's entry into WWI initiated alliances among the federal government and American manufacturers (e.g. steel and chemical giants like Bethlehem and Dupont). Prior to this need to "catch up," government was responsible. President Dwight D. Eisenhower is credited with institutionalizing this term by warning the nation of the dangers inherent in an unbridled military-industrial complex.

[2] The Allied Powers included Australia, Canada, Ceylon, Egypt, New Zealand, India, South Africa, Russia, Japan, and Italy. The Central Powers include Germany, Austria-Hungary, the Ottoman Empire (Turkey), and Bulgaria.

[3] German submarines sank ten American-flagged merchant ships between Germany's February 3, 1917, announcement of their resumption of unrestricted submarine warfare and the United States declaration of war on April 6, 1917.

[4] The trench warfare fought between German-held territory and the rest of Western Europe was commonly referred to as the Western Front.

[5] MacLean, Casey, "World War I on the Homefront," *National Marine Sanctuaries*, NOAA, May 2018. The war would end eighteen months later, but not before America lost 200 U.S. merchant ships, 53,000 troops on the battlefield, and 63,000 more in hospital care. More devastating still would be the hundreds of thousands of deaths due to an influenza outbreak that the war would fan into a global pandemic.

[6] In 1911 Mexican liberals overthrew the military dictatorship of Porfirio Diaz. This development—one less tyrant the better—fit neatly into Wilson's progressive [meaning pacifist] worldview. Soon thereafter, Mexican conservatives in a coup led by Victoriano Huerta overthrew

Mexico's new liberal government. This did not fit into Wilson's worldview. He declared Huerta's government illegitimate and insisted there be democratic elections. Of course there was not. Nevertheless, Huerta was forced to flee the country and Venustiano Carranza replaced him. More to his liking, Wilson recognized the Carranza government in October 1915. Wilson approved of Carranza, but a veteran Mexican General by the name of Pancho Villa did not. Civil war ensued. In short order Villa destabilized Mexico. Unintended or uncaring, he also destabilized the American southwest. Unwisely, in early 1916 Pancho Villa's forces raided Columbus, New Mexico. "Enough was enough."

7 Wilson's pacificist nature weakened with the sinking of every merchant ship. Stepping closer to the interventionist camp, he lent his voice to the "preparedness movement," first by addressing the pitifully weak condition of the army and navy. With his blessings if not vigorous promotion, in June 1916 Congress passed the National Defense Act of 1916 followed by the Naval Act of 1916. By April 1917, in the wake of renewed submarine atrocities and Zimmermann's telegram, Wilson was all in and civil rights American's were accustomed to were on their way out. Trench warfare volunteers were slow in coming—a military draft was implemented. So were increased taxes, loans to Allied governments, rationing of foods and fibers, and greatly expanded industrial and agricultural production. More alarming, Wilson was quick to expand his new found powers. He created the War Industries Board to dictate manufacturing priorities and practices. He appointed future President Herbert Hoover to lead the Food Administration tasked with rationing essential commodities that included sugar and cotton. The Federal Fuel Administration introduced daylight savings time and rationed petroleum products. A war bond program along with a trade board was launched. Unappreciated at the time, Wilson pressed his advantage and greatly increased the size of the budget and thus the federal bureaucracy. In fiscal year 1916 the federal budget was $1.0 billion. In 1919 it was $19.0 billion, not including massive loans to assist allied countries finance their war efforts. Fully appreciated at the time, the country including remote San Juans mining communities began to experience firsthand what a wartime economy was going to look like.

8 Reed, Stephen B, "One Hundred Years of Price Change; the Consumer Price Index and the American Inflation Experience," pgs.1-2.

9 "Woodrow Wilson," Wikipedia.

10 Colorado WWI Centennial Commission, pgs.2-3.

11 Hafen, LeRoy, *Colorado and Its People*, Vol. 1, p.540.

12 Hafen, LeRoy, *History of Colorado*, Vol. III, pgs.1008-1009. Historian Hafen capped his glowing account of Colorado responses to Wilson's war with more emotion-rousing zeal. Left unsaid here but not unforgotten in Hinsdale County, the Lake City community also contributed their fair share.

"Colorado in the World War" was a wonderful spectacle, a whole state converted into a smoothly running powerful machine for winning the war. It was a moving sight to see rich and poor, country and city people alike, accept the draft, give up their sons, some of them to die, without a murmur or protest. For the time, there were no parties or classes. It was a unit moved by the single purpose to make the power of this state felt to the highest degree in destroying the enemy of civilization. It was a great sight to see a great people aroused, to see all their bad qualities in abeyance, to see them rise to the high level of unselfishness and service. Everybody within the boundaries of the state did everything he could. No sacrifice was too great. All shared in the fine spirit of the Council of Defense. With these latter it was never too early, never too late-when the governor called, all dropped their own work and hurried to his aid, and this without a penny of expense. The state went beyond all expectations. All loans and other funds. were oversubscribed; all quotas exceeded. Governor Gunter is justly proud of the record our people made and as he said in an interview: "It was the greatest experience in the life of the state." Pg.1013.

[13] The war officially ended with the signing of the Treaty of Versailles on June 28, 1919.

[14] Barry, John M., *The Great Influenza*, pg. 169. Barry believes circumstantial evidence points to Camp Funston by way of Haskell County, Kansas. "In the last week of February 1918, Deal Milson, Ernest Elliot, John Bottom, and probably several others unnamed by the local paper traveled from Haskell, where 'severe influenza' was raging, to Funston. They probably arrived between February 28 and March 2, and the camp hospital first began receiving soldiers with influenza on March 4. This timing precisely fits the incubation period of influenza. Within three weeks eleven hundred troops at Funston were sick enough to require hospitalization. Only a trickle of people moved back and forth between Haskell and Funston, but a river of soldiers moved between Funston, other army bases, and France."

[15] Ibid., pg. 5.

[16] Twitty, Eric, *Basins of Silver*, pg. 293. Eric shines a bright light on Silverton's dark experience. "In October, the beginning of a long winter, the Spanish influenza pandemic arrived with force. The flu spread like wildfire through Silverton and some of the large mine boardinghouses. Many individuals were struck low, and the doctors and volunteer nursing committees quarantined and attended to the sick. Most of those who contracted the illness languished for weeks then recovered, but a significant number died, which instilled fear throughout the Animas River drainage."

[17] Ibid., pg. 345.

[18] Ibid.

[19] Ibid., pg. 346.

[20] Ibid., pg. 348

[21] Ibid., pg. 293.

[22] Ibid.

[23] Ibid., pgs. 293-294.

CHAPTER 6

Hitting Some Hard Traveling

I've been hittin' some hard-rock minin',

I thought you knowed,

I've been leanin' on a pressure drill, way down the road,

Hammer flyin', air hole suckin', six foot of mud

And I shore been a muckin'

And I've been hittin' some hard travelin', Lord. [1]

Then I looked on all the works that my hands had wrought,

And on the labor that I had labored to do:

And behold, all was vanity and vexation of spirit,

And there was no profit under the sun. [2]

On September 12, 1918, when John York pledged his willingness to deliver his kick to the Kaiser, he could never have imagined the magnitude of the cost, nor the cost of the Kaiser's kick in return. Nor could he have imagined how long the proverbial jury would take to deliver a verdict on whether the New Place was going to be a bonanza or a bust. He was fully occupied with his problems underground and his problems with his owner in Denver. They defined the courtroom of his daily life for the moment. WWI and influenza would have their say before Judge Reaper's bench at a time of their choosing, but not yet.

Little if at all appreciated at the time, two weeks after York registered for Wilson's war the Meuse River-Argonne Forest offensive unleashed an unprecedented Allied army assault along WWI's entire Western Front. The assault, resisted by an undermanned but determined remnant of the Kaiser's still frightful military, would continue until November 11, 1918, when exhausted by death and disease the greatest armies the world had ever fielded would lay down their arms. This forty-seven day offensive would be the deadliest campaign in United States history, costing 26,277 American lives. It would only end when WWI ended — Armistice Day celebrated thereafter on November 11th memorializes the nation's gratitude to all who served. But the war's traveling companion, life-threatening influenza was not so readily defeated. Nor were John York's troubles in the "New Place."

York would have thought little about worldly matters on September 12th when he returned underground to pick up where he and Rowland Ewart had left off in the New Place. Nor would he know for months to come that his service to his country would not be needed. But he would have known if he read the *Lake City Times* that seventy-two other Hinsdale County patriots were serving. Seventy-two enlistees was a remarkable percentage given a county-wide population numbering less than 538 men, women, and children. Sadly, four of the seventy-two did more than enlist — they would give their lives in the line of duty. George Cameron, James E. Dilley, Edwin P. Pickett, and Russell Steinbeck would not return home. There is no doubt that Henson Canyon miners knew more about them than simply their names. Hinsdale County may have been remote, but its citizens—young and old—did not turn a blind eye to the troubles of others. They identified with their tragedies, shared what little they had with the widows and orphans of its victims, and would take to the streets with joyous merrymaking the day they learned the war had ended.

York completed his September 15, 1918 weekly report with a familiar mixture of exhilarating accomplishments, encouraging signs, and a demoralizing accounting of shortages and setbacks. "Not much to report," he wrote to A.E., perhaps trying to manage his owner's expectations.[3] He and Ewart had lost sight of the high grade ore streak they had been following. They only had three hundred pounds of powder and one hundred feet of fuse on hand. That was it. What was so newsworthy about that? York's September 22nd report was not much better. He reported that they were in 32 feet, but "after cutting through that quartz streak that crossed the drift, the quartz we have been following quit us as well as the ore we had." York wrote that they were still in a stratified formation; the only "vein" is a small "gouge." He ended with a gentle reminder that they would be out of coal and powder by the first of the month.[4]

On October 6, 1918, York reported that the drift was in 46½ feet. The "footwall is opened up for twenty feet; two feet next to the foot is a ground up quartz and gang rock. This is what I think will be the vein." He added no doubt with considerable reluctance that no mineral was in sight in the breast. He had picked up "several pieces of lead in the muck;" and they could run until Wednesday, the 9th, then be forced to shut down. On balance, not a report likely to encourage A.E. Nor would his letter to the Denver office three short days later.[5]

Wednesday, October 9th, dawned to an idle mine, but not an idle John E. York. He had busied himself typing Reynolds' Denver office manager, J.P.M Humphrey, a terse accounting of time for September: "York 28½ shifts; Ewart 24 shifts." In long-hand he wrote, "We must have some money." Apparently, A.E. was again "up against it" financially and "the boys" apparently had concluded that they would do better appealing to Reynolds' office manager than to the king himself. This approach may have been successful. For the balance of the month there was no further mention of money and York and Ewart continued their hunt for treasure.[6]

The New Place was stingy when it came to clues much less treasure. More encouraging, A.E. had accepted Van Horn's July 17th invitation to visit the mine and go fly fishing while there. A.E. traveled to Henson Canyon the second week of August to inspect the work. There are no accounts of his visit, but it is clear he was comforted for a time by what he had seen underground. No doubt York and Ewart had been on their best behavior. No doubt the surface plant and the underground workings had been in as tip-top condition as a seasoned albeit penniless crew could have made them. No doubt A.E. had found time to fly fish and catch his fair share. Based on the tone of John York's subsequent reporting to A.E., no doubt goodwill if not funding between owner and workforce could prevail for the balance of 1918. Faith in ultimate success also prevailed.

On October 18, 1918, York testified to this belief. He reported that:

> *our drift is now in 61½ feet and that ore streak I think is at least 100% better than when you were here. It is now in one solid streak five inches wide in the bottom and six inches on the top. Through the center of this streak is some waste and on the whole the streak will hardly pay yet but on one side of this streak is one inch of solid ore and about half of this one inch is gray copper and the other lead. Then between nearly every strata is knife-blade seams of quartz with mineral through them. All of them bearing towards the foot wall;" water is running out of the 'lifters next to the foot.*

The "lifters" referred to the lowest bore holes drilled into the breast of the drift. The "foot" referred to the floor of the drift. A typical drilling pattern on the breast of a drift might include twenty or more bores each of which could be three feet deep. "Powder," meaning sticks of dynamite or nitroglycerin, would be packed into the bore holes and detonated in a specific order. The charge in the "lifters" was intended to send a shockwave upward and raise ever-so-slightly the three-foot thick section of the breast above it. A bore hole in the center of the pattern of holes would be left empty to give the energy created by the explosion a predetermined place to go. The net effect of this procedure when the composition of the dirt [hard rock by another name] cooperated was three feet more of tunnel with a relatively clean-cut floor, ceiling, and sidewalls.

If all went as planned, the force of the explosives would fracture the face of the drift into fragments called "muck." Ideally the muck fragments would be small enough and light enough for a laborer to shovel into mine cars to be pulled to the surface for dumping or sorting. High-grade ore would be shipped to a mill. Low-grade ore would be set aside for future sale should silver prices warrant doing so. In the case of the Vermont/Ocean Wave, experienced miners like York and Ewart could assess the likely value of the face before it was reduced to muck.

On October 20, 1918, York wrote to A.E.: "We have cleaned up the third round since you were here. The character of the rock in the breast is changing and between the strata is knife-blade seams of almost solid gray copper." He noted that there was less ore showing in the breast than before. Now nearer the footwall a small streak of quartz was "coming in next to the foot and looks as though we might have some ore there in a few more rounds." [At last, so it seemed, "gray copper" and "some ore in a few rounds" sounded really encouraging.]

York went on to report that he picked up 25 lbs. of ore in the muck, "some pieces four or five inches square and an inch thick almost solid gray copper." Happily, he also reported that Williams delivered 5,500 pounds of coal, "Baldwin nut" [hardest soft coal in the market, probably from Crested Butte]. Unhappily he added that there was only enough powder for one more round the next day in the breast. Until he got more he had two days outside work to do, fixing track on the dump and "putting the dam in the creek." [When ice formed on the surface, they needed a pool of water to feed the boiler that was deep enough to escape freezing. The dam would be washed out by high water in the spring, thus having to be redone each fall.]

Just two days later, usually a sign of elevated excitement or concern, on October 22, 1918, York reported that the drift was in sixty-eight feet. They "still have a small streak of ore on the hanger and a little mineral scattered over the breast and small seams of lead and copper coming in that gouge next to the foot wall." With palpable excitement detectable in his words, York continued:

> *I do not think there is any doubt now but what we have the hanger, while it is still broken up it is plain and well defined. Shows the slippage next to the ore streak. The hanger that is showing up has about the same dip as the foot and about four feet from the foot. In putting that air-line in the shape you suggested we will need two reducers from four inches to three inches and one reducer from 3 inches to 2 inches and I think we can make it all right.*

Deep into the mountain, but still short of opening an airway overhead into the Ocean Wave's "Dago Tunnel," ventilation had become a serious issue again. Extending the air-line that had served them thus far was an expedient but far from optimal remedy. Failure to mitigate the lethal health effects on the crew threatened further development of the New Place. Equally threatening were the equipment breakdowns especially typical of private mines increasingly in need of someone else's' jack. John York's next report was not encouraging.

On October 31, 1918, York apparently did not have any underground progress to point to, and no treasure clues to titillate the front office—nothing. Instead, he reported that he had fixed boiler flue leaks, unglamorous but symptomatic of a surface plant long past its reliable life. He reported that he had telephoned Lake City to order two more tons of coal but Williams only delivered half a ton. [Williams explained that a one-foot snow caused him to unload most of the shipment as he progressed up the county road to keep from bogging down, thus only a small fraction could be delivered. Usually short-orders meant Williams was not being paid for prior deliveries.] York wrapped up his tale of woes with war-related news. He had pulled all the brass pipe out of the mine, and had stripped it off the "old Rand compressor." Boxed up along with the pipe, it was ready to ship off to the War Department to be manufactured into munitions.

November started out on a sweeter note. On November 3, 1918, York wrote,

> *We shot in the breast today noon and find a very material change for the better. That streak of high grade is going ahead and looks better than it did. There is a streak of about two feet that has considerable quartz scattered all through it and small bunches of mineral through the quartz. The breast is also showing more moisture than it did. It seems to me that streak of gray copper should lead us to ore worthwhile. While we have not the solid hanger yet I do not believe we will have to go many feet farther until we have the side wall.*

Returning to surface plant issues, York continued that the flue on the boiler was leaking worse than ever. He may need to put in a new flue if copper "calk" he used did not fix it. As for coal, no shortage there. The brass that he mentioned in his previous report? York wrote that he shipped it all to the Morse Bros. in Denver: 47 pieces of pipe, one 2½ feet long. "I protected all the ends save one. I

Direct-Acting Steam Air Compressor. One of Rand Drill Company's most popular compressors, it was designed for the conditions found at the Vermont/Ocean Wave site. *(Rand Illustrated Catalogue)*

also sent with the pipe that heavy round iron." There was no mention of the brass stripped off the old Rand compressor.

John filed his second November report on the 8th. The drift was in a respectable seventy-four feet. The "streak of ore" they have been following was still with them. What appeared to be high-grade grey copper was less but the vein was larger. They needed more engine oil but were in good shape concerning coal. Notably absent was any mention of war much less any hint that it might be about to end. The news that spread around the world at the speed of light, that would bring the residents of Lake City into the streets and forever impress old and young alike, was on its way up Henson Canyon but had not reached the Vermont/Ocean Wave yet. When it did, oddly enough we would not learn about its impact from York. Thankfully, we would from young Herman T. Heath. Through his twelve-year-old eyes he captured the moment for us.

The exciting news of the Armistice reached Lake City early on November 8, 1918, and the entire town spent the day and well into the night venting their elation over this long awaited news.

Lake City was under considerable stress at the time due to the Spanish Influenza Epidemic which was causing so much illness and death across the country. The official Proclamation placing Lake City and Hinsdale County under quarantine was not issued until December 2, 1918, but the city officials were attempting to break up gatherings of more than two or three people. In spite of this, all able-bodied men, women and children in Lake City, jointed in a day of rejoicing over the wonderful news.

All available ammunition in town was expended that day. Gun shots could be heard all day and late into the night. Some of the men hung a circular saw blade from the front of the Pueblo House hotel and spent the day beating on it with a hammer – a delightful sound. The older men set off round after round of dynamite charges from the Hogback above the Catholic church.

I was 12 years old at the time and well remember joining my young friends ringing the fire bell and the Baptist and Presbyterian church bells. We kept that up long after most people had heard all the bells they desired for some time to come, and until most of us had blisters from pulling on the ropes. Oh, but it was such fun at the time.

Paul Ramsay recalls joining a group of young people and assembling at the Ocean Wave smelter at the north edge of town to chew the fat and express their elation over the good news and to ponder on what the future held. They soon found out as the sheriff caught up with them and sent them to their respective homes.

There was no other celebrating other than this that I can recall, but it provided a way for everyone to express the joy of the day and left us all with a peaceful feeling and a great sense of relief that the fighting and killing was over.

There was very little activity on November 11th [the official Armistice date, now celebrated as Veterans Day]. All the ammunition and energy had been expended. [7]

Like the mine accidents and avalanches that too often hit close to home, so too the heart-wrenching price paid for the victory took a similar toll. The loss of anyone from the community never went unnoticed. These patriots would be honored in yearly ceremonies for their sacrifice and scores of others for their service for decades to come. Only then could daily life return to its mundane normal.

John York mentioned none of this in his reports to Reynolds. Why not is anyone's guess. He may have considered it too hallowed to include along with his routine activities. He may have assumed, rightly so, that A.E. perched in his Denver office did not need a Henson Canyon miner to report national news. Whatever the explanation, there is no known record of such a communication, not then, not ever. York's next report dated November 13th was all business. "Not much of a material change in the last two rounds; however there is some change, I think for the better." He adds that there is a little more water in the lifters, that the soft gouge streak is mostly quartz with mineral scattered through it, and that the small streak of lead and copper about an inch wide in back of the drift is still with them. They are still in a stratified formation, but need to be in a solid one. [York and Ewart had driven the north drift a distance of 125 feet through a stratified formation, but they had predicted that this drift after being in eighty feet would be shorter.] York concluded his report with good news. The boiler was in fairly good shape. "I made a thin steel wedge and drove it in that crack in the boiler head and calked (sic) it with copper the best I could."

York sent A.E. three more updates in seventeen days including Thanksgiving [a day of no particular consequence until the U.S. Congress declared it a national holiday in 1941]. The first update was a distress call, the next two were more encouraging.

IT IS OVER "OVER THERE." What better news than that. America's toll would not be as high as most other combatants, but it was high enough to horrify most San Juan residents. Nor would there be much comfort in the aftermath. (*Courtesy of the* Silver World)

On November 18, 1918, York wrote that the only change was more moisture in the heading, that there was only a pint of engine oil left, and that there was enough powder for one more shot "and then we are down until we get some." On November 24th he wrote that the drift was in ninety-three feet and "we have a little better showing than we have had for quite a while." He reported that a foot of ore looked pretty good but not enough to pay [given the low price of silver]. He continued, "The streak is wet all up and down the breast and dripping from the top." There still was no oil, but apparently it was on the way. In the meantime, York had found some in the mine to keep them going.

Three days later, on November 27th, no doubt with joy in his heart that he could not wait to share, he wrote that the drift was in one-hundred feet and

> *the breast looks far better than at any time yet. I shot in the breast tonight and went in and picked down. There are small seams of lead, gray and yellow copper with good sized bunches scattered all over the breast. Next to the hanger there is about ten inches of gouge matter mixed up with quartz and mineral scattered through it and gradually showing more moisture. [Apparently in this case "moisture" was a good thing.]*

He was not finished. "Since you were here I got 300# of powder and have driven 45 feet and have used just 150# for the 45 feet and have 150# left; there is about twelve cars of muck in the breast and I will be able to get 150# or maybe 200# of good ore out of the muck as we are mucking."

Anticipating Reynolds' concern over how long accomplishing all this

---

GREATER LOVE HATH NO ONE THAN THIS

James E. Dilley
Private, United States Infantry
October 5, 1918
Missing in Action
Meuse-Argonne Offensive

George Cameron
Private, 3rd Division, 30th Infantry Regiment
October 9, 1918
Killed in Action
Meuse-Argonne Offensive

Edwin P. Pickett
Private, United States Army
October 21, 1918
Died of Flu-induced Pneumonia At Sea

Russell Steinbeck
Private, United States Army
November 1, 1918
Killed in Action
Meuse-Argonne Offensive

Hinsdale County Honor Roll. From a population never exceeding a thousand pilgrims except during brief "rushes" if then, this silent memorial standing in the shadow of the courthouse exemplifies their generation of public servants. *(Author's Collection)*

was taking, York set aside the temptation to remind his owner of the fresh clues pointing to treasure ahead and instead ended on a humble note. "My man quit tonight so I am alone and will be until Harry can come down. I have been trying to get the health board to allow him to come but do not know yet whether they will or not." [8]

What? "The health board?" Yes, the war may have been over but its hand-maiden was just beginning to make her rounds. The deadly horrors of the Spanish flu were reaching everywhere, Colorado and the San Juans not excepted. They were terrorizing military installations and large cities. They reached Denver on September 27, 1918—a Denver University student named Blanch Kennedy reportedly was first. [9] She died a few days after returning from a visit to Chicago. Soon scores of others suffered the same fate. Restrictions on movement and assembly followed that. Effective October 6, 1918, Denver's Manager of Health and Charity, William H. Sharpley, and Denver Mayor Mills, closed

all schools, business colleges, churches and Sunday schools, clubs, lodges, pool halls, movie houses, theaters, reading rooms, Red Cross work rooms, dance halls, and colleges (except those under government supervision), and (banned) all music rehearsals, public indoor funerals, fraternity and lodge meetings, and all other places of public assembly (defined as two or more people). Workplaces with large numbers of employees were to be inspected by the health department and all suspected cases discovered would be segregated, and those buildings found to be poorly ventilated would be ordered closed. The order would go into effect at 6:00 am on Sunday, October 6. For that day only, Catholic churches would be allowed to hold their early mass, as there was no way to contact members of the congregation before they began arriving. [10]

Denver's resolve wavered but did not break until well into the new year, and the deadly serious nature of the matter was not lost on most Colorado jurisdictions albeit some were quicker to act and some were prepared to act more aggressively than others. Hinsdale County's neighbors fell into both camps. On the western side of nearby Engineer Pass, as noted earlier, Silverton had adopted a largely liberal stance and paid the piper with a disproportionately high death toll. Western and southern travel through there would have been foolish and in any case had been prohibited. Gunnison, on the other hand, the nearest population center fifty miles to the north of Lake City, had implemented a total quarantine that was totally effective. Hinsdale County would order an equally tight quarantine early in October that would not be relaxed for six months. As far as John York was concerned, Harry, visiting family in Fort Lupton for the Christmas holidays, was trapped on the wrong side of this. Made-up of the same stock as York, he was thankful to be in Fort Lupton but nevertheless expressed sincere regret that he could not be of some help to John.

As for John's situation, "my man quit tonight so I am alone and will be until Harry can come down?", this simple statement revealed deep-seated emotion rarely expressed by men like him. It spelled real trouble, trouble well beyond fixing even with the skills of a jack-of-all-trades. A lesser man would have called it quits long before this, but John York was not a lesser man. This one, single anguished cry would summarize and end any loneliness or self-pity he must have been feeling. Accepting his lot in life as no better nor worse than the ordinary man, he knew only one response. He had a God-given duty to serve with perfection. His duty at the moment was to serve A.E. Reynolds. He had no choice but to do what he could do, to work the mine alone in the dead of winter if necessary. Yes, he would work Reynolds' last best chance regardless of being short of supplies, short of pay, and short of help—actually without any help at all.

Harry's visit to Denver would not be brief. York would see ice melt off El Paso Creek before he would see Cousin Harry again. As for "my man" who quit, that would be faithful friend Rowland. York harbored no animosity there. In addition to being his faithful friend, he also was responsible for wife and children alone in Lake City who were ever-desirous of his loving care. And Christmas was not just another day. We see the heart of the man in a July letter Rowland wrote from the mine to his sister Lizzie at home in Weldon, England.

My dearest Lizzie,
I received your letter with the sad news of dear Father's death. I was not surprised. I also heard from Hannah. I am glad you feel the way you do about it. Father's end was glorious. Two passages of Scripture came to mind, as I read your letter "Precious in the sight of the Lord is the death of his Saints," "And may my last end be like his", our loss is his gain. Katie and the children are all well. They were all up to see me the other day, they did enjoy the day riding

in an auto it was a picnic for them. Little Helen wanted me to go home with them, she does not understand why I should stay away from home, all the time she came to me the last time I was at home & said, "Daddy stay home you're her husband you don't have to go away," so seriously I was highly amused. Hoping you are well with fondest love from your loving brother,

Rowland

Even so, and despite being "over" working without pay, Rowland did not rule out rejoining York after a Christmas break. That said, he too was quarantined. Those outside Lake City's town limits could not come in. Those inside could not get out. Reynolds' dream became York's nightmare. What soon was recognized as a pandemic that would kill 500,000 Americans and perhaps fifty million others worldwide was sentencing him to a solitary winter at the mine. He had drawn a joker from the deck of life just as Reynolds' last best chance to make a mine was on the cusp of unearthing paydirt.

While the pandemic surged around the world in 1918 and 1919, Lake City escaped the worst of it. Dr. Cummings, County Health Officer and Lake City's sole physician, with the help of Hinsdale and Gunnison County sheriffs, sealed off the entire region. Unknowing visitors were greeted by the sheriff at the train platform and escorted to a room at the schoolhouse set apart for such occasions. Here they remained for observation for five days before being allowed to proceed into town. Soon word spread and visitors ceased. Work at Reynolds Tunnel did not cease. In a December 4, 1918, note to Harry, York wrote,

I have been having the devil's own time here keeping things from freezing up and have not done a very good job of it either. Top of the lubricator froze and bursted (sic) and the end of the intercooler froze and bursted. I had every drain valve open and drained as well as I could drain everything. [He discovered the end of the intercooler was clogged with rust and sediment and held water instead of draining.]

This morning after putting the wooden end on I concluded to try a round in the breast so got up pressure and started to drill at eleven o'clock and at a quarter past three I had my round in and shot. I only had to come out once during the round to fire up and get the pressure up and everything worked fine. I was in the mine a few moments ago: more quartz, more water, hanger more solid, gouge streak next to hanger wet and sloughs off, lifters and holes next to hanger wet, roof drips so that in drilling I got quite wet.

York ended with what sounded like hopeful thinking. He had no way of knowing how long the quarantine might last, but he advised his friend it was still in effect yet still possible to get to the mine. The town had *fixed up some of the rooms in the school house so that if anyone wants to come in they take them there for four or five days before letting them go up town. Bill Spencer, the man you played billiards with died in Calif. with the "flu" and Mrs. Gardner went to Grand Junction and died with the "flu" there. There has not been a single case in Lake City up to date.*

With that, York pivoted to a progress report. He would keep mucking and sharpening steel and blasting "for if I don't work, up here alone I would get nuttier than a pet coon." He concluded with:

Mrs. McPolin sent me up a quart of preserved pears and they are certainly fine and I have some cider so if you want to get in on them you had better hurry along for they are tasting (sic) mighty fast. I heard that Williams and Mendenhall had a foot of solid gray copper in the Bell of the West. [Back to business, he suggested A.E. see son-in-law Bradish Morse about a set of new tubes for the intercooler.] [11]

As Christmas 1918 approached, York sent Reynolds a not so subtle reminder of the conditions he was dealing with at the mine. Dated December 15th, he wrote:

I have been unable to get a man so have been going it alone. I get up a pressure and then beat it for the inside and drill till the air goes down then repeat the dose until I get the round in. I shot in the breast last night and have been mucking today and will be mucking all day tomorrow; then will have to sharpen the steel, lay track and pipe.
[The breast shows] little more mineral and getting wetter; ore streak about one foot wide three and a half feet from the hanger that has considerable yellow copper some lead and some gray copper through it and a little mineral scattered all over the breast. One round will show considerable ore and may be the next will show but little. Three rounds back I got four powder boxes full of fine gray copper and lead. [12]

News of gray copper was always good news, even a harbinger of better news to come, but it was not yet the treasure York and the boys had been searching for so long. Harry, still safely quarantined with family in Fort Lupton, still took an interest in the hunt. He also believed the motherlode was near and friend John was working a vein that would lead to it. Apparently A.E. was similarly inclined. Unmoved by York's plight and appeal, as was his practice he was about to present York with new terms for continuing work in the coming year.

As matters at the mine stood, in Reynolds' opinion current clues pointed more conclusively than ever to paydirt close at hand. He too still believed in his vision for his tunnel project, so convincingly that he succeeded in persuading Cousin Harry to return to the hunt. His only question, "what was his jack-of-all-trades willing to commit to?" Not one to dawdle, Reynolds was quick to share his latest thinking with Harry. Harry, still smittened with the great adventure he and York shared, was eager to re-engage. In the role of friend and honest broker, he did not take long before testing A.E.'s latest thinking on York. York's response to Harry's inquiry, given the hardships and setbacks he had endured thus far, revealed the heart of a faithful servant willing to continue serving a noble cause. His response also reflected a miner's curiosity, the curiosity motivating every adventurer on a quest for treasure. In his response to Harry dated December 16, 1918, York sat in his cabin and composed on his old typewriter:

> *Your letter received today and contents carefully noted in regard to the cost per foot. While the ground is fairly good, both drilling and breaking it is much tighter than it has been. If the two of us pull 40 feet per month we will have to have good luck all the time. Considering everything I do not think it can be broken for less than $15 per foot. At that I do not believe we can make over $4.50 per day and then we will have to go some to do that.*
>
> *I have just about worked the tail off myself the past three months and I am on the rugged edges from every point of view. However, I am willing to make most any sacrifice to push it ahead a little farther. [York predicted ore on the level he was working would be another 50-75 feet ahead] but it is my belief that we will have to raise to find much ore. [By "raise" he meant driving a shaft upward, overhead, to a level closer to the surface.]*
>
> *The breast looks now very favorable, much better than it did the last round. [He reminded Harry that he was at the location where A.E. on his visit said he would have to advance seventy-five feet more to find ore.]*
>
> *Dr. Cummings [administrator of the quarantine] said that you would be permitted to come direct to the mine without going into quarantine in Lake City. It is certain good judgment to take all due precautions against the "Flu" for it is no respecter of person. [York advises Van Horn that there is enough coal for three weeks steady running, that the weather is still unseasonably warm, before closing with what is really on his mind.] I certainly hope the "Flu" will not find where you live or you find it.* [13]

Harry's interest in resuming an active role in the project, and A.E.'s willingness to adjust their compensation, did not diminish John York's interest in settling up overdue accounts. Reynolds owed him [and others] back wages, a great deal of back wages. In the past, accounts eventually would be settled. That remained York's expectation, after all he still worked the mine alone. Nevertheless, his patience was wearing thin, thinner and thinner as his own stack of unpaid bills thickened. On December 19, 1918, York wrote A.E. a heart-felt letter appealing his case. Interestingly, he did not mention his isolation or the local effects of the pandemic. More interestingly still, he gave no indication of any animosity concerning the long-standing fact that back pay was owed and mounting. Instead, he simply reported his circumstances.

> *I am on the ragged edges financially unless I can raise about $300 immediately. [He explained he bought land/farm with a brother and needed to pay principal on a note coming due. Reynolds was no stranger to this problem, nor was he likely to be sympathetic to others with it.] That is the way I am hooked up. [York advised A.E. that he was willing to work on to make a paying mine; he wanted $1,793.65 to get caught up, but would settle for $1,313,90 cash and the rest in stock. Stock? Stock that could only be redeemed with future earnings was another testimony to faith in treasure ahead.]*
>
> *I shot in the breast last night and there is but little mineral showing although there is a change in the rock in the breast. Water still runs out of the quartz seams scattered over the breast and dripping from the roof of the drift. [He is now in 112 feet.]*
>
> *Back where we started the raise [Reynolds took his December 16th advice] there is three feet of ore that does not lack very much of being pay ore and I believe that to go up there 50 feet or 100 feet we would have pay ore. I think from 50 ft. to 100 ft. farther on this level we are driving will just about demonstrate whether there is any ore on the level.* [14]

Reynolds could be fully consumed by circumstances at the mine. but there is no evidence he was ever interested much less consumed by York's personal circumstances. Not so with many of the folks in town. Mrs. McPolin's early Christmas gift to John of a quart of her preserved pears was but one example. On December 26th, in the afterglow of the Christmas spirit, the *Silver World* editor provided another example for which we are grateful.

> *For real grit and nerve to stick to a purpose in mining commend us to John York at the Ocean Wave. When John's helper quit and the quarantine barred Harry Van Horn from coming in for a time, did John give up and shut down? Not much! Mr. York would get up a head of steam in the morning, go in and run the drill while the steam lasted, then go out 2500 feet [3500 feet actually] and fire up and then go back and drill again, in that way getting in the round of shots. That's what we call grit.* [15]

A.E. had his own way of lifting up others. On December 31, 1918, he welcomed in the New Year by formally offering the Ocean Wave company his third new deal for exploiting his Reynolds Tunnel properties. He began his lengthy letter—a concise summary of the project to-date—with his typically formal, frosty salutation:

A.E. to Harry Van Horn and Others: You who originally undertook to develop the Ocean Wave vein above Lake City and to put in both time and money, should now look carefully over the situation and see if you do not all feel encouraged to contribute a reasonable amount each to complete the work which you originally undertook.

The work being done now is approaching immediately under where the old workings [meaning the Ocean Wave's Dago Tunnel] had ore 450 feet above this level, and you are having all the time now a showing of small streaks of high grade ore such as the workings above produced, a small amount of water such as the vein would be expected to carry, and to all appearances, after going another 100 feet you should begin to come immediately under where the ore was in the old workings, and you will have ahead of you the full length of ground to open, in which the ore was taken out above. [The issue, he continued, would be solved in the next 300 to 400 feet of work.]

You have the advantage now of knowing that ore does go down to this level and that when it is found the quality is good—probably as good as it was in the old workings which were celebrated for high grade ore. [16]

Fair enough so far, but then kingly ire kicked in as he recounted the trouble with their "enterprise" thus far. Simply put, he blamed "the boys" for abandoning the true vein and wasting 500 feet of money and effort before realizing their error. At that crucial decision point, they were just twenty-five feet beyond the point where they left the proper vein. The long and short of his reasoning was that he did not believe he should have to pay for their mistake, meaning John York and Rowland Ewart were not going to get most or any of what they were owed. The only path forward that made sense to A.E. was to continue developing what was being called the "New Place," the true vein—already proving to be fruitful—which brought him to his 1919 third new deal. Reynolds' letter continued:

Mr. York and one other man [Rowland Ewart] have run about 120 feet in this direction, and he is there now alone, single-handed, trying to do his own firing and drilling and mucking, and it has got right up to the point where we have either got to quit for an indefinite period, or take hold and furnish the money for 300 or 400 feet of work. [Surprise, A.E. did recognize if not exactly appreciate York's single-handed efforts.]

My personal opinion is that our chances are just as good as they ever have been in this undertaking, and that this expenditure is well worth doing and doing right away without having to wait six months or a year or an indefinite period; and the question is now, will each of you who have done so well in the past in helping, take hold and make fair contributions, all pulling together, to enable us to put about five men, all told, at this work and determine the question within about the next ninety days, of whether we are to have a mine or not. Mr. York is entirely worn out with the situation as it is now, and he ought to either get help or quit at once.[17]

Imagine Reynolds' thought process. On the one hand he declared he was unwilling to pay for five-hundred feet of "wasted money and effort," meaning no backpay would be forthcoming. On the other hand, he sought from these same men an estimated $3,000 to $4,000 to pay debts [not their past wages, of course] and muck out 300 to 400 feet more dirt. With no detectable sense of this irony, he went on to explain work would be funded by selling shares [primarily to them] at $0.50 each. Their shares, once the mine was producing, could be redeemed for cash before any other payments were made. In street language, Reynolds needed someone else's jack, someone else to share the risk. His heart and ego urged him on, what about his crew? Thus ended Reynolds December 31st letter. Thus began York's and Van Horn's new year.

Reynolds had understated the costs of the mine and overstated the proximity of the prize, but his estimates would not matter. The annual *Colorado Bureau of Mines Report for 1919*, available to John York if its estimates would have mattered to him, provided a more accurate assessment [not necessarily paid] of expenses to date. Reynolds Tunnel costs were put at $64,383. The "Ocean Wave Development Tunnel," in the Bureau's term, meaning the crosscut drift leading from Reynolds Tunnel to the workings in the New Place, was put at $34,346 for a total project cost of over $98,729. This accounting did nothing more than remind shareholders what they had invested in sweat and mostly their own cash, and the risk of committing more of both. Only York and Van Horn would respond to Reynolds' New Years Eve proposition. Only York and Van Horn signed on to Reynolds' third New Deal. How much jack was pledged—almost surely all Harry's—is unknown, but it was enough.[18]

On January 15, 1919, Cousin Harry successfully navigated pandemic quarantine restrictions and joined jack-of-all-trades York in Henson Canyon. Absent since August, we have no details about how he occupied his time away, but we do have first-hand insight into the details of his trip back. Harry reported them to A.E.:

I left Denver Friday night as intended, and upon reaching Sapinero Saturday, called up Dr. Cumming, chairman of the Health board of the county, and obtained permission from him to come on in and go direct to the mine. The train was two hours late, and upon arriving in Lake City at eight o'clock, I was met by the City Marshall who had a saddle horse ready, and I stepped from the train and got on the horse and came direct to the mine, reaching here at ten o'clock at night. I am the first one to come to Lake City to escape the quarantine. They usually keep them in quarantine for five days, at an expense of $7.00 per day, I am told, so I was very fortunate to get permission from the Health board to come on to the mine.[19]

Like York, much of the mine's surface plant was on its last legs. Van Horn and York began repairs by replacing parts on the compressor. Then they spent two days "tearing out that old rotten chute and building a new one." The location of the chute was not mentioned, but given their focus on the New Place it probably was there and connected an upper and lower drift. Eager to start drilling, a ruptured pipe had to be repaired first. Not to be forced off their self-imposed schedule, they managed to get in a round of explosives and shot late that same night. They were working the New Place, in 114 feet, perhaps a level above the main Ocean Wave drift. Harry was eager to report what they were encountering.

> *I find upon examining the old drift that the stratified formation continues about 135 feet from where we started the new drift, so it is very probable that we will have to go from ten to twenty feet yet before we get out of it, and I do not look for any ore until we get into the solid, however the indications at present are very promising as there is a good vein, and considerable of moisture. Do not know the result of our shots to-night. [He concludes with a request for more coal.]* [20]

On January 26th Van Horn reported twelve shifts and 13 feet progress. One foot per shift would impress no one, but would not be a surprise either. Neither would the ground that was very hard, tight, stratified, and with no ore. On February 2nd Harry reported:

> *Since writing you last Sunday, we have advanced the breast nine feet, making it now 136 feet, and we now think we are just getting out of the stratified formation;*" small streak of "*high grade gray copper with us all the week, and it still shows in the breast; it was only about one-half an inch wide, but it looked like the pure stuff.* [21]

On February 9th Van Horn was again a bearer of bad news. In addition to freezing water lines, he came down with a "bad bilious spell" that prevented him from working for two days. "Bilious" was a term used to describe food poisoning or a gall bladder attack. As a result, they only advanced the breast seven feet [143 ft. total on their new contract]. No ore was observed. They encountered a great deal of water, still considered a good sign provided it did not get any worse [22]

Two days later Van Horn responded to a letter from A.E. he had received while recovering from his "bilious spell." Unstated by either party, it suggested that Reynolds was having some success attracting new investors. Also unstated, new investors meant a fresh infusion of jack to pay for supplies and hopefully wages. Spanish flu restrictions remained a problem.

I have your letter of the 8th in which you state that there will probably be four men leave Denver the 16th for Lake City, to look over the work on the Ocean Wave mine, and in reply, I have made the following arrangements for their care and comfort, while in Lake City, which is the best I could do under the circumstances, as the town is still under quarantine, and up to date, no one has been allowed to enter the sacred precincts of the city, without going into quarantine for five days.

The men will not be allowed to go to a hotel, but upon their arrival at Lake City, they will be met at the depot by the Health Officer and conducted to a room or rooms, where they will be provided with comfortable beds, and their meals will be brought to them; on the following morning a team will be provided to bring them to the mine, and take them to town again in the evening, when they will be allowed to depart on the train the following morning, or if they wish to stay longer than one day, suitable arrangements will be made to meet their wishes; in other words they will be in quarantine or placed by themselves, while in the city, but will be allowed to come to the mine, and depart when they have finished their stay, and not be required to remain in quarantine the usual five days; we can arrange to feed them all right at the mine, provided they can put up with bachelor cooking such as we have, but we have no bedding sufficient for their comfort at night. [Van Horn added that they should pack lunches for train travel—there were no "eating houses" open to the public in Sapinero and Gunnison was totally off-limits. At the mine they could climb the hill to the old workings—there was no snow on that side of the mountain.] [23]

The day appointed for A.E.'s Denver visitors came and went without visitors and without apologies or explanations. On February 20, 1919, Van Horn could not stand the suspense any longer. He wrote A.E. that he had not seen or heard from the Denver "mystery men" [as if A.E. did not know that]. He reported that a snowstorm and slides had closed the road to all but horses, as though that could explain why they never showed up. [Reynolds did not bite. He did not respond.] Harry did not miss a beat. He reported that they were again into the "hardest ground we have ever encountered… and dry as a bone." If water was encouraging, none of this sounded good. They were in 155 feet, but they needed coal. That did not sound good, either. On the legal front which was rarely a consideration, A.E. was reminded that the Ocean Wave Company charter would expire in the middle of March and needed to be renewed. [24]

On February 26, 1919, Van Horn was the bearer of still more bad news. With a hint of self-doubt and a contrite heart, he wrote:

Breast of our drift is now in 161 feet, and the ground is as hard as it is possible to make it. [He confesses that there is "no showing, just good hard rock."] We have no walls, and I am of the opinion that the true foot wall must be to the left of us. The outlook is very discouraging at present. Do you think we should continue on as we are, or should we turn more to the left? Back at the receiver, which is about 1100 feet in, there is a good foot wall, and it has never shown up any place since, and the ground is oxidized, but where we are now oxidation is not present.[25]

As if developments underground were not ominous enough, surface conditions were worse. In the past, asking A.E. what to do when tunnel conditions were befuddling usually resulted in a stop-work order. On this occasion, work would cease due to equipment failures—most serious being the boiler—and snow slides. With or without an answer from Reynolds, irrespective of enticing clues or lack thereof, their work week was done. They needed Reynolds' approval to replace the boiler, and they along with every other miner in Henson Canyon needed a miracle to clear the county road of avalanche debris. Expecting neither anytime soon, Harry made his way back to Ft. Lupton. Even John York laid down his tools and retreated to Lake City.

The question of which direction to tunnel aside, surprisingly A.E. was quick to address the failed boiler. He authorized equipment repairs including boiler replacement that would amount to more than $2,000. Apparently the lure of near-certain treasure remained strong. York, however, remained in town until March 14th albeit with thoughts of returning to the mine. The mine had become his only real home and he longed "to see if anyone has been prowling around."

Van Horn began a search for a replacement boiler. Replacing the old boiler also would require tearing down the masonry shell surrounding it and rebuilding it once the replacement boiler was set on a new foundation. Not only was finding an appropriately sized boiler a challenge, finding stone masons and materials to rebuild the shell would not be easy. All of this translated into lost work days, lost capital, lost momentum, and lost morale. All of this also translated into the specter of A.E. having second thoughts and issuing another stop-work order, or worse yet, a permanent shutdown. On May 1st Van Horn, still in Ft. Lupton, updated A.E.:

> *As yet, have heard nothing in answer to my inquiry of the Endner Lumber Company, at Gunnison, in reference to their prices for cement, fire-clay and lime. We will need ten sacks of cement, seven sacks of fire-clay and eight barrels of lime, and it should be ordered from somewhere at once otherwise we will be laying around here waiting for it.*
>
> *There is a smokestack that seems to be in a pretty fair shape, and is just the size and length (45 feet high, 2 feet diameter) we want, standing on a boiler at the old Crook Smelter at Crooks' Falls, Lake City, and is owned or controlled by T.B. Stearns, of Denver.*[26]

Harry suggested that A.E. should "take up the matter of its [the smokestack] purchase with Mr. Sterns (who was in Denver)," but reconsidered. Instead, he determined that the stack on the boiler at the nearby Lellie Mill would work if they could get it down in one piece. Meanwhile, masterful innovators that they were, York and Van Horn managed to scrape together everything they needed to restore steam power to their compressor.

The Crook Smelter turned out to be a bust, but the abandoned Lellie mine and mill was the source of almost everything, notably the boiler and stack. Just a mile or so down the county road from the Reynolds Tunnel, a Godsend really, transporting the heavy equipment seemed like it would be a simple matter. Not so simple. The early-Spring snowslides—two massive avalanches actually—still stood in the way. Unfazed by such complications, not to mention surviving a train wreck on the way, Van Horn was back at the mine on May 4th reporting progress to A.E.:

> *I arrived in Lake City Monday night at eleven o'clock, part of our train on the Lake City branch jumped the track, and we had to finish the trip in a box car, and remained in town over Tuesday looking up a jack screw and some other things we needed to do the work. [Van Horn and York took down and moved out the old boiler; completed excavation for the foundation of the replacement boiler; went "up the hill" and found a good "gin-pole"; prospected for sand; and took down the stack at the Lellie. Harry added that the] snow slide is pretty solid yet, but I am afraid it will not remain so long, and [it] would be easier to get the boiler over it just as soon as possible. [His thought was it would be easier sliding the heavy boiler over snow and ice than dragging it through mud.]* [27]

On May 20th the boiler was no closer to Reynolds Tunnel than on May 4th. Using their gin pole and borrowed pulleys, York and Van Horn had managed to get the boiler on timbers, but they needed a team of horses, and more work on smoothing a path over the top of the two snow slides. They had shoveled frozen snow for eight days on one of them alone. Worse yet, the second slide was melting into mud, and the creek was rising and would soon cover the bars where they planned to get their sand. They were in better shape when it came to masonry needs. Lime, cement, and fire-clay were scheduled for delivery, and "I have a man engaged to brick-in our boiler as soon as we are ready for him, and I trust I will be able to pay him as soon as his work is completed." [Alas, there always was that pesky money problem.] [28]

On May 25, 1919, nearly three months after all Reynolds Tunnel and Vermont/Ocean Wave work had unexpectedly ceased and unexpectedly revived, Van Horn was able to strike an upbeat albeit sheepish note in his weekly A.E. update. He also felt confident enough to forecast that all necessary work would be completed by the end of the week.

Heavy Work. Moving a typical boiler to the Revenue Tunnel mimics the effort required to move a replacement boiler into place at the Reynolds Tunnel. A major difference: the grade was steeper and obstructed by two avalanches at the Reynolds Tunnel. *(Amon Carter Museum of American Art, Fort Worth, TX — Public Domain)*

Since writing you last, we have screened and hauled our sand and gravel; got up our gin-pole; hauled the brick and small stuff from the Lellie Mill; put in the cement foundation; put the skids under the boiler and got it started out of the building.

We have a team up to the mine to-night, and will have to do a couple of days work on the road leading to our power house, and then get the boiler about 250 feet up the road to the foot of the snow-slide, then Williams will send up his heavy outfit to haul the boiler.[29]

Just thinking about this struggle could have been debilitating. In fact, it seemed to be wearing on Harry's soul. On June 1st, a week into the move, Van Horn was no longer confident. A sizable portion of the 1919 mining season was behind them and they had precious little to show for it. Prospects for improvement were no more encouraging. Note Van Horn's return to "Dear Sir," no longer "Cousin A.E.", in his routine report.

Dear Sir: — Since writing you last Sunday we have spent 2 days in the road with a team and man; got it in good shape to haul the boiler; spent 2 days getting the boiler out of the Lellie Mill and onto the road; spent 1 day hauling rock and smoothing off the snowslide; spent last 2 days with Williams, and to-night we just succeeded in getting the boiler over the snowslide, and it will take another day to get up to our place, then of course, it will have to be unloaded and put in place.

We simply had one dickens of a time for the past two days getting the boiler over the slide, and in addition to our troubles, the weather has been stormy and windy making it very unpleasant. [As it turned out, Van Horn also needed another section of stack, fortunately available at the Ute/Ulay. He also needed paid for May: York, 31 shifts; Van Horn, 31 shifts.][30]

On June 3rd Van Horn was in a better mood and could report that the boiler was finally in place in the Reynolds Tunnel power house. "We had ten horses on the boiler to bring it up the hill, and they had all they could do." Harry was awaiting the Lake City mason. Two days later Harry was still awaiting the Lake City mason and was no longer in a good mood. He sent A.E. a short note stating that the mason probably was not coming and he doubted he could find anyone else in Lake City. He would try Gunnison or Montrose a hundred miles away, but needed assurance he could pay the man when work was done. He and York had done all they could themselves. He signed the note, "Hastily, Harry Van Horn."[31]

Surely a change was coming and both Van Horn and York sensed it. On June 17th come it did in the form of the customary A.E. Reynolds stop-work order. On June 20th Van Horn acknowledged the curious language it contained "in which you [Reynolds] say that as soon as we get everything dispatched here that we can do, it will be necessary to close down until arrangements are perfected." Harry's response, equally curious, took full advantage of the lack of specifics and the absence of a hard and fast deadline. He wrote:

> In reply, will say we have undertaken the setting of the boiler; will take 7 or 8 days to complete that except putting up smoke stack; need to patch building since we took it apart to get boiler in; then gather up tools; will be about July 1st before able to leave it in good shape.

Resigned to their fate, York and Van Horn nonetheless were committed to an "orderly shutdown" which would serve Reynolds—and maybe themselves—well regardless of Reynolds next move. As for the boys next move, Van Horn asked Reynolds if they could "get a few dollars" to get out of town and pay their grocery bills. He asked if there was work in Creede at the Commodore, still owned by Reynolds, maybe a lease for them at the No. 3 Commodore Dump. Common practice of the day was to rework mine waste hastily discarded during glory days, but usually containing some paydirt considered low-grade in the sorting process.[32]

Not lost on Van Horn and York, this stop-work order looked different than others they had experienced. It was. It ended Reynolds' third New Deal and development of the New Place. But it did not end Reynolds' last best chance to make a mine. Frontier entrepreneurs did not become mining kings by being croakers and grumblers. And some men of character were inclined to remain believers in visions no matter the costs. Reynolds was just such a man, and so were John York and Harry Van Horn. Not only did they endure injuries in the mine, they endured insults in their relationships with A.E. Yet, through them all they remained committed to their internal work ethic and loyalty to employer and co-worker alike. On every occasion they placed the interests of those they were responsible for above their own. York's treatment of Rowland Ewart was a perfect example of this quality. York was his mentor and often ensured he was paid even if it meant York must go without. York's mentor, Cousin Harry, was just the same.

ROWLAND EWART

Rowland married Kate, born Mette Katrina Hansina Urup, a native of Denmark, on December 30, 1901, in Lake City's St. James Episcopal Church where they faithfully attended. They birthed two sons and five daughters. Rowland was a long-time friend and sometimes partner of fellow countryman John E. York. Ewart, a native of Weldon, England, emigrated to Lake City in 1890. He was a noted boarding house cook as well as miner. A mother's loving letter to her emigrant son provides another glimpse into Rowland's character that helps explain why ordinary San Juan pilgrims accounted for extraordinary American exceptionalism. It also explains the likely source of his cooking skills.

My dearest Rowland, I was very pleased to hear from you the other day. I should love to see you all. Now I hartily (sic) wish you all a happy new year. I do hope that it is better....I will copy my recipe for jock pies. 3 lbs. or 4 stone of flour, 1 lb. lard, pt boiling water, teaspoon full of salt. Pour boiling water and lard over the flour. Cook for half an hour then let it stand for an hour or two before raising , as it is so much easier. The meat should go through a sausage machine or cut into small pieces the size of dice—add pepper, salt and a tea cup full of water...more lard...boil feet, tail and anything of a rindy nature for several hours till it sets to a stiff jelly. Let it stand till cold...You can copy... recipe book. Butterscotch can be made with granulated sugar. Well butter a sauce pan, 2 cup to a pound to every pound full 1 table spoon of vinegar and 2 of water. Aunt Ruth now makes hers of moist sugar which is...nice. 1 lb. sugar—slowly melt—then boil till it sets. They require no stirring—the latter recipe is much the best. Much love to you, Katie and the little ones...E. Ewart. (Courtesy of Ewart Family)

After leaving the Ocean Wave a few months before York and Van Horn shut it down, Rowland found work a short distance away at the Golconda. In February 1920 he was "brought down" from the Golconda, a victim of the flu pandemic that rebounded twice since its outbreak in 1918. Rowland and John were kindred spirits. Loss of a close friend to the Spanish flu was deeply troubling to a man like York. Having lost his own young wife years earlier, he was cheered by the family life his friend enjoyed. The loss of friend Rowland and the loss of his Vermont/Ocean Wave home did not augur well for the jack-of-all-trades.

York and Van Horn completed their orderly shutdown of the Reynolds Tunnel and Vermont/Ocean Wave surface plant and departed Henson Canyon early July 1919. In early August York was staying at the Occidental Hotel in Lake City. The Occidental was managed by P.J. McPolin, husband of Mrs. McPolin of "preserved pears" acclaim, both dear friends of John. On Occidental Hotel stationary John wrote another sad but amazingly gracious note to A.E.:

> *Mr. A. E. Reynolds, Denver, Colo. – Dear Sir: — I would like to know what prospects there is of resuming operations on the Ocean Wave mine? I am very much in need of some money and would appreciate very much if you can send me some. Very truly yours, J.E. York.* [33]

How Reynolds responded if at all is not known. In either case, York's next move, out of character, out of desperation, was a legal one. At the Hinsdale County Courthouse on July 29, 1919, he filed a mechanics lien on the Ocean Wave for $3,296.84 in unpaid wages. For a man like John York, this must have been painful. But for anyone, $3,296.84 was a lot of jack to walk away from.

Consistent with York's Quaker upbringing and his unwillingness to burden himself with ill-will toward others, and as contrary to logic as going back to work for an employer that failed to pay his workforce, John York did just that. A few short weeks after filing his mechanics' lien, York along with Friend Harry was again hard at work in Creede at Reynolds' Commodore Mine. And as though nothing unpleasurable had occurred, on September 4, 1919, Van Horn was back to writing progress reports to Reynolds in keeping with yet another new deal.

In step with Reynolds' typical business approach, Van Horn, York and a handful of others were to work for shares in a Commodore lease. Their wages would be a percent of profits from ore they produced and shipped to the Pueblo smelter. One comforting feature of the lease was J.P.M. Humphrey, Reynolds trusted office manager, was in for a 15% share. His contribution was cash, always a sorely needed asset no amount of sweat equity could replace. His involvement also was much needed testimony to the integrity of the venture. Maybe Reynolds would settle past accounts as soon as his finances were able. Maybe his Vermont/Ocean Wave vision was not dead. [And do not forget, he had signed an option to purchase outright Hendrie's Vermont presumably brimming with proven high-grade ore still held in reserve.] [34]

Meanwhile in Lake City, Reynolds enlisted the legal services of H. A. Avery to help York "settle accounts" on scrap metal and timber from his abandoned Ocean Wave smelter located on the north edge of town. Reynolds was reluctant to part company with the lumber. He informed Avery that he wanted to keep it for "use at the Ocean Wave Mine," a sure sign that he was not yet ready to cut and run from his prized elephant. Avery persuaded him to sell the planks which were not suitable for the mine and leave the timbers that were too heavy to be stolen. [35]

Reynolds also enlisted the services of York to find a buyer for the boiler at the Ocean Wave mill [not to be confused with the boiler at the mine]. Despite their impasse regarding back pay, faithful York diligently complied. On July 24, 1920, from Creede York wrote to A.E. that he had made a deal with a Mr. S.C. Dickey to buy the boiler for $600 "onboard the cars at Lake City." On August 17th H. A. Avery advised Reynolds that the boiler "went out Wednesday morning consigned to S.C. Dickey."[36]

John York did his duty to the bitter end. In June he put Reynolds Tunnel and its surface plant in safe, potentially long, cold standby. In July he brokered surplus equipment for A.E. Reynolds. In September he worked the Commodore "on shares" with friend Harry. In October, having never regained his strength and natural immunities from his months working the Vermont/Ocean Wave project alone, he died from the Spanish Flu in Creede.

Unlike Pike Snowden before him, drover turned wealthy locator of the Ocean Wave who died in obscurity, John York, jack-of-all-trades and master of some, died among friends largely because of the Ocean Wave. On October 23, 1920, the *Creede Candle* honored his service to his fellow man.

> *John Elmer York, well known and highly respected in this community for a number of years, died Sunday morning at age 52 of the flu. John York was born in 1868 in Davis county, Iowa and came to Creede from Lancaster, Missouri, in 1897. He has since resided here and in Lake City, in both of which places he had mining interests. He was a man of sterling qualities; always friendly, ready with the helping hand and if he had an enemy it was not known. In all his dealings he was upright and always had a pleasant word for everyone. The deceased comes of a family of eight boys, six of whom are still living, and three girls. Mr. York's father, aged 93, is still living. C. M. York, a brother, now living at Lancaster and formerly Superintendent of the Creede schools from 1898 to 1901 inclusive, came on to attend the funeral which was held Friday afternoon from the Congregational church. Internment was at Creede Cemetery and under the direction of the Knights of Pythias, of which he was a Past Chancellor and a number of times Representative to the Grand Lodge. Mr. York had a host of friends both here and at Lake City and his relatives have the sympathy of the entire community."[37]*

Pike Snowden was dead. Rowland Ewart was dead. John York was dead. Work on the Reynolds Tunnel was dead, comatose at the very least. But as long as A.E. was alive his vision was alive. Vermont/Ocean Wave treasure awaited someone able to decipher its clues, someone willing to lay their money down. The universal truth of the matter: treasure's allure does not weaken with trials or time. Someone would resume the hunt.

Notes – Chapter Six: Hitting Some Hard Traveling

[1] Woody Guthrie, "Hard Travelin'."

[2] Ecclesiastes 2:11, KJV.

[3] September 15, 1918, MSS 1220, Box 19, FF 1372.

[4] September 22, 1918, MSS 1220, Box 19, FF 1372.

[5] October 6, 1918, MSS 1220, Box 19, FF 1374.

[6] October 9, 1918, MSS 1220, Box 19, FF 1374.

[7] Herman T. Heath remembrance written during Operation Desert Storm, January 16 – February 28, 1991, courtesy of Grant Houston, Silver World.

[8] October 18 – November 27, 1918, MSS 1220, Box 19, FF 1375-1379. ["Lifter" refers to one of the holes for explosives drilled into the breast or face of the tunnel closest to the floor. When detonated, the force of the explosion "lifts" the rock face, hopefully creating a relatively clean separation from the surrounding rock.]

[9] "Denver, Colorado and the 1918-1919 Influenza Epidemic," pg.1. Cited from "Denver's First Death from Flu Reported", *Denver Post*, 27 September 1918. "it is likely, of course, that influenza was already circulating in the city. There were already nearly 100 cases in nearby Boulder, for example." Pg. 6. Also see Barry, John M., *The Great Influenza*, pg. 345.

[10] Ibid., pgs. 1-2.

[11] December 4, 1918, MSS 1220, Box 19, FF 1380.

[12] December 15, 1918, MSS 1220, Box 19, FF 1381.

[13] December 16, 1918, MSS 1220, Box 19, FF 1381.

[14] December 19, 1918, MSS 1220, Box 19 FF 1381.

[15] Lake City *Silver World*, December 26, 1918.

[16] December 31, 1918, MSS 1220, Box 19, FF 1382.

[17] Ibid.

[18] Colorado Bureau of Mines, Report for 1919.

[19] January 15, 1919, MSS 1220, Box 19, FF 1384.

[20] January 15, 1919, MSS 1220, Box 19, FF 1384.

[21] January 26-February 2, 1919, MSS 1220, Box 19, FF 1385-1386.

[22] February 9, 1919, MSS 1220, Box 19, FF 1386.

[23] February 11, 1919, MSS 1220, Box 19, FF 1387.

[24] February 20, 1919, MSS 1220, Box 19, FF 1388.

[25] February 26, 1919, MSS 1220, Box 19, FF 1388.

[26] May 1, 1919, MSS 1220, Box 19, FF 1395.

[27] May 4, 1919, MSS 1220, Box 19, FF 1395.

[28] May 20, 1919, MSS 1220. Boz 19, FF 1396

[29] May 25, 1919, MSS 1220, Box 19, FF 1397.

[30] June 1, 1919, MSS 1220, Box 19, FF 1398.

[31] June 3-5, 1919, MSS 1220, Box 19, FF 1398.

[32] June 20, 1919, MSS 1220, Box 19, FF 1400.

[33] August 4, 1919, MSS 1220, Box 19, FF 1404.

[34] September 4, 1919, MSS 1220, Box 19, FF 1407.

[35] November 5, 1919, MSS 1220, Box 19, FF 1413.

[36] July 24-August 17, 1920, MSS 1220, Box 19, FF 1433-1435.

[37] *The Creede Candle*, October 23, 1920.

CHAPTER 7

Elephants and Prairie Dogs

"Elephant Corral is Denver city's first hotel, inn, cottage camp,
mercantile business and corral, combined, and was built and
open for business in 1859."
— *Steamboat Pilot* [1] —

"That summer my father took up a ranch where the town
of Lake City now is. We built a cabin just back of the
Elephant Corral, which he built later."
— Eugene Bartholf [2] —

Strange as it may seem, A.E. Reynolds also had an elephant corral. Associating elephants with treasure hunts, prospecting, and mining was a well-engrained artifact of nineteenth-century American culture, and "going out to see the elephant" was often a polite brushoff in casual conversation, easier to swallow than "my planned journey is none of your business." The term was common street chatter for embarking on what might seem like a fool's errand—prospecting and mining especially—to see or experience something others were rushing to see or do. As for prairie dogs, their behavior reminded at least one pioneer of the boardinghouse chatter of miners after a hard day underground.

An "elephant" on the frontier was also understood to mean a reckless or frivolous activity, certainly a dangerous one best left to the young, hardy or foolhardy adventurer. Porch dogs remained on the porch, but 1850s America was populated with hunting dogs. Fertile free lands and rich mines were waiting on the far side of the prairie. California and Colorado gold was lying around everywhere, no easier elephants could one hope to find. Pay no attention to the empty-handed "go-backers" with "We have seen the Elephant" ironically painted on the canvas of their returning wagons. In A.E. Reynolds' case, he saw and acquired hundreds of such elephants and had a corral full—a portfolio full of claims—to prove it. [3]

A.E. was a young man when eastern living became intolerable to him. Pike Snowden was no older than sixteen. John York was in his early twenties. Men and women who went looking for their elephant soon discovered more hard work and risks than they ever imagined. Some did see the elephant, or at least the hind quarters of one, but most returned home or died trying.

Associating "corral" with elephants was also a rich frontier custom. Whatever the logic, looking for elephants required livestock and corralling livestock was a necessary feature of a frontier store of any consequence. Livestock pulling wagons across the prairie needed cared for until traded for pack animals better suited to mountain trails or no trails. In Denver's case, when Colorado gold seekers reached what quickly became the Queen City of the Prairie, they were steered to Denver's elephant corral. Ask anyone how to find it and they could point the way. That was no great feat, actually, given the "city's" size. Or ask everyone why it had such a name and no one thought it odd. Everyone knew its purpose. In fact such a question would be sure to prompt a laugh.

In the words of the earliest adventurers and the chroniclers that ferreted out their journeys, the "Hoosiers, suckers, corn crackers, buckeyes, red-horses, Arabs, or Egyptians," hoping to get rich and get out, owed their survival to Denver's Elephant Corral. They arrived half-starved and ready to exchange their teams and wagons for provisions and mining equipment. Freighting and commercial haulers soon followed, but first they needed a depot. Charles Blake and Andrew Williams saw the opportunity and built one. Their Elephant Corral so named quickly grew into a thriving trading post serving teamsters, gold-seekers and the region at large.[4]

According to the *Colorado History Gazette*, the Denver Elephant Corral started as the largest building in the Denver and Auraria settlement. It was thirty-two feet wide and one hundred feet long. It was soon enlarged to include a livery stable, stockyard, mercantile shops and "of course", a brothel.

> *The front of this large building contained the bar and gambling tables. This made for an easy exit thru the cotton covered windows if someone started shooting. Behind the bar, six bedrooms were rented to anyone needing overnight accommodations. Horace Greeley spent a single night in one of these rooms before pre-empting a cabin to escape the barroom noise that lasted all hours of the night. It is said that Blake and Williams advertised along the main routes to Denver and often sent employees out to meet the wagon trains and escort them back to the Corral. Around 1860, Blake and Williams sold the business to Robert Teats who enlarged it and named it the "Elephant Corral."[5]*

Not all Elephant Corrals featured shops and services and entertainment. A traveler could board his horse or oxen or himself in Spartan sleeping quarters. He could buy a drink and join a game of Faro. He could glean the latest news from

GOING OUT TO SEE THE ELEPHANT

Will Bagley tells of twenty-six year old William Stinson hired to lead a party of Forty-Niners across the plains. In addition to his scouting skills, according to Bagley, Stinson also was a marketer, promising his wards "a sight of all the elephants on the route, in other words, of all the interesting objects on our journey." [6] As the rush to California gained steam along the 1850 banks of the Missouri River, Bagley writes that an 1850 anonymous journalist reported on the "wagon-art" he observed. Painted on nearly every canvas top were the names of owners, various devices and mottoes, "quaint, odd, and appropriate:"

> *Gold or a Grave, Lucky Trip or Long Absence, Never Say Die, and Root Hog or Die [perhaps intended to evoke fond images among hog farmers.] Covers sported images of a sprawling eagle, a huge elephant, a tall giraffe, a rampant lion, a stately ox...* [7]

The origin of "to see the elephant" can be traced at least to April 13, 1796, when sea captain John Crowinshield brought the first elephant to America. Will Bagley writes:

> *Hachaliah Bailey made a fortune exhibiting a series of elephants, beginning in 1815 with the exceptionally talented Old Bet, who met a violent end when a New England farmer shot her for defiling the Sabbath. The saying appeared as early as 1834, and an 1872 compendium of Americanisms explained that it meant "to have seen all and to know everything...." Once elephants began appearing in circus parades in the late 1830s, the phrase spread like wildfire.*

Different people saw the elephant in different ways at different times—during the Civil War, it described a soldier's first experience with the savagery of combat. The expression "roughly meant 'to see it all,'" David L. Bigler noted. For gold seekers, the phrase captured the romance that drew them west. [8]

the claims and make the acquaintance of his next prospecting partner. Many prospecting adventures had their birth in the Elephant Corral.

In the American West, associating "elephants" and "elephant corrals" with gold rushes had a rich history. Denver's 1859 elephant corral was legendary—even tiny Lake City boasted of one in the mid-1870s. Many mining camps could, but like Lake City most were whimsical, nothing like Denver City. Mining camp elephant corrals usually were simply corrals and basecamps for organizing assaults on the High Country. Whether in search of information or companionship or a convenient livestock pen at the edge of town, Lake City's Elephant Corral at the mouth of Henson's Canyon served as a jumping-off place for the adventuresome.

Merchandising was left to the General Stores, entertainment to the saloons and brothels just a brief walk away.

A.E.'s corral of sorts was an artifact of his mercantile days, one capable of arousing expectations among the adventuring class. It was a one-stop shop for those who were worn out searching for claims of their own. Reynolds' Denver office—populated with his claims properly recorded in a Government Land Office—some patented and some not, promised rewards beyond belief. In their rawest state, they pointed to buried treasure. Best of all, the hardships of searching for it were almost over. The elephant could be purchased or leased for a pittance, or maybe not much. As a goodwill gesture, along with the elephant came maps of the underground workings, and assayed samples, imagine that. Only a little jack was lacking.

But not all elephants were created equal. Some were proven bonanzas. Some were marginal producers. Some were probably depleted. Some were no more than a glint in a visionary's eye awaiting development. Some were like the Vermont/Ocean Wave, a mixture of "wildly productive" and "buyer beware."

When all was said and done, all of A.E.'s elephants were for lease or sale. He preferred leasing. He had a hard time parting with anything. Stock sales were best of all, but those days were over. Reynolds' lease terms would be stiff, but the price would be framed by global supply and demand, by the whims of the marketplace. Wilson's war years inflated demand and metal values. Postwar

Elephant Corral. Jargon for a frontier mercantile, General Store by another name, that often included a livery stable and stockyard to outfit treasure-seekers with all manner of provisions they were not likely to find anywhere else. (*J. Harrison Mills,* Harper's Weekly)

years saw the opposite effect. Recovery of war-ravaged economies accompanied by an explosion of new industries—motorized vehicles and commercial flight and consumer products in particular—would help. Prospects looked bright until the Great Depression of the 1930s turned down the lights.

Miners being miners, adventurous treasure-seekers at heart, global calamities were far from their thinking when in search of a rich mineral vein to work. Investors were not much different other than their ability to factor global pricing into their risk calculations. The greater the risk, the greater the near-term return needed to be. Conversely, in the case of purchasing a claim, for example one of A.E.'s elephants, the greater the risk, the lower the price needed to be.

Of all the elephants in his corral, A.E. had his darlings, chief among them the Vermont /Ocean Wave group. That was where he had put his jack down in 1899. That was where he expected to get it back and more in 1920. Despite directing Cousin Harry and John York to shut down Vermont/Ocean Wave work in 1919, the wisdom of considering this elephant his best chance to redeem his fortune and his reputation was never seriously questioned. Yes, he ordered the shutdown, but it was to be orderly and accomplished in a way that would enable an efficient restart. Yes, the deaths of his trusted crew, the boys who tried to fulfill his vision more than once, would be difficult to replace, but he had always managed to recruit capable men in the past. What these setbacks did was force a change in strategy. He would step back from the front lines, after all he was eighty-one, and he would rely exclusively on leases rather than stock shares to fund the work. Tactically, he would turn over his kingdom to son-in-law Bradish P. Morse, husband of daughter Anna. The net effect would be less stress on his aging frame, and more financial certainty relying on lease payments instead of mill returns. The net would not be hunting for treasure with his own jack.

Whether unwisely influenced by his father-in-law or not is impossible to say. What is clear is that the Vermont/Ocean Wave and its impressive Reynolds haulage tunnel was Bradish's darling as well. And he, too, saw the greatest chance for financial rewards in the so-called "New Place." If the option of selling the Vermont/Ocean Wave properties was ever discussed, doing so was handily dismissed. Sale of other elephants was another matter. They were fair game. In the meantime, abandoning mines to local authorities for past-due property taxes, or preferably leasing mines with stringent conditions and sizeable royalties, was the chosen route to financial survival.

The Vermont/Ocean Wave was an appealing candidate for leasing. Its mineral characteristics had been extensively profiled albeit high-assay veins remained elusive. Dead-work required to exploit them, presumably largely accomplished already, could be easily exploited by others willing to marshal their capital and their labor for a while longer. The Vermont/Ocean Wave elephant was tangible, not a mirage dancing on a distant horizon. The irony of the matter was having to share certain treasure with others or recover no treasure at all.

Generally speaking, early twentieth-century San Juan miners and mine owners were comfortable if not excited with leasing practices. The lessees paid the
mine owner [lessor] a fee and/or a royalty for the right to work the property. The
nature of the compensation varied. Often it was a percentage of the net profit at
the smelter. Often it was a flat fee paid in cash up-front. Often it was a complex
cost and revenue sharing arrangement in which the owner agreed to maintain the
infrastructure and the lessees agreed to fund operating costs [e.g. consumables
like powder and coal]. What was considered infrastructure and what was considered operating costs was negotiated. A twenty percent fee was typical, revenue
shares also were negotiated. The local market for labor and silver governed, but
the estimated quantity and quality [assay] of ore played their part.

Lessees embraced the notion that the potential return on their labor would
far exceed hourly or daily wages. Better yet, striking high-grade ore was a bonanza
they could expect and should also profit from. Of course there were pitfalls for
both parties. The mine owner was apt to misrepresent the certainty that rich ore
was just a few rounds of powder farther in, that adequate dead work had been
completed, and that the surface plant was well-maintained. For their part, the
lessees were tempted to under-report production levels or ignore good steward-
ship of the infrastructure necessary for a mine's long-term wellbeing or safety.
Damage to the surface plant or underground workings through selfish practices
that left them in need of costly repairs was commonplace.

Even when the owner and lessee were honorable, another common practice presented additional risks. Often the lessee found that subleasing specified
blocks of ground or lengths of drifts or levels of the mine to other miners was
more lucrative and far easier than working the lease themselves. In this scenario,
diligence of both owner and the prime lessee was of the utmost importance. A.E.
was well-experienced in all these matters. He drove hard bargains which resulted
in few leases. Son-in-law Bradish, heir-apparent when it came to business affairs,
could be counted on to do the same.

Along with the worsening of 1920 weather came the worsening of A.E.'s
health. Warning signs turned out to be heart disease. On March 20, 1921, A.E.
ended even nominal control of his elephant corral. Son-in-law Bradish P. Morse
would be chief corral-keeper going forward. On March 29, 1921, Colorado's
mining king was dead. His passing, typically inconvenient for the heirs as well
as the deceased, presented B.P. with problems that would ultimately take his life
as well.

Befitting his once prominent role in Lake City affairs, his dogged commitment to regional mining and his Denver philanthropy, his obituary earned a place
in Colorado's prestigious *The Trail* journal: "Eighty-one yrs. old, pioneer mining man, cattle man, Indian trader, trustee of the Denver University and one of
Colorado's most outstanding figures, [Albert Eugene Reynolds] died March 29
at Nashville, Tenn., of heart disease following an illness lasting several weeks.[9]

The king earned even more royal treatment in both the *Silver World* and the *Lake City Times*:

NOTED FIGURE OF STATE PASSES

Denver papers of Monday announce the death in Nashville, Tenn., of Albert E. Reynolds, one of the notable characters of the settlement and development of Colorado. Mr. Reynolds was 81 years old when he died. He was born in New York, but came to the West in early-life and soon became identified in post trading with the Arapahoe and Cheyenne Indians, subsequently becoming associated with the famous Lee & Reynolds freighting outfit, one of the most notable of the lines of transportation over the Santa Fe Trail and its lateral lines in Colorado.

He came to Lake City in the early eighties and thereafter became heavily interested in mining enterprises. He was the moving spirit in development of the Virginius mine on Mt. Sneffels near Ouray and of the great Revenue tunnel by which the deeper parts of that mine were worked. He also opened up the Commodore mine at Creede, deriving a fortune from that property. In connection with the Gold Link property at Ohio City the company of which he was head owned over 600 mining claims in Gunnison County.

Mr. Reynolds held large interests in Hinsdale county, including majority interests in the Ocean Wave and Frank Hough groups and minor holdings in the Palmetto group, the Ophir, Golden Fleece and other properties, but aside from the Ocean Wave he has paid little attention to these interests for many years, though he did organize a company and do quite an amount of work [Vermont/Ocean Wave Group] under the superintendency of J.D. Fisher several years ago.

The remains were brought to Denver for internment. A daughter, two sisters and two brothers survive the deceased, the faithful wife having preceded him to the Great Beyond several years ago. With his passing goes one of the notable figures of Colorado's reclamation, settlement and progress." [10]

Impressive tribute, would you not agree? Never mind that such extensive holdings were bound to have a number of troublesome loose ends. As executor of the estate—chief elephant herder—son-in-law Morse soon discovered that the estate was in chaos with several thousand patented and unpatented mining claims as well as farm properties owned and leased totaling over 30,000 acres. He knew a lot about the "good" elephants, but he had no idea there were thousands of others maybe not so good. And 30,000 acres of farms?

Properties with a history of productivity were the Revenue Tunnel located at Sneffels, Ouray County; the Commodore at Creede, Mineral County; the Golconda at Summitville, Rio Grande County; and the Gold Links, Gold Cup, and lesser properties at Pitkin, Ohio City, and Tin Cup, Gunnison County.

Promising mines included the May Day near Hesperus, La Plata County; the Emma at Dunton, Dolores County; the Frank Hough, Ocean Wave, Vermont, and Palmetto near Lake City, Hinsdale County; and the Parole and Forest King at Platero, Conejos County. Other mining claims were located in Boulder, Pitkin, and San Juan Counties.[11]

The root cause of the estate's problems was not record-keeping. That was excellent due to the incredibly conscientious Denver office support provided by J.P.M. Humphrey. The root cause was the sheer volume of debt, contract obligations both honored and derelict, and overdue invoices some of which spanned years and longer. Always short on cash, all of this and more had to be juggled in order to keep the sheriff at bay and at least some work going in the better mines. In general, Reynold's' ventures as a whole generated considerable cashflow. In general, they also generated considerable expenses, more than overall cashflow could keep up with. The short-term solutions that evolved into a way of life was to short-pay Peter in order to short-pay Paul. Creditors and laborers were paid not according to date due, but according to availability of funds and their place in the line of creditors. Priorities were set by operational requirements or legal proceedings. The most threatening demands were addressed when a carload of ore or lease payments provided funds. Sadly for some, first come-first served was not an A.E .Reynolds business practice. Along with the elephants, estate Executor Morse inherited this legacy, too.

Bradish Morse, more commonly known as Brad or just "B.P.," devoted most of his day every day for the remainder of his life trying to stay one step ahead of a court judgment or tax sale or lease default or in all likelihood a creditor with a gun. Despite advice from high-rollers and scam artists who knew what they were talking about to let creditors repossess properties, B.P. was determined to preserve the good reputation of the Reynolds. His goal was to pay all debts owed. Sadly, there was no cash to pay much of anything. Sadder still, there was no priority placed on back wages owed other estates, notably the York estate, or to Rowland Ewart's widow. Reynolds' largest business obligations, mostly unpaid loans from Denver and Pueblo banks, amounted to about $150,000. In addition, taxes had not been paid on many of the mining properties, in some instances for ten or more years. Amounting to as much as $40,000 on the Revenue Tunnel properties and $29,000 on the Gunnison County claims, these debts could not be negotiated away. County governments forever in need of money were eager to sell tax certificates for properties on which payments were in arrears. Worse yet, annual tax bills alone for all Reynolds properties increased the estate's total debt by another $50,000 each year.[12]

In fact, B.P. enjoyed some success. One-stop shopping at Reynolds' corral of elephants appealed to the moneyed class. By the end of 1921 Bradish had negotiated contracts for the sale of four major properties and leases for several others. He disposed of the May Day on a two-year lease-and-purchase option at a price of $125,000, with $10,000 in cash. He leased and bonded the Commodore for $75,000, $5,000 in cash. A fraction of a claim at Ouray netted $900 [small but still real jack in 1921 – enough to buy a good car]. He sold the Ely-Revenue Copper Company's lands at Ely, Nevada, for $70,000, payable in early 1922. Purchasers of the Revenue Tunnel properties were obligated to pay $50,000. Leases were being negotiated for the Vermont and Ocean Wave Group, as well as for the Gold Links Tunnel at Ohio City.[13]

Morse's first year managing the Reynolds estate promised a bright future. The family bank account increased by more than $135,000 with purchase options totaling an additional $200,000. Royalties on ore sales from the leases were expected to add tens of thousands more. On paper, life looked good. The year 1922 was going to be the beginning of another prosperous chapter in the Reynolds' legacy. In fact, the family bank account stagnated and evaporated as assets were triaged to creditors. There would be no ore sales that amounted to anything, and none of the purchase options were exercised. The lease or sale of Reynolds' corral of elephants was proving to be more difficult than expected. Yet once again, the Vermont/Ocean Wave with its Reynolds Tunnel resurfaced as the last best chance to redeem the Reynolds fortune.

Like A.E.'s famously successful Virginius/Revenue Tunnel above Ouray or Nevada's Comstock/Sutro Tunnel, Reynolds' Vermont/Ocean Wave tunnel set the Vermont and Ocean Wave on a pedestal. Soon known simply as the Reynolds Tunnel, it was a serviceable and efficient haulage and ventilation corridor into the depths of a proven, mineral-rich mountain laced with Vermont and Ocean Wave silver-rich veins. This fact was indisputable. Great wealth had been extracted during prior decades and all signs pointed to great wealth remaining still. This, too, was indisputable albeit difficult to deliver.

Moreover, the surface plant was intact. And the mineral reserves were proven [well, sort of]. You can still hear B.P.'s sales pitch echoing off the mountains: "Why not capitalize on the tremendous investment and work

Heavy-Duty Trucks. WWI also advanced the development of a new mode of transportation. In 1917 a consortium of manufacturers rolled out the Class-B Standardized Military Truck, "Liberty Truck" for short, that soon became a common site at the nation's mines. *(U.S. Signal Corps – National Archives)*

already accomplished. You can be the one to see the elephant and take credit for the prize. A great treasure, the motherlode, has to be close at hand."

Like his father-in-law, Bradish Morse never lost faith in this vision. Faith of the average miner was another matter. Needed were miners, speculators at least, that were not average. Needed were men with jack to spare, with prospector hearts, and with prairie dog instincts. That's right, prairie dogs. Burros and elephants were not the only companions of lonely men that entertained them with their simple ways.

Both the Vermont and the Ocean Wave were labyrinths of tunnels, shafts, winzes and stopes. Beginning in the 1880s, leads were opened and set aside time and again in the course of locating and extracting high-grade ores. In 1921 these opportunities for further gain were bewildering temptations. More than one imaginative pilgrim saw curious similarities between treasure-seeking miners willing to dig more dirt, and ever-active prairie dogs. In fact, the common traits of prairie dogs and miners with prospector instincts are not just humorous, they are prophetic.

> *In their habits, they are clannish, social, and extremely convivial, never living alone like other animals, but, on the contrary, always found in villages or large settlements. They are a wild, frolicsome, madcap set of fellows when undisturbed, uneasy and ever on the move, and appear to take special delight in chattering away the time, and visiting from hole to hole to gossip and talk over each other's affairs—at least so their actions would indicate.*[14]

When it came to working underground, the prairie dog lived in tunnels, the miner tunneled to live. Both hollowed out drifts and stopes. The dog harvested roots. The miner harvested veins. While the prospector delighted in locating a mine, the miner with prospector instincts delighted in rooting out high-grade ore in the mine. Harry Van Horn, John York, and Rowland Ewart were of this ilk. Bradish Morse needed to attract more of the same. Put in safe and secure long-term shutdown in mid-1919, Reynolds' last best chance to make a mine sat unattended until 1921 when another generation of

Brotherhood of Burrowers. Some who have spent a lot of time in the wild see similarities in the nature of prairie dogs and miners. If asked, the dogs would likely protest. *(Wikipedia)*

prairie dogs came on the scene. A.E. Reynolds was gifted with an ability to discern this trait in a miner. Son-in-law Morse was fairly-well gifted in that regard as well.

On August 5, 1921, B.P. sensed he was close to securing a lucrative lease. In a *Dupont Private Wire* addressed to E.B. Hendrie he wrote:

> *We have had a number of applications for lease and bond on the Ocean Wave property in Lake City. Knowing that you own the Vermont and of the relations that exist between you and Mr. Reynolds as covered by an option on the property which you gave him when he thought that he was going to be able to do something with this and which option has expired—I am writing to ask if you would care to continue this option to the estate so that we could incorporate it in negotiations looking toward the leasing of the Ocean Wave. The two properties are so closely connected that I feel that we could put both under a lease and bond as well as one, and that the proposition would be more attractive covering the two to a prospective leasor (sic) than just the one. Trusting that I shall hear from you in regard to this. I am yours very truly, B.P. Morse.*[15]

B.P. did not have to wait long. Hendrie, a man of few words and limited patience, wrote back on August 8, 1921: "Dear Sir: I have your favor of August 5th regarding the option upon my property above Lake City. Will say that I will be very glad for you to handle those interests down there in connection with your Ocean Wave property. Very truly yours, Edwin B. Hendrie.[16]

Nor was B.P. one to dawdle. With clear rights to the Vermont in sight, he followed up with Hendrie and his prospective leasee, J.M. Kerr. As such matters were apt to unfold, J.M. Kerr had teamed up with A.J. Reynolds, a nephew of A.E., and nephew Reynolds was well-acquainted with the Vermont/Ocean Wave Group. In an August 12, 1921, *Dupont Private Wire* to J.M. Kerr, B.P. wrote:

> *Dear Sir: I am in receipt of your night letter of the 10th and we are wiring you as follows: Will give you lease and bond on Ocean Wave and Vermont three year bond. Three hundred thousand for both. Graded royalties to apply on purchase price. Usual lease terms and conditions. Will hold open if you agree to make examination at once. I think that this is plain, and I understand from Mr. [A.J.] Reynolds that you want both a lease and bond on Ocean Wave and Vermont. I have included both of them in this proposition. This makes it a much better scheme to handle for both properties as the Vermont has been a good producer as well as the Ocean Wave and the property is so that you can work both of them as the tunnel connects with the Vermont shaft. I hope I will have word from you that you will go ahead with this property as I think it is one offer of especial merit and that you will make some money with it. Yours very truly, B.P. Morse.*[17]

On August 12th B.P. also wired E.B. Hendrie: "Dear Sir: Acknowledgement is made of your letter of August 8th in regard to your property above Lake City. I will advise you if anything comes up in regard to Ocean Wave, and as I am figuring with several people on the Ocean Wave I hope to have something to report to you shortly. Yours very truly, B.P. Morse." [18]

J.M. Kerr was equally motivated. Like our industrious prairie dogs, the Henson Canyon mining community was similarly communal and industrious when it came to sharing good news. J.M. knew the history of the Vermont/Ocean Wave Group and also was reasonably sure there was treasure to be found. Had not the U.S. Geological Survey and the trustworthy *Silver World* routinely reported as much? On August 16, 1921, replying to J.M.'s telegram, B.P. responded in kind:

> *Dear Sir: We are in receipt of your telegram of the 14th and note that you will make an examination of the Vermont and Ocean Wave at once, and we will hold this open until you have this opportunity which we will limit to thirty days, so that the matter will be definitely settled by that time. I wish I were there to go over this property with you as I have made quite a study of it from Bancroft's bulletin and am just as well satisfied as can be that the work was done on the wrong vein and that they never have been on the Vermont vein at all. I also believe that the Vermont and the Ocean Wave veins are the same. If you can possibly do it, I would go up the raise to the old Vermont shaft and see what the vein looks like at that point, as there is undoubtedly good values in the Vermont. Trusting that you will find things interesting enough to go into the proposition. I am yours very truly, B.P. Morse.* [19]

Whether J.M. Kerr took up B.P.'s suggestion that he climb the Reynolds Tunnel raise to the Vermont shaft is unknown, but we do know that J.M. remained sufficiently interested to make a counteroffer. He proposed a longer lease term and a lower price. Again, B.P. promptly responded with an August 26th *Western Union* telegram. He was not interested in increasing the proposed term of the lease to five years, but he was willing to lower the price to $250,000 if paid outright and royalties were increased, which should not be an issue, he added, since they were paid out of ore proceeds. [B.P. explained that the reason he could not agree to a five-year lease was that his lease with Hendrie was only for three years.] B.P., well-schooled by his father-in-law in proper lease arrangements, also reiterated that the leasee must commit to ninety shifts per month, thereby ensuring that a minimum of three men would be working underground. B.P. was not interested in a deal that did not move dirt, but instead might serve the lessee simply as collateral for some other fraudulent scam.

Not to be badgered too much, Kerr proposed a $100,000 bond in keeping with arrangements he [probably including partner A.J.] had discussed with A.E. Reynolds just before his death. B.P. countered that the $100,000 bond A.E. once offered Andrew was not valid because A.E. was dead. B.P. needed $300,000. Overall, he continued, A.E. would insist on harsher terms if the bond was low. He wrapped up his pitch with another reference to Bancroft's bulletin, just in case that was relevant to Kerr's thought process. B.P. took exception to a Bancroft statement that the Vermont vein "bottomed out" at the Reynolds' Tunnel level, but otherwise he liked to cite it whenever he could. He also liked to stimulate action by sharing with Kerr and A.J. that there was another interested leasee by the name of John Cortellini from Leadville, Colorado. B.P.s exception to Bancroft's report, short and not so sweet, was drafted with the same purpose in mind:

> *We struck two pockets of ore and it was a fine high grade ore as you would see anywhere showing that mineral is there. As far as the present tunnel is concerned, it is not bottomed ore... [John Cortellini] is anxious to take a lease on account of there being some of his employees who formerly worked on the Ocean Wave and are very anxious to get a hold of it.*[20]

Nothing more was heard from or about John Cortellini. It did not matter. On September 7, 1921, the Vermont/Ocean Wave Group lease was negotiated and on its way to J.M. Kerr and A.J. Reynolds for signatures. Two days later it

---

USGS BULLETIN 478 [21]

Published in 1911, this scholarly work served as a preeminent guide to Henson Canyon mines for decades. The Vermont and to a lesser extent the Ocean Wave were featured. Vein material "consisted chiefly of Argentiferous tetrahedrite and galena, with smaller quantities of sphalerite, chalcopyrite, and pyrite. The main output of the mine has been silver and lead." Any savvy investor capable of serious due diligence would consult this bulletin before purchase or lease.

The value of the ore from the upper workings in 85 shipments of 25 tons each ranged from 33.9 to 253.10 ounces of silver, and 7.5 to 59 percent lead. The average silver and lead content for these 85 shipments was 84.53 ounces of silver and 27.96 per cent lead, giving an average value, computed on the present [1911] market prices, of $44.80 silver and $12.06 lead, or a total average gross value of $56.86 per ton of ore mined. In 1894, 63 tons mined yielded $4,965, an average of about $79 per ton of ore. Two later shipments of 16,078 pounds and 10,504 pounds, in 1895 and 1896 respectively, yielded an average total value of $22.67 and $22.78 per ton each.

was returned unsigned. It needed modified. B.P. telegraphed his attorney with these instructions:

> *Make lease and bond Kerr and Reynolds five years on Ocean Wave and three years on Vermont, ninety shifts per month stop raise royalties a little stop two hundred thousand Ocean Wave, one hundred thousand Vermont. Hendrie has promised to give extension lease on Vermont and have asked John [J.P.M. Humphrey] to get it.* [22]

Kerr and Reynolds signed their lease but Hendrie insisted on changes to his B.P. lease of the Vermont. Office manager Humphrey broke the frustrating news to B.P. on September 16th. In a brief note, J.P.M. informed B.P. that Hendrie now required a $6,000 payment due April 1922, and that he would not budge on this point. On September 17, 1922, Morse received Hendrie's letter conveying the altered lease agreement.

> *Dear Sir: I am enclosing you two copies of Lease and Bond upon the Vermont Group. Will say that I think there is also a millsite with it and I own half of the tunnel which was run by Mr. Reynolds. Now, if this is all right, and you will kindly sign both and return to me, I will sign one copy and return to you. Hoping that you will be very successful in handling this. I am Very truly yours, E.B. Hendrie.* [23]

B.P. was not "successful in handling this." He advised Hendrie that he rejected the Vermont lease sent to him, and that he knew nothing about the mill site or question of half ownership of the Reynolds Tunnel. This might have been true, but probably not. In any case, B.P. told Hendrie that he would have Humphrey research the matter and that he would go forward if Hendrie sent him a lease like the one he had signed with A.E. in 1899. On September 23rd Hendrie replied. He informed Morse that he was surprised the Vermont lease was returned unsigned, stating that it was the one Morse had sent him. Obviously confused, he said he would await the arrival of Humphrey to point out changes. He ended by saying he wanted to "make it satisfactory." [24]

Meanwhile, John Kerr and A.J. bided their time. No one ever said herding elephants was easy. John York would have said aligning everyone's legal interests was enough to make a man "nuttier than a pet coon." Kerr and A.J. were steadfast in their belief that the only lease that made sense was a lease that included both the Vermont Group and the Ocean Wave, and of course the Reynolds Tunnel and the surface plant. The interdependent features of the entire property was obvious to even the dullest of investors and J.M. Kerr and A.J. were a country mile from "dull." B.P. was of like mind. While Humphrey ironed out wrinkles with Hendrie, Kerr and A.J. traveled to Lake City to inspect the mine. On October

6th Kerr, just back from Lake City, advised B.P. that he was ready to begin work as soon as they got their lease. "This is most important as I believe that the Vermont claim is the key to the entire proposition." He also reported that someone was constructing a dam and powerline "on your property in order to take the water from El Paso Creek… these people are going to work the Lellie mine just below our property." Nice to know, but of no consequence to B.P. Getting back on topic, it turned out Kerr was ready to get their lease, however it needed more modifications. He wanted "shifts" clarified – this should be understood to mean eight hours, and to apply to either the Vermont or Ocean Wave, not exclusively the Vermont. He also needed abstracts and copies of the leases for his investors. Ending on a high note, he planned to start work no later than October 14th and wanted the lease to reflect that fact.[25]

The October 14th start date came and went without a signed lease agreement, but November 11th marked more than the end of Wilson's War. E.B. Hendrie, J.M. Kerr, A.J. Reynolds, and B.P. Morse had finally signed their leases and work was finally underway. A.J. joyfully advised B.P.:

> *Mr. Kerr and I think we may make some money out of this mine, and surely will do so if the money is in it. [In other words, if we secure enough investor cash.] We have hardly gotten well started yet but will have things going good in a few days and will keep you advised of progress. Are trying to open up the upper workings and also connect with the ore body from the lower tunnel.* [26]

Joy is a fickle soulmate. A.J.'s joy fled when he glanced at the abstracts requested by investors and noticed that there was a mechanics lien on the property that would interfere with payment for any ore they shipped from the mine. The lien in the amount of $3,296.84 dated July 29, 1919, was John York's lien for unpaid wages and accrued interest. This was a surprise even to office manager Humphrey. A similar lien for far less back wages filed in the name of Rowland Ewart had been known and had been resolved in short order. Attorney Ralph C. Horton acknowledged the same in a courteous note to B.P.: "Dear Sir: yours of the 14th received and thanks for settlement. As I know this will be a real Christmas present to the Widow [sic.] at this time." [27]

After further investigation and considerable legal advice, efforts to get out from under the York lien had not fared as well. Although John York and subsequently his heirs had failed to pursue their claim in accordance with Colorado statutes, the York estate was not without remedies. For his part, B.P. had not disputed the fact that York's claim was a valid debt, but he also had not been moved to honor it in light of the relief Colorado law provided him. Kerr and A.J. were comforted by this knowledge. Charles York, John's closest relative, beloved older brother, and practicing attorney, also surprised by the discovery of the lien, had not been comforted. He had engaged Dr. Samuel McKibben residing in Creede, Colorado, to serve as estate administrator empowered to pursue the matter. Dr. Sam had done his job well. Along with supporting documentation, he had informed Morse and Humphrey that he was aware the Vermont/Ocean Wave was back in operation, and that the York estate was entitled to royalties from Vermont/Ocean Wave sales until the debt to the York estate was paid in full.

On January 18, 1922, Humphrey had mounted a spirited counteroffensive: "most of the work so far I understand to be in getting ready for work and cleaning out the tunnels that had badly caved in some places, and up to this time there have been no shipments of ore, and I have not been informed that they have found ore in sufficient quantities that they are able to make any shipments," he had written to Dr. McKibben. He had then cited another paragraph from the same document Dr. McKibben was basing his request. The indebtedness of the *Ocean Wave Mining & Reduction Company* to J.E. York was an obligation which was "collectible only out of the proceeds of ore from that property, or out of any moneys received by that company from a sale of said property, but is not payable in any other way." Humphrey had concluded his defense by trying to claim the high ground—the Reynolds estate "could not agree to preferable treatment of the York estate since many similar claims had been made, but that he was hopeful that the property in question would pay and that they would be able to settle all claims in due course." [28]

Sounded fair. Final. With a glimmer of hope to help the medicine go down. But the difference between how the York estate had been handled compared to the Ewart estate was stark yet understandable. First, the magnitude of the difference between the claims was great. Second, the York heirs lived in Iowa. The Ewart widow with six young children lived in Lake City.

With a favorable legal opinion regarding the York lien and a signed Vermont/Ocean Wave lease in hand, and a respectable start on shareholder funding, the newly organized *Henson Creek Mines Company* bolted out of the chute. Company offices were opened in La Junta, Colorado, a reasonable distance by train to Lake City. Company officers were elected: A.J. Reynolds, President; Fred A. Sabin, Vice-President; Rufus Phillips, Secretary-Treasurer; and John Kerr, Manager. Reynolds and Kerr held majority shares. Phillips, an A.E. Reynolds trading post associate, decades-long family friend, and La Junta banker, provided $10,000 cash of the initial $100,000 operating budget at $1.00 per share. A.J., an attorney soon to become a prominent politician [Deputy District Attorney for Denver], became the face of the company and apparently the focal point of miner derision if their tunnel graffiti was any indication. Kerr justified his favored ownership position by virtue of his mining experience. Phillips and to a lesser extent Fred Sabin ponied up the jack.

As an afterthought, on January 18th A.J. asked B.P. to make two corrections to their lease. Proper ownership of the Reynolds Tunnel was the Ocean Wave company, not B.P. Morse, as the lease read, and use of the tunnel should be noted in the lease, which it was not. B.P. agreed. With administrative matters thus settled, the *Henson Creek Mines Company* treasure hunt began. Within days their first reported ore sample was bismuth silver assaying at 721 ounces per ton, a very encouraging beginning to be sure.[29]

On February 21, 1922, A.J. reported more good news. In addition to being appointed Deputy District Attorney for Denver, no doubt a subtle reminder he was not to be trifled with but of no relevance otherwise, he also proudly announced that the *Henson Creek Mines Company* was making great progress at the mine. Kerr, the only company officer with any practical mining experience, had shipped ore from where they had collected the bismuth silver sample. They were following a vein with a narrow streak of the rich ore and two feet of lead and copper. Their crew was twelve men strong. They planned to build a small con-

Tunnel Graffiti. Deputy District Attorney for Denver A.J. Reynolds, mossbacks Kilvert and Ramsay included, were not too busy to leave their marks on the tunnel wall. *(Author's Collection)*

centration mill near the tunnel portal to better deal with abundant low-grade ore. Their La Junta subscribers [investors] were in agreement save for one pesky detail. They wanted to see a return on their investment first. [30]

In Henson Canyon mining, good news often had a short lifespan. On April 10, 1922, B.P. noted what he believed were troubling storm clouds building on the horizon. A.J.'s company board meeting scheduled in La Junta only had one action item on the agenda: finances. Just three months into their lease, B.P. was getting concerned that this dog was not going to hunt. He wrote A.J., "Will be glad to hear from you as to how you make out at La Junta as I am anxious to see that work go ahead on the Ocean Wave. You are too near success to drop it and I hope you have made arrangements to go ahead with it." [31]

Too impatient and troubled to wait for A.J.'s reply—A.J. probably too befuddled to reply in any event—B.P. traveled to La Junta the next day to meet with Rufus Phillips. He documented his impressions concerning the visit in a note to office manager Humphrey. "Dear John: While in La Junta, I had quite a number of talks with Mr. Phillips, who is the real backer behind the Ocean Wave property and he is willing to go ahead and put up the money to develop that property." B.P. went on to say that he and Phillips agreed that they needed someone who knew what they were doing at the mine. Clearly concerned about John Kerr's abilities—if not John, who?—B.P. suggested an acquaintance by the name of Jim Lyons. He asked Humphrey to follow up with Lyons. If he was interested, "ask him to write Mr. R. Phillips, First National Bank, La Junta, to work out the details." Phillips, for his part, also an impatient and impulsive man, obviously riled up by B.P., booked a train ticket to Lake City that same day.[32]

On April 21, 1922, Rufus Phillips freshly returned from Lake City, shared his observations in a letter addressed to both "A.J. Reynolds, Deputy District Attorney, Denver, and John Kerr." He stated that he had just spent three days at the mine. He expressed appreciation for what it took to work through the winter. He stated that despite disappointing results and a lot of money spent, a lot had been accomplished. Always a gentleman if not always sincere, he shifted gears: "While we have made a good many mistakes I do not want to find fault." Then he dropped the hammer. Their debts must be paid, then more funds invested. They should abandon their present plan and "open up the Dago Tunnel. This tunnel is nearly a thousand feet long, and I have an estimate of $1,000 as the cost of opening it up... I think too, we must sooner or later put in a mill, but this is a good way in the future yet."

The Dago Tunnel? Really? The Ocean Wave's lowest-level tunnel John York and Rowland Ewart had been driving a raise on and had nearly reached a few short years earlier? And a mill? Was the mill they had just put in not sufficient? Yes, all of that. And banker Phillips had more on his mind. He wanted to reorganize the company to better reflect where company funds were coming from. Nothing personal, of course, he just thought it fair to expect A.J. and Kerr to each ante up $10,000 cash or relinquish shares and thus control in favor of Rufus. For obvious reasons, Rufus failed to mention any thought of relieving John Kerr of his manager responsibilities in favor of Jim Lyons.[33]

Jim Lyons was not interested. His hunting dog days were over. Of all the elephants remaining in the Reynolds Estate corral, he agreed the Vermont/Ocean Wave Group was likely the last best chance to make a mine. But he was not up to climbing long ladders, or coping with stale air. Besides that, he suffered from "neuritis," a little understood condition promising blindness not far down a short road.

B.P. had a Plan B. He informed Rufus that Robert Sayers was a competent engineer and "a good clean young fellow; you would get good satisfaction from his work and the property would be in safe hands."[34]

On April 29th, emboldened by the knowledge that B.P. saw matters his way, Rufus Phillips presented his Plan B. He thanked B.P. for introducing him to a new mine manager candidate and shared with him a suggestion by A.J. that "we" buy out Kerr. Phillips did not think Kerr had anything to sell. In fact, he had his doubts about Andrew and said as much to B.P. Andrew had overspent their budget and banker Phillips was offended by his fiduciary irresponsibility. Rufus wrote B.P.:

> *Messrs. Reynolds and Kerr not only overreached that amount [$10,000], but had all of the money spent practically by the 1st of March, two months ahead of time. While I suppose they will not admit it, yet it is clear to me after my trip that there has been some very poor management, and I think without exaggeration, twice as much money spent as should have been.* [35]

B.P. agreed. In a May 3rd reply to Phillips he expressed support for reorganizing the ownership of the *Henson Creek Mines Company* to give control to the La Junta investors. Doing so should be fair to A.J. and John Kerr. Always a wily negotiator, B.P. added, "Of course with all this you cannot forget that both Reynolds and Kerr had good salaries out of this $10,000 and that they suffered no loss and have had a good job when jobs were hard to get." Without being specific, B.P. was referring to the nationwide recession and the abysmal state of mining in Henson Canyon.[36]

John Kerr did not seem troubled by Plan B, but it was not welcomed by A.J. Reynolds. Probably without malice of forethought, maybe in a careless hurry, but maybe as a reminder of his political weaponry, a reminder of his prideful perch, he responded on "Office of the District Attorney" stationary with a counterproposal. Then it was Rufus' turn to be offended, either by the stationary or with the implicit rebuke or both. Rufus pushed back hard, including expressing his disdain for A.J.'s "fat salary." He invited Reynolds and Kerr to La Junta—in effect to the proverbial woodshed—for "negotiations." B.P. also received an invitation, observer-status to be sure.[37]

Increasingly Phillips was in close consultation with Morse. On May 11, 1922, he shared his frustrations with B.P. He had been unsuccessful in getting Kerr and A.J. to meet him in La Junta. He was adamant about the "La Junta crowd" taking control of the company. He was equally adamant about replacing Kerr with Robert Sayre or someone like him with instructions to produce "high values" by developing the abandoned Dago Tunnel. B.P. had his doubts, not about replacing Kerr, but about reopening the Dago Tunnel. Rufus went to considerable lengths to explain his thinking. His thinking also reminds us why this treasure hunt has been so challenging, and why this elephant has remained a darling in the corral.

> *There are four tunnels on the upper works of the Ocean Wave and the Dago Tunnel is the lower one of the four. It is in this tunnel that Mr. Reynolds*

[A.E.] had given a lease to some "Dagos." He found that they had began (sic) understoping on a vein that showed, I understand, very good values. He immediately cancelled the lease and fired them off of the premises [not the case, but their good fortune was]. This was the last work ever done on the upper works.

As five or six years or more have gone by, the tunnel has caved in very badly in a number of places, and although we knew of this caving, our first plan was to open up this tunnel and try to get some shipping ore that would help pay expenses as we went along. When Reynolds [Andrew J.] and Kerr went up to the mine to go to work, they made an inspection of the Dago Tunnel, and without consulting the rest of us, gave up the idea of opening it, and began spending money right and left putting the compressor and pipe line in condition, and removing a tremendous amount of dirt that had caved in at the extreme end of the lower crosscut tunnel [meaning the "New Place" last worked by York, Ewart and Van Horn].

Although I went up into the [ore] chute on my recent visit, I cannot tell you very much about it. It is about 30 feet wide east and west on a vein, and the upraise extends perhaps 25 or 30 feet. Mr. Clark [A.J.'s mine superintendent] told me that soon after opening up the chute, they ran into a small body of ore, and he remarked to Andrew, "That looks to me like a million dollars." Their hopes, however, in this regard were short-lived for the streak of ore played out in a short distance and they were up against a blank wall, which I think they called a "horse." They went right ahead, however, and the vein is opening up again just about like it was at the start. Andrew thinks that this is the Ocean Wave vein, but I could not get Mr. Clark to say that he thought it was, although he admitted that there is that possibility.[38]

When Rufus finished with him, B.P. was a believer. In a May 16th letter B.P. wrote that the attitudes of Kerr and Andrew were unacceptable, and he would cancel their lease and write a new one for Phillips if they could not agree to reorganize the company. As for the Dago Tunnel,

I think that it would be a good idea to follow out the line you suggest… a winze can be sunk from the Dago Tunnel and give a good stoping ground so that you can begin to get out ore and ship and help carry things along. It can then further be sunk to the tunnel [meaning the Ocean Wave crosscut where York, Ewart and Van Horn were working the "New Place"] and you will know whether you are on the vein or not when you get to the tunnel. It might of course be well to follow the ore chute we have on the tunnel level and I think that the opinion of Robert Sayre or someone familiar with operation of this kind would be advisable in this respect. [as B.P. was fond of saying and illustrated by his own frustrations, he closed by writing that he was "anxious that this work proceeds and amounts to something." [What he meant was he needed their lease payments as much as they needed a return on their investment.] [39]

Executing Phillips' plan promised another immensely valuable benefit. Just as connecting the Reynolds Tunnel with the upper abandoned Vermont workings had provided natural ventilation to the Vermont leg of the lower tunnel crosscut, connecting the Ocean Wave leg of this crosscut with the Dago Tunnel would naturally ventilate that extensive section of the mine. That this obvious improvement, well within reach, had not been pursued on day-one much less discussed is mystifying. Regrets aside, it was on the front-burner now and would be stirred to life once one last detail could be attended to—Rufus had to get Andrew onboard or throw him overboard. Given Andrew's high opinion of himself, treating the political Denver prosecutor like an incompetent mining executive could be unwise and thus avoided, handled with care at the very least. Rufus was not unwise. He paused long enough for ally Morse to run interference. On May 16th B.P. delivered. He informed Andrew that the *Henson Creek Mines Company* lease would be cancelled if he and Rufus did not agree on reorganizing the company. Phillips' proposition was fair, he said. He [B.P.] could not see any role or use for Kerr. Silent on Andrew's future role, B.P. did remind him as if that was necessary that neither he nor Kerr had any jack in the game, and that they both had received handsome wages in the meantime. Before returning to Kerr, B.P. drove one more nail into Andrew's coffin. Phillips' reorganization plan would result in less ownership for him, but less was better than none. As for John Kerr, B.P. continued,

> *I cannot see for the life of me where Kerr comes in for any consideration in this matter at all [implying Andrew was different]. He left the property the minute that the money didn't come to pay his wages and he got good wages for all he did when there. He didn't raise a cent of money and I haven't a bit of use whatever for him in this matter.* [40]

With that, out came B.P.'s carrot and stick. First he praised Andrew for putting the company together including their compensation package, then he warned Andrew that he had others interested in the property.[41]

Amazing what a not-so-veiled threat could accomplish. Within a week Phillips reported to Reynolds Estate Executor Morse that he, Reynolds' nephew Andrew, and Company Manager John Kerr had met that Saturday afternoon in La Junta for 3½ hours and had reached an agreement. "Everybody seems to be in a good humor and is ready now to work together on the proposition." The "La Junta interests" would have 40,000 shares of stock, Kerr & Reynolds 25,000. Thirty-five thousand shares were for sale, 10,000 at $0.50 each to be sold immediately to raise $5,000, enough to go on. Phillips would instruct Mr. Clark to begin work on the Dago Tunnel and to go ahead and build a bulkhead in the Vermont-end of the Reynolds Tunnel crosscut in order to install an air line as far as the receiver and stope in the Ocean Wave-end. [As always, ventilation was a problem. This remedy would make-do until they succeeded in connecting the Reynolds and Dago tunnels, a total distance of over three thousand feet most of which had already been completed.]

Superintendent Clark promptly and joyfully replied with a telegram announcing completion of the bulkhead, and that two men were at work cleaning up the Dago Tunnel. Phillips [remember he is a banker, not a mine "engineer"] would visit the mine to supervise the start of work in the stope at the receiver. [The "receiver" was a large tank that served as a reservoir used to better control the air pressure between their outdoor compressor and their drills.] Their short-term goal was to eliminate using their compressor to ventilate the stope, relying instead on the bulkhead and lengthy air line. If successful, not only would the crew breathe easier, the compressor could be devoted fully to powering their pneumatic drills. Contradicting himself almost in the same sentence, Phillips confessed that Kerr and Andrew still opposed use of the Dago Tunnel. Reality also contradicted the banker. Executing the Dago Tunnel strategy would cost $3,000, not the $1,000 that Phillips was forecasting.[42]

True to his word, Rufus visited the mine. True to his nature, he stayed in close touch with B.P. On June 3, 1922, he reported to Morse that he had just returned the previous night from his eight day trip to Lake City. Not content with overseeing the work, he had "chased around" the countryside looking "for some pipe suitable for an air line with which to ventilate the lower workings of the Ocean Wave." He had checked every junk yard between Pueblo and Salida, also old mines on Henson Creek, and had bought 1,000 feet of 10-inch pipe about eight miles from the mine "which we have to transport a distance of two miles on burros getting it down to the road, and from there it is an

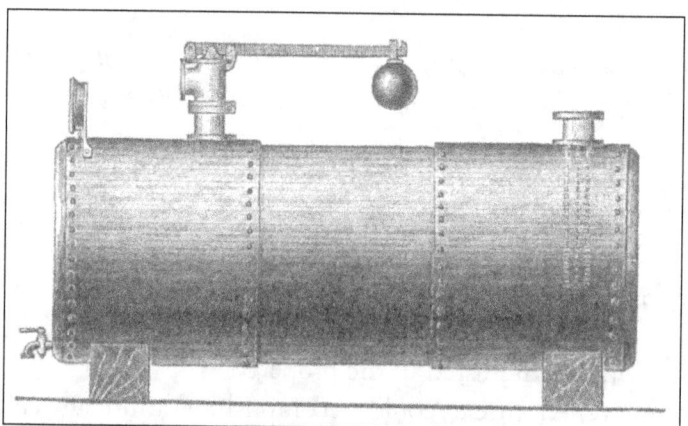

Rand Air Receiver. Maintaining constant air pressure needed to properly operate pneumatic drills required what amounted to a pressurized tank located between the steam-driven air compressor outside the tunnel and the drill. A "reservoir" of pressurized air served to dampen the peaks and valleys of pressure resulting from the cyclical operation of the air compressor. *(Rand Illustrated Catalogue)*

easier haul up to the mine." Three of Superintendent Clark's boys were installing it. Noting the ventilation provided by the upraise to the old Vermont workings, Phillips repeated his expectation that the airtight bulkhead intended to seal off the main Reynolds Tunnel, and the 10-inch air line serving like a stovepipe leading from the bulkhead to the far reaches of the lower-workings of the Ocean Wave crosscut, would also succeed there.

Phillips wrote, "that is, we do not expect to use a fan or compressor, although I am inclined to think that a fan will be necessary by the time we get the air line extended the full distance of the Ocean Wave crosscut. I do not at first expect to even use the air compressor for running the drills." What? That's right. It turned out he had more to share. He continued by explaining that the *Colorado Power Company* might run their transmission lines from Ouray to Lake City down Henson Canyon. As A.E. Reynolds envisioned in 1899, electric power, if ever available, would be a game-changer for the Vermont/Ocean Wave. Phillips believed it could be purchased for 1.25 cents per kilowatt-hour. If so, he would convert to electricity, and he would no longer have to rely on a boiler and steam-driven compressor.

Rufus ended his report with a suggestion he and B.P. meet at the mine in late July to discuss these developments. As an afterthought, he added that three men had been working for the past three weeks on opening up the Dago Tunnel.

> *They succeeded in dragging an ore car up to the tunnel [accessing the upper workings of the Ocean Wave] over a mighty poor trail and are laying a track in the tunnel as they go along. By means of some hip boots, Mr. Clark and I got in the tunnel for a distance of 350 ft. where there is an upraise extending to tunnel #3. It is quite evident, therefore, we will have no difficulty in getting plenty of ventilation. [He also repeated his belief that $1,000 was enough to achieve this objective. He also ratted out Kerr and Andrew concerning their new concentrating mill recently built outside the Reynolds Tunnel portal.]*
>
> *Messrs. Kerr and Reynolds had accumulated something like 15 or 20 tons of ore, which I had hauled in to Lake City and the car will go out either today or tomorrow. There were 90 sacks of concentrates and I am satisfied that this ore is mighty poor stuff. I think the mill they erected has washed what gray copper ore there was out into the creek and we are shipping a good quality of iron. [To confirm his suspicion, he sent samples to an assayer.]* [43]

As bank presidents go, Rufus Phillips was sharp-eyed when it came to valuing assets and minimizing risks, a gift that apparently included evaluating paydirt or the lack thereof. In a *June 15, 1922, Bureau of Mines Report*, Inspector Robert Innes confirmed his assessment. Innes wrote that "a small shack equipped with a jig and Wilfley Table was installed during the winter, as no crushing was done, I presume only the values in the fine ore was saved, if any." He also reported

Wilfley Concentrator. The mechanical separation of silver ores from "muck" made mining low-grade material profitable. Pulverized ore washed across a sloped vibrating table with riffles gave up its heavier (silver) components. In the case of Vermont/Ocean Wave ores, when if ever a mine-mouth mill was used to pulverize ore is not clear. *(Public Domain)*

he "was informed the ventilation was bad in the Vermont tunnel…." He confirmed that three men were employed "mostly on surface," at present putting track in the Ocean Wave tunnel.[44]

Not so sharp-eyed when it came to ferreting out ventilation pipe, Rufus had thought he had a deal for pipe from the Sunflower Mine farther up Henson Canyon, likewise for delivery by a man with a "forty-burro train." High water, not explained, had nixed that plan, forcing Phillips to turn to the Golden Fleece Mine located on the other side of Lake City up the Lake Fork of the Gunnison River. On June 24th Superintendent Clark wrote that track had been laid and the Dago Tunnel had been cleaned out for a distance of 350 feet, happily for less money than they had thought.

Not so happily, not so good news followed on July 3rd. Only 540 feet of the Golden Fleece 10-inch ventilation pipe was usable and installed. That said, Superintendent Clark noted that there was "a draft at the end of the pipe that would blow out a carbide lamp, and that they could notice the effect of the suction for several hundred feet back into the tunnel." Returning to the Sunflower, Clark had purchased six-hundred feet of additional pipe and had installed it as far as the raise leading up to the Dago Tunnel. Phillips advised B.P. that "I have told Mr. Clark to push the work in the Dago Tunnel as far as the point where Mr. Reynolds [A.E.] stopped the Dagos understoping," no doubt hoping that they could also recover paydirt from that location by the time they both arrived in late July for a proposed site meeting.[45]

Their "late July" site meeting at the mine slipped into the uncharted future. So did the viability of the *Henson Creek Mines Company* piloted by banker Rufus Phillips. Phillips did return to Lake City on August 2nd, and on August 5th he had reported his observations to B.P. Five men were working. The Dago Tunnel had been cleaned out for 350 ft., and track was in 250 ft.:

We have reached the up-raise that connects with the next tunnel above. There has evidently been a lot of stoping done at this place in the Dago years ago and now the back filling is caving down so any further progress is worse than digging a new tunnel. In the lower workings [referring to the Ocean Wave crosscut] we have put in 1,100 ft. of air pipe so the air at the stope at the receiver is about as good as it is outside. They have taken a lot of rock out of this stope, but not much ore. They have gone up on the vein 50 ft. and the length of the stope on the vein is about 50 ft. I have had a lot of samples of the ore assayed, but they do not show much change one way or the other. The ore is not continuous, but seems to be in pockets here and there. There is certainly not enough of it yet to pay the cost of getting it out.

While over there, I investigated further the question of sub-leasing and this is what I want to talk over with you. After returning home, I wired Clark to lay off all his men as I am now fully convinced that our next move is to try to get some development done by sub-leasing. Another thing quite evident is that there is no prospect whatever of finding anyone who will sub-lease and pay the royalties stipulated in our lease.[46]

Reality had taken its time in arriving but arrive it did. Silver prices had plummeted. Inflation had soared. And A.E. Reynolds' notion of a fair lease—carried forward by son-in-law Morse—had driven [as it always had] the leasee to despair. Phillips lamented to B.P. that he had learned that the highest royalties in the district were 20%, some between 8-15%, far lower than what their lease called for. His recommendation was to sub-lease the lower workings at a small royalty. If successful, raise the royalty for the upper workings since high-grade ore seemed more likely closer to the surface or at a greater elevation.[47]

On September 1st B.P. rendered his verdict. Apparently distracted by Reynolds Estate matters in Tennessee unrelated to mining, and wearied by Lake City matters, he advised Rufus that he was making arrangements with a Mr. J.F. (John) Robinson who worked for him in Gunnison County to look after his affairs in Henson Canyon. If Phillips had any illusions about his own role in this regard, B.P. dispelled them when he stated that Robinson would inspect the property promptly, and that he believed the root problem was incompetent mine supervision and thus a great deal of wasted effort. As for royalties, they were not too high, but "very reasonable." "What I need is to get a good leaser on the work rather than have 'old moss backs' that lay around Lake City that would do no work even if they had to pay no royalty."[48]

Maybe B.P. was nearing the end of his own rope, do you think? Surely he was overreacting. Not all "mossbacks" were lazy—most were incredibly industrious and knowledgeable due to their age. And surely Rufus had been offended. But no, at least not outwardly. He may even have been encouraged. After all, he had provided most of the company's operating funds. Instead, he was eager for Robinson to inspect the site and recommend improvements. So was B.P. In a long September 23rd letter to Robinson B.P. explained his concerns and in so doing revealed his underlying motivation. "Do not forget about the Ocean Wave and Mr. Phillips at La Junta. He will spend some money there if he is talked to right and feels that he knows what he is doing." Ah, that money thing again.[49]

A week passed without Phillips hearing from Robinson or Robinson inspecting the mine. B.P. again urged Robinson to set aside the comforts of Gunnison and

> *run down to Lake City [sixty-mile train trip] and look at the Ocean Wave and advise Mr. Phillips in regard to his proposition. He is waiting to hear from you and I have promised him you would write to him in regard to it. I wish you would give this your attention as it is important that we get this property to working and not have it lying idle. That they have had someone there who understands mining and they have frittered away a great deal of money without accomplishing anything.[50]*

On October 13, 1922, two weeks later, Robinson responded to Morse, if not respectfully, at least with a respectable report:

> *Dear Sir: As per your instructions, I have examined the Ocean Wave-Vermont Mine on Henson Creek near Lake City. [John Kerr had met him at Sapinero and accompanied him to the mine. He reported that Kerr had given him "his aid and assistance."] Mr. Clark also gave me information about the surface and underground workings. After going over the conditions on the surface and in the tunnel, it appears to me that the lessees have the property in excellent shape for development and operations.*

B.P. was not expecting good news of this nature, and actually it was not so good. If poor return on investments was not due to poor management, the next most likely explanation was that it was due to lack of paydirt in the first place. But there was more encouraging information in Robinson's report that shoved this possibility aside. Robinson also noted that the Lellie vein with extensive workings just below the Ocean Wave that opened onto the county road merged into the Ocean Wave vein near the East end lines of the latter claim, and that the Ocean Wave vein in all probability joined the Vermont/Alabama vein at or near El Paso Creek. Clues? The Vermont/Ocean Wave challenge had always been successful underground prospecting for at least one of these proven veins. Robinson was using treasure-hunt language, an encouraging change from whines about where the next dollar was going to come from. He saved that for last.

From the best data I could obtain on the dip and strike of the Vermont/ Alabama vein, it appears that the main crosscut tunnel would have to be driven 25 to 50 feet further to intersect this vein. I would therefore advise driving the main tunnel this distance. The Easterly and Westerly drift from the crosscut tunnel is apparently on the Ocean Wave vein. At a point 1100 feet East of the tunnel, a stope has been started, this is probably the same ore shoot that shows on the surface and in the "Dago" tunnel. It would be advisable to continue this stope or to drive a raise at the east end of it. I think this development would open an ore body of consequence and that the values would increase going up.

Mr. Kerr tells me the first car out of this stope ran $30 per ton and that the second car ran $40 per ton and Mr. Clark tells me that a recent assay out of the back of the stope ran $60 per ton, indicating an increase in the value of the ore going up. [If the market value of silver was $0.50, roughly speaking $60 per ton suggests its silver content was 120 ounces per ton, not a great baseline considering transportation and mill costs yet to be deducted.]

It would be advisable to develop the two small veins that show on the tunnel level, the first at a point 80 feet north of the Ocean Wave vein in the main tunnel and the second at its crossing of the cross or blind vein. Ore shoots are short as compared to the length of veins and some drifting on these small veins might open one in pay quantity. In order to develop this property as outlined, it would be necessary to properly ventilate the workings, preferably by a continuation of the larger ventilating pipe that leads from the raise and old shaft [leading to the Vermont upper workings]. In case the old shaft workings are caved and closed, ventilation could be had by pipe line from the outside, operated by an air jet or small fan.

[Now the money thing: good ore showed] in places on the surface, and subleasing should be adopted.... The best method of handling this would probably be the "split or 50–50 system".... $15,000 was a reasonable working fund to accomplish his recommendations.] In conclusion I will say that my observations lead me to believe that further explorations would result in the discovery of important ore bodies.[51]

Idle since August and with winter fast approaching, battle lines hardened. B.P. was looking for cash generated from his lease with A.J., John Kerr and the "La Junta crowd." Rufus Phillips, chief among the La Junta crowd, was looking for a sweeter deal on royalties and bond from B.P., and assurances from a respected mining engineer [Robinson would have to do] that the Vermont/ Ocean Wave Group was worth further investment. Both Morse and Phillips were looking for a competent mine superintendent. With less than Solomon-like wisdom, Robinson had pronounced the project "worthy", in effect had affirmed the competence of the current superintendent, and had proposed splitting the financial baby equally. Robinson had supported Phillips' request that Morse reduce the lease royalties, and he had supported Morse's demand that the La Junta crowd must invest additional jack in developing the mine. The ingredients for a workable path forward seemed reasonable to Robinson. From B.P.'s perspective, they were not even close. With his back up and a ghost from Robinson's past in tow, B.P. plotted yet another course.

B.P. Morse and A.E. Reynolds had more in common than with Anna Reynolds Morse. Both did not compromise on much of anything, royalties and bonds in particular. This should have been well-understood by Robinson and a seasoned bank President like Rufus Phillips, but apparently hope does spring eternal. While reluctantly seeing eye to eye on Phillips entering into sub-leases to leverage funds and spread risk, B.P. and Rufus were nowhere close when it came to squeezing sub-lease royalties into Phillip's lease royalties. Instead of B.P. agreeing to increase his royalty percentage, the exact opposite would be the case— Rufus's royalties would be reduced by the amount agreed to with the sub-leasee.

Knowing that B.P. was anxious to see work resume, Phillips played his best hand. On November 3rd he informed B.P. that despite what he or Robinson thought, the only way a sub-lease was affordable given his royalty structure was at a flat 15% royalty rate which was not likely to attract competent investors. He, Rufus, needed relief, otherwise seeking sub-leasers was a waste of time. With a sense of urgency and a tone of disdain, he added that he had kept Mr. Clark on as a watchman up to this point but was informed that he was moving on and therefore the risk of pilfering would rise. "Will you please let me hear from you at length and in detail as to the foregoing, at your convenience, and oblige, Yours truly, R. Phillips." [52]

Morse's sharp response was not long in coming. On November 7th he wrote, "would say that I would not reduce the royalties on the proposition as they are sufficiently low at present." He also rejected the notion that royalties expected by sub-lease investors were too high to be accommodated. By way of proof he suggested Phillips consider subleasing to a Mr. Bell who had expressed interest in such a proposition. In the meantime, and in any case, his curt response was clear. Clearly frustrated, neither was it kind.

> I do not think that this [sub-leasing] would be possible perhaps with the gang that is over there [Lake City], but I do not believe they are worth bothering with anyway; you have got to have someone there who is willing to work and I do not believe there is over three people in Lake City who has this disposition.
>
> Trusting that I have made myself plain in regard to the matter. I am Yours very truly, B.P. Morse. [53]

On November 11th the matter of royalties was settled. The settlement was not the last nail in the *Henson Creek Mine Company's* coffin, but it was close.

In somewhat formal fashion, Phillips promptly replied: "I am very glad to get your favor of the 7th answering my letter of the 3rd regarding the Ocean Wave, although it does not contain very much comfort." As much by way of face saving as duty, he asked how to get in touch with Mr. Bell, and what exactly was meant by "a split or 50-50 basis" proposed by Robinson. He also reported that Mr. Clark locked up tools and the surface plant and was in Lake City willing to "check on things regularly." [Common culture in that day tolerated helping one's self to anything thought to be abandoned at mines idled for any length of time.] Phillips, also exhibiting an elevated degree of frustration, seconded B.P.'s opinion of the quality and character of miners in Lake City, including Mr. Clark among them.[54]

T.J. Reed would hammer home the final coffin nail. Reed had been A.E. Reynolds' trusted mine engineer and superintendent at his highly profitable Virginius/Revenue Tunnel above Ouray. As divine appointments go, Reed had made the acquaintance of Robert H. Sayre while working for A.E. on another project in Creede. Sayre's father also had been a business associate of Reynolds. Young Sayre was a mine engineer and one of Rufus Phillips' La Junta investors. For reasons unknown, one day while Reed and Sayre were discussing common ties, the Ocean Wave and J.F. Robinson came up. Also for reasons unknown, Reed documented the conversation.

> *Jim Robinson made the poorest report on the work [at the Red Jacket mine] that any man could have made... I had a dream that night before I got your last letter. I saw a long spotted snake, it crawled around parties that were with me and didn't offer to bite, it finally started off and I followed it and found it all coiled up, I had a newspaper in my hand and struck a match and got the paper on fire and throwed it on the snake and woke up and the first person I thought of was Jim Robinson. Some dream.*[55]

The ghost, a snake or simple dream if you insist, had surfaced at a decisive moment. J.F. Robinson's credibility was compromised and 1922 ended with no additional work executed at the Vermont/Ocean Wave mine. Reynolds Tunnel and the surface plant were locked down. With J.F. Robinson's rosy assessment of the project tarnished by T.J. Reed's uncomplimentary assessment of Robinson, the La Junta crowd balked. Any thought of further investment froze in place. Moreover, the absence of relief on royalties and bond fees stifled the search for sub-leasers. Andrew Reynolds and John Kerr had claimed they could attract someone else's money but had failed to deliver. B.P. Morse had claimed he could find more treasure-hunters out to see the elephant but had failed to deliver. Letters and propositions would churn throughout 1923, but nothing would come of any of them. Somehow Robinson returned to grace with Rufus, no doubt because Morse somehow remained loyal to him, but that did not matter either. 1923 would end no differently than it began, but the Vermont/Ocean Wave with its impressive Reynolds Tunnel and functioning surface plant would be no less alluring than in A.E. Reynolds' day. As disappointing as the previous two years had been, B.P. remained convinced that this elephant remained the Reynolds Estate's best chance to make a paying mine. It would consume his time and energy to the point where the other elephants in the Reynolds corral were afterthoughts at best. All that was missing at the Vermont/Ocean Wave were Henson Canyon miners with prospector instincts, treasure-seekers with prairie dog zeal, investors with jack to spare.

Notes—Chapter Seven: Elephants and Prairie Dogs

[1] *The Steamboat Pilot*, "Elephant Corral Has Helped Make History," July 3, 1941.
[2] *Silver World*, October 9, 1931.
[3] Gehling, Richard, "H - The Fifty-Niners," pg. 18.
[4] *The Steamboat Pilot*, July 3, 1941.
[5] Ibid.
[6] Bagley, Will, *With Golden Visions Bright Before Them*, pg. 31.
[7] Ibid., pg. 253.
[8] Ibid., pgs. 31-32.
[9] *The Trail*, April 1921.
[10] *Silver World & Lake City Times*, March 24, 1921.
[11] Scamehorne, Lee, *Albert Eugene Reynolds*, Colorado's Mining King, pg. 209.
[12] Ibid., pg. 210.
[13] Ibid.
[14] Kendall, George Wilkins, *Texan Santa Fe Expedition*, pg. 192; Wikipedia — "Prairie Dogs."
[15] August 5, 1921, MSS 1220, Box 20, FF 1471. Part of the surface plant of what became the Vermont/Ocean Wave Group was Edwin Beard Hendrie's Burro Cabin lode. He was the "first" owner of two or three [depending on who is counting] cabins there. He established the Hendrie & Bolthoff Machinery Co. of Denver about 1900. He maintained a number of mining interests in Henson Canyon including ownership of the Vermont Group and an agreement with A.E. Reynolds for rights to the Reynolds Tunnel. The option to purchase this property may never have been fully executed despite Reynolds' order to do so, and in any case had expired when B.P. Morse acting as executor of the Reynolds Estate was in the process of leasing the property. Hendrie's ownership position also explains why there was no development work undertaken by Reynolds in the Vermont despite its likely high-value reserves.
[16] August 8, 1921, MSS 1220, Box 20, FF1471.
[17] August 12, 1921, MSS 1220, Box 20, FF1472.
[18] Ibid.
[19] August 16, 1921, MSS 1220, Box 20, FFi473. B.P. is referring to USGS Bulletin 478, *Geology and Ore Deposits Near Lake City, Colorado.*
[20] August 26, 1921, MSS 1220, Box 20, FF1475.
[21] Irving, John Duer & Howland Bancroft, USGS Bulletin 478, pg.86.
[22] September 9, 1921, MSS 1220, Box 20, FF1477.
[23] September 16-17, 1921, MSS 1220, Box 20, FF1478.
[24] September 23, 1921, MSS 1220, Box 20, FF1478.
[25] October 6, 1921, MSS 1220, Box 20, FF1480.
[26] October 29-November 11, 1921, MSS 1220, Box 20, FF1483-85.
[27] December 17, 1921, MSS 1220, Box 20, FF1489.

[28] January 18, 1922, MSS 1220, Box 20, FF1492.

[29] Ibid.

[30] February 21, 1922, MSS 1220, Box 20, FF1497. Eric Twitty in "Ocean Wave Mine Site 5HN1082" explains that the *Henson Creek Mining Company* leased the Reynolds Tunnel but unlike prior ventures, was not interested in ferreting out the main vein. Instead, it was content to work the low-grade ore bodies that previous operators located but ignored. The company rehabilitated the critical areas underground, developed the low-grade bodies, and built a small concentration mill near the tunnel portal in 1922. The low-grade ore proved to be too troublesome for the simple facility and the company abandoned it. See *Colorado Mine Inspectors Reports: Ocean Wave, Mineral Resources of the United States,1922,* for additional details.

[31] April 10. 1922, MSS 1220, Box 20, FF1503.

[32] April 11, 1922, MSS 1220, Box 20, FF1504.

[33] April 21, 1922, MSS 1220, Box 20, FF1507.

[34] April 22, 1922, MSS 1220, Box 20, FF1507-08.

[35] April 29, 1922, MSS 1220, Box 20, FF1511.

[36] May 3, 1922, MSS 1220, Box 20, FF1512.

[37] May 9-10, 1922, MSS 1220, Box 21, FF1516-17.

[38] May 11, 1922, MSS 1220, Box 21, FF1518.

[39] May 16, 1922, MSS 1220, Box 21, FF1522.

[40] Ibid.

[41] Ibid.

[42] May 22, 1922, MSS 1220, Box 21, FF1526.

[43] June 3, 1922, MSS 1220, Box 21, FF1532.

[44] Innes, Robert, *Colorado Bureau of Mines Report*, June 15, 1922.

[45] July 3, 1922, MSS 1220, Box 21, FF1546.

[46] August 5, 1922, MSS 1220, Box 21, FF1552.

[47] Ibid.

[48] September 1, 1922, MSS 1220, Box 21, FF1556.

[49] September 23, 1922, MSS 1220, Box 21, FF1562. The term "mossback" could refer to an elderly person considered wise, or to a person of any age considered lazy.

[50] October 2, 1922, MSS 1220, Box 21, FF1565.

[51] October 13, 1922, MSS 1220, Box 21, FF1570.

[52] November 3, 1922, MSS 1220, Box 21, FF1577.

[53] November 7, 1922, MSS 1220, Box 21, FF1578.

[54] November 11, 1922, MSS 1220, Box 21, FF1579.

[55] November 15, 1922, MSS 1220, Box 21, FF1579

CHAPTER 8

Mossbacks

The young man knows the rules,
but the old man
knows the exceptions.

— Oliver Wendell Holmes —

By three methods we may earn wisdom:
first, by reflection, which is noblest;
second, by imitation, which is easiest;
and third by experience, which is the bitterest.

— Confucius —

B.P. Morse, as executor of father-in-law A.E. Reynolds estate, tended to hundreds of mining properties standing idle in Reynolds' anecdotal elephant corral. Yet he was fixated on just one. The Vermont/Ocean Wave Group with its Reynolds Tunnel was his darling. Like his father-in-law, he believed it was the last best chance for the estate to make a mine and retire its debts. Sold "as is", it was worth hundreds of thousands of dollars. Properly developed, it would produce millions of dollars' worth of silver. There was treasure there, he knew it. All he needed to prove it were savvy miners with old-fashion prospector instincts. They were found among the mossbacks, a class of ordinary souls accomplishing extraordinary feats. He also needed someone else's jack. On New Year's Day, 1924, Mr. Richard Kilvert wrote him a letter that suggested his prayers were being answered.

The letter was in longhand on *Golden Fleece Tunnel Mining & Leasing Company, Lake City, Colorado* stationery. Unbeknownst to B.P., Richard Kilvert was just the sort of mossback he had been looking for. Unbeknownst to Kilvert, B.P. was just the sort of owner he could get excited about working for. Little

New Technology At Last. One can only imagine the joy this power equipment brought to the "boys." Hand-drilling was a brute-force artform. The pneumatic drill, Waugh or Rand did not matter, was both science and a Godsend. *(Rand Illustrated Catalogue)*

could he imagine he also was about to be ushered into a suspenseful Reynolds-world vision dancing with other-world challenges.

Kilvert's letter informed B.P. that he had purchased a "Waugh Clipper Drill" from a Mr. Clark at the Vermont on a trial basis. It had not worked for him at the Golden Fleece and he wanted to know where to return it. Although he had gotten it at the Vermont, "as I am told everything has been carried away [meaning sold or stolen] from there." He wisely concluded returning it to the Vermont/Ocean Wave was not a good idea. This news was not how Morse was hoping to start the New Year. But Kilvert was not finished. He also asked if it was possible to get a lease and bond on the Vermont/Ocean Wave Group including Reynolds Tunnel. Now B.P. was interested.

Kilvert continued. He had not been in the "Vermont mines" and did not know what they looked like, he had only heard from others. "I am told the last time it was operated it was not managed right – to be made pay." He wrote he would take a look when weather was favorable if a lease was possible. "As the Compressor plant would have to be started up to put air in As the air is very bad I have been told." Kilvert's command of the King's English was spotty and his writing style omitted punctuation, but his intent was clear. Ignorant of Kilvert's capabilities, mining or financial, B.P. was undeterred by his mishandling of the English language. He had learned long ago that rough bark was no gauge of how sweet the fruit the tree could bear. B.P. welcomed the man's interest.[1]

RICHARD JOSEPH KILVERT

Richard Joseph Kilvert, like John E. York and Cousin Harry and so many others in that day, was a self-taught Henson Canyon "mine engineer." He would have been included in the "over-the-hill" chapter of Lake City's "mossback" class, the chapter Morse and Phillips wrote off as lazy and dull. But Richard Kilvert was not in that chapter, obvious to anyone who cared to ask.

Richard was born in the fall of 1859 at Ellesmere, Shropshire, not far from the border of Wales. Shropshire was the heart of the British Empire's industrial revolution. His father, Joseph, age 36 when Richard was born, was a blacksmith. Mary was his mother's name. The family name and probably home dated back to the thirteenth century, and before that to the Norsemen who colonized Northern European coasts hundreds of years earlier. Richard also was a blacksmith and worked with his father until sometime after 1893 when he emigrated to the United States with his wife, also named Mary, and young daughter Myrtle.

If Kilvert did not work the mines before he left for America, he surely worked them soon after his arrival. If his port of entry was New York, he arrived before recordkeeping on Ellis Island. More likely he came by way of Boston or Philadelphia and moved directly westward to the promising San Juan mining districts of south-west Colorado. He and family were residents of Lake City at the time of the 1900 U.S. Census. In 1920 the Census listed his residence as Ft. Lupton, Weld County, in northeastern Colorado. In 1920 his declared age was fifty-two, but more likely he was sixty. His declared occupation was "goldminer." His wife Mary confessed to being age fifty-five. Daughter Myrtle was twenty-eight. The census-taker spelled their name "Hilvert." In 1924 Richard Kilvert worked if not lived back in Lake City. He and Cousin Harry, also with home in Ft. Lupton and employment in Lake City, likely knew each other well. Like Harry, obviously very intelligent, he had managed to accumulate enough wealth to lease mines, not just labor in them.

On January 9th Morse followed up on Kilvert's inquiry first, consistent with his nature, with Rufus Phillips regarding theft of equipment. He wrote that he had evidence the watchman at the Ocean Wave, "your man Clark, whom you employed as watchman," took away "considerable machinery and material." He directed Phillips to pay for it or find Clark and get it all back. To Richard Kilvert he wrote that the Waugh clipper drill belonged to the Reynolds Estate and that "they had a man named Clark who was looking after the property here and undoubtedly he took the drill." As for a Vermont/Ocean Wave Group lease,

I believe there is a good chance to go right into the Ocean Wave and open up some shipping ore. The last work that was done there opened up an ore chute

I think about 15 or 20 feet long. You will have no trouble with the air to get in there and look at it; there is good air all the way in the tunnel as there is an upraise connecting it with the Vermont shaft. [2]

On January 15th Kilvert wrote B.P. that he would keep the drill and other equipment "with me stowed away until we see what we do about the mine." He reported deep snow around the Vermont. All Henson Creek mines were closed at the moment. He was told that the only thing left at the Vermont/Ocean Wave mine was the compressor and the boiler. "I wish we could catch some of those light-fingered people and put them through for it. It may help to put a stop to some of this stealing." He added that he would like a lease and bond if royalty terms were reasonable. He proposed 5% on ore up to $35 per ton. B.P. countered with 10%.

Concerning the air in the mine, the air was probably good in the main tunnel all the way into the Vermont upraise. From that point to where the ore was encountered was 1600 ft. and at that distance acceptable air quality probably required forcing it in with the compressor or a fan. The ten inch ductwork leading from the Vermont shaft needed mechanical assistance. To examine the property, the compressor could be started and fresh outside air forced in. Afterwards, to work the property safely, the ductwork would have to be upgraded.

Kilvert advised B.P. that he could not start work until April or May because of the snow. Concerning the royalty, he explained that he started at 5 percent on ore up to $35/ton because he would have to throw it on the dump. It would not pay to ship and treat it. "Now Mr. Morse I will leave it to you to give me as good deal as you can on it." He concluded by saying that the deal could be terminated if work was suspended for 60 days unless due to snow slides or weather. [Mr. Kilvert was a mossback with business savvy as well as mining experience.] [3]

B.P. also heard from Rufus Phillips on January 15th. Concerning "his employed watchman" and the missing equipment. Phillips was uncertain if Clark was still in Lake City, and otherwise sidestepped the matter of pilfered equipment.

I have had no word from Clark since last fall sometime when he wrote that the water had been backing up in some places in the mine and thus filling the air pipes and the water was flowing out through some outlet in the compressor. He said as there was danger of this freezing up in the winter time he had disconnected some of the pipe and drained all of it where there was any danger of freezing. I have had no word from him since. [4]

B.P. was not impressed with Phillips' report on Clark. On January 19th he reiterated his belief that Clark had taken equipment to the Golden Fleece to sell. He also informed Phillips that he had asked Kilvert "to go over to the Ocean Wave and see how it looks," and that he would explain more after Kilvert reported back to him.

Three days later Phillips responded to B.P. He had received a letter from Clark stating that he had stored some of the material with "Mr. Kibbert at the Golden Fleece." He also had stored a lot of material with Harvey Youngman in Lake City and he enumerated the various articles. He stated that a lot of the other "stuff" had been put in the office at the mine and the office had been nailed up. He further stated that Van Buskirk, "the man who hauled our coal," had stolen 13 bars of new steel which he had sold to the *Silver Main Mining Co.* despite Clark's protest to the mine manager. He claimed the Silver Main manager had told him he did not have anything to do with the Ocean Wave and bought the steel from Buskirk anyway. "He [Clark] also says that he hid a lot of the small stuff in the boiler and is inclined to think that it is there yet." The next day, January 23rd, B.P. doubled-down. Kilvert had visited the mine and had reported to him that the place was practically stripped "including all the trimmings on the compressor and boilers." B.P. again exhorted Phillips to get hold of "your man Clark." [5]

On January 23rd B.P. pivoted back to Kilvert. Ever alert to an opportunity to restart work and hopefully reap royalty payments, he suggested that Kilvert contact Andrew. His idea was simple. A.J. Reynolds could raise funds and Kilvert could operate the mine. B.P. expressed his confidence in this arrangement in a short note to A.J. advising him of the same.

A long winter month later, on February 27, 1924, Kilvert replied to Morse. He summarized an exchange of correspondence with A.J. who thought that $10,000 to $15,000 was needed to carry on the work in a meaningful way. Kilvert thought $5,000 would be enough to get started, but he still had not been able to get inside the mine to make a proper assessment. Nevertheless, he was eager to get started and said so. "I wrote Mr. Reynolds the snow is going fast—And the price of metals good. The quicker the better to get going." [6]

As usual, despite considerable correspondence nothing came of Morse's efforts to broker a deal between A.J. and Kilvert. However, B.P. and Kilvert were able to agree on lease terms in May. On June 3rd Kilvert wrote [forgive the absence of punctuation] Morse that he had not succeeded in securing financial backing, an ominous sign to be sure, but that he had been back to the mine the day before and had finally been able to inspect the underground workings.

> *Now Mr. Morse I was up to the Ocean Wave mine on Monday, the 2nd Would have been up there before only I met with accident The mule kicked me on the knee and sure it laid me off & put me in bad shape though I get round now with a stick. I found things at the mine in bad shape The worst of all is about 30 ft. inside the portal of tunnel it is caved in One or two sets of timbers so I could not get in It looks as though some one had blasted them in as the timbers is splintered. Compressor I found a great deal better shape than I expected to find it Also the Boiler is all right These 2 can be fixed up in running order*

quickly Almost all Drill steel gone some few short pieces left Find 2 stoping machines One looks in fair shape and the other is stripped of everything. I find 9 cars out side (sic) and Coburn the Sherif say (sic) that there ought to be 21 or 23 cars So there must be some left inside the tunnel.

Anvil and some few tools left in blacksmith shop though not much good Everything is gone out of the Boarding House only 2 tables and the cooking range and small bedsteads & springs Bunk House all stripped all but the stoves in each room Office find 4 mattresses 2 stoves 1 small desk 1 bed steads All dishes is gone There is some kind of a small ore washer they had to mill the ore it is too small for anything I found the doors of the power house all open also in the Mill the same We shut and nailed everything up before we left Now I have a good idea of the mine inside from a friend of mine who worked in the mine when it closed down and I feel sure the mine can be made to pay if it is handled right The only thing that is worrying me is the money to get going My Chicago people is hanging me up too long I would not wait a minute on them if I could get the needed funds else where (sic) As you say a man ought to have $5000 to start in with Though I believe & feel sure that the mine would be paying before we used $2500 of the money The main expense is & largest to start would be the air pipe Out side (sic) of that I won't be afraid of getting through with $1500 If a man had $5000 behind him he would be sure Though I am sure it is not needed. P.S. I am sending a sample or two of ore which I took from ore house—to have tried Will write you to Denver.[7]

Always someone else's money, and from subscribers located in Chicago? The Chicago monied class had funded Henson Canyon mines in decades past, before then Kansas City and even London investors, but those sources had dried, another consequence of WWI. Improbable as it was, Kilvert and Chicago subscribers were back in touch. [When it came to other people's jack, A.E. Reynolds fared better in New York City.] More preferable, Kilvert continued to look to local sources and familiar faces to pony-up operating funds. When that appeared unlikely, he was so filled with expectations that he was willing to work for nothing save a share of profits should there be any.

Moreover, Kilvert was willing to pay wages with his own funds to two others with no assurance that investors, Chicago or New York or locals like Rufus Phillips or A.J. Reynolds, would partner with him. From B.P.'s vantage point, Kilvert's commitment was both admirable and alarming. How much jack could the old mossback have at his command? Generally inclined to back away from such uncertainty, in Richard Kilvert's case he was willing to accommodate the same uncertainty he was not willing to accommodate regarding A.J. and John Kerr. "Why" is a good question. A good answer is that Richard Kilvert was honest, selfless, and knew mines and what it took to make them profitable. B.P. also was wearing out, to the point that he was even willing to continue appealing to

Phillips to back Kilvert. Toward this end, B.P. proposed rescheduling the long-delayed meeting at the mine.

Another month passed without progress on securing additional financial support. With a shoe-string budget and perhaps expectation of a meeting at the mine, Kilvert had taken matters into his own hands. On July 5th he advised B.P. that he had moved up to the mine and was "bussie cleaning up getting ready for work. I am going over the upper workings to day." He wrote:

> *Have been looking up things which had been removed from the mine. Have found about $400 to $500 worth of all sorts of things such as pipe cutters and dies hose 1 Bar – some fittings Also I got all the mine maps Though have not found half yet – as things is strawn all over the country. The worst is the cave in the mouth of the Tunnel That will take me a week to get cleared out and timbered up. Yours truly R. Kilvert. [He added that he had not seen Phillips, he hoped he would invest, and he wished to show B.P. "some things" when they all "meet soon."]* [8]

On July 10, 1924, Kilvert reported to B.P. that he was still cleaning up the main drift with one more week required. Two day's work in the power house also was needed. The cave-in he reported earlier had required sixty to seventy-five carloads of debris "to take out besides the timbers is all in. Though we are getting along with it nicely Can't work fast as the ground keeps running on us. Though we will have it well in hand by tomorrow night." He had one man working with him. He had resisted the idea of going to La Junta to see Phillips – it was better if Phillips visited the mine and he used the travel money to pay his workers. He proposed that both B.P. and Phillips visit together. "I believe you could do more with Mr. Phillips than I can, as I am a poor talker, though I can assure him he will have a good honest partner if he goes in with me." Kilvert ended by saying he would keep working at financial risk as the season was short and he needed to get ready for winter. [9]

Working at financial risk was one thing, working at risk of asphyxiation was quite another. Kilvert needed money to buy coal to fuel the boiler to drive the compressor that pumped outside air into the mine. By the end of the month he would need money for just about everything else a mine needed to operate. On July 17th Kilvert reported to B.P. that Phillips still had not committed to working with him. While waiting for coal, he busied his one-man "crew" with cleaning out the lower [Dago] tunnel.

> *I had to put car and track in to do this. By so doing when I get in it will give me the course of the ore shute – I don't think we are on the right ore shute (sic) in lower tunnel. Then if the coal is in we shall start timbering up stope in Lower Tunnel 2400 ft. in It will take 10 or 12 days to timber up stope & put in ore shute (sic) Can't do this until coal is in so we can have air to work*

*with Have been looking for you in here Hoping you will give me a call soon.
Yours Truly R. Kilvert.* [10]

Four days later B.P. responded. On July 21, 1924, he informed Kilvert that
he was spending most of his time in Tennessee preoccupied with untangling
Reynolds estate matters there. His neglect of "elephant corral" affairs including
his darling Vermont/Ocean Wave Group was beginning to show. His disinterest
in his long-promised visit to the mine and La Junta also had begun to show, but
B.P. reluctantly reengaged. He informed Kilvert that he now planned on visiting
the "first part of August and am going to make arrangements with Mr. Phillips
to see if I cannot get him to go down there." Sounded certain, no? But B.P. would
go to La Junta first. [11]

Kilvert responded to Morse on July 30th. Writing on brown paper with
handwritten letterhead that read "Ocean Wave Mine, Lake City", Kilvert began
by saying he was glad to hear B.P. and Phillips were coming down. He reported
that the tunnel was open and clean all the way to the first stope, 2400 ft. in "I
judge." He continued,

> *Finding the timbers decayed and dropped down letting down about 10
> cars of rock Passing over this to the second stope I find all timbers have decayed
> and dropped out letting down about 20 cars of rock. [He had to run the com-
> pressor for 5 days] before I could get in for the bad air It was very bad... Then I
> had to make some temporary ladders to get up into the stopes took some samples
> which I have sent out for assay. I had to buy some coal enough to let me get in
> and look the work over. Now I can't go any further until I get help from some
> one (sic) to go a head (sic). [Kilvert added that he also would need to buy some
> timbers for stopes and a carload of coal. There was a large air receiver at the
> farthest stope that was ok, also two more cars and one water tank for the drill-
> ing machine, but he needed Mr. Phillips, meaning he needed jack.]* [12]

B.P. and Rufus did not come. Neither did the needed jack. Yet Kilvert had
soldiered on in apparent silence, just as friends York and Ewart had done a half-
decade earlier. Believing in eventual success to the point of self-financing the
quest, A.E. Reynolds' vision of treasure still had legs. Finally, on November 20,
1924, even faithful Kilvert, like faithful York and Ewart, reached the end of himself. As usual, it hardly mattered to anyone other than Kilvert and his family.
Winter weather would soon end Henson Canyon's 1924 mining season. The end
of the 1924 mining season erased what was left of B.P.'s confidence in Vermont/
Ocean Wave treasure. Kilvert wrote B.P.:

> *Not hearing from you for so long a time I thought I had better write to let
> you know how things is going with me. Well we are digging away taking out*

some ore we hope to have a car ready soon. Work is taking longer than planned have retimbered stopes and chutes… We also had a great deal of caved ground with the old timbers caved down with it so it made it bad handling. Mine is in good shape. Ore body is not large and the ore is in and out in the vein. Hope it will get more continuous. They are not working on the Ocean Wave vein, that will take a crosscut 35 ft. to cut the right vein. [Kilvert also had reached out to Phillips. He asked when B.P. was coming, noting that Phillips also was waiting for his visit. He ended with a sad plea.] As far as putting up any money, if he would put up a little now it would be a great help now. To put coal in for winter also Timbers I have stayed with it & put money & labor into it. [And the road may not be open much longer…] [13]

B.P. was pleased to hear news of progress at the mine despite not seeing any lease revenues. Actually, there was no signed sub-lease between Kilvert and Phillips, but that did not seem to matter either. Both parties had trusted that each would act in good faith until signatures could be executed. That had not materialized. Fortunately for B.P., Kilvert's working at risk benefited the owner. Had he been dishonest or irresponsible, matters could have turned out differently. As it was, reports of responsible property maintenance and continuing development work were comforting to B.P. If sub-lessors [Phillips] performed, the lessor [B.P.] was happy. Since the lessor in this case was bypassed by a diligent sublessor [Kilvert], B.P. was indifferent for the time being. Without royalties from Phillips or a signed lease [and royalties] with Kilvert, he could not have been happy, but at least he was not harmed. Nor was he defrauded out of royalties earned on ore sales at the mill. Unsigned lease agreements notwithstanding, there had been no ore sales.

Kilvert was a bright light in B.P.'s otherwise gloomy life. He said as much by way of encouraging Kilvert in a December 5th reply to his progress [really lack of progress] report. He began by saying he was glad to hear Kilvert was working. "I hope you will certainly be able to get out enough ore to make it up." He said he would try to visit the first of the year [how many times had he promised this?], adding that he could do no more with Phillips by writing letters. "I wish you could get him to put up sufficient money so that you could run the crosscut and do that work, but keep pegging away and I will do the best that I can for you. Yours very truly, B.P. Morse." [14]

How interesting. An uncooperative lease holder was being pressured to ease the terms of his sub-leases from above and below. Rufus Phillips [and his La Junta "crowd"] were about to feel heat from B.P., their owner above who would not budge an inch on their contract, and from Richard Kilvert, their sub-leasor below who could not continue funding actual work without someone else's jack. Squeezed from top to bottom, the ball was back in the La Junta banker's court.

As usual, with winter came typical stagnation on all fronts. Kilvert retreated to town and occupied himself with family matters until renewed churning on leases, financing options, and the weather improved. Judging from experience, the new year typically ushered in new opportunities, pent up plans born out of too much holiday leisure at home in front of the wood stove. Sure enough, in mid-January both Phillips and B.P. showed signs of reborn interest in the mine. On January 14, 1925. B.P. advised Kilvert that he was preparing a new 5-year lease for Phillips. It would have work requirements in it. He believed Rufus would find it of interest, and that it would motivate him to negotiate a sublease that would be satisfactory to Kilvert. As promised, B.P. wrote Rufus that same day.

> *I am enclosing you a letter from Mr. Kilvert [probably one that had been received months earlier]. It looks to me that you people ought to get in touch with him and get in on this proposition before he makes a deal with other people. He has ore there and I think that a very little money will place him on his feet so that he can make a profitable proposition out of it. He has, he says, better than a car of ore loaded now and with the present price of lead he is going to be enabled to ship a much lower grade of ore than formerly. You will note what he says about the ore body being better grade as they go up on it.* [15]

Kilvert replied to B.P. on January 20, 1925. Barely noting the matter of leases, at the outset that is, he focused on why there had been no progress for months. He explained in great detail in his punctuation-free style why he had stopped work in December, and all that he had done by way of development work prior to then. In December progress ended due to

> *water freezing up for the boiler The frost is very sevear between 30 & 40 below zero The water in the dam, in the creek is not deep enough though The water in the creek is froze up so we had to stop work until the weather moderates a little and the snow slides come down. On digging out for a post on the tunnel level underneath the second stop we encountered some good Sulphide (sic) ores it is a small streak about 4" thick it may be the top of a (sic) ore shute (sic) going down – samples from same gives assay values: Gold=0.05; Silver=35.0; Lead=43.8; Copper=5.0 Value $85.90 This would have to have a winze sunk on it.*
>
> *We got into the cave stope the other day found the air very bad had to get out right away Took ore sample from cave down ore which give return of: Gold=0.12; Silver=68.5; Lead=15.9; Copper=15.6 Value $88.99 [He added that they needed air from Vermont upraise which must have been insufficient at this point...this location] is where a upraise has to be put through distance 460 ft. [meaning vertical distance to the Dago Tunnel] The ore streak in top of stope where we have been working is small so far though I believe it is on the point of opening up and will get stronger though as far as we have raised up on it the ore seems to have better values last samples from top of stope give*

value: Gold=0.50; Silver=56.2; Lead=31.0; Copper=3.3; Value $89.00 per ton.

Now if the ore bodie (sic) was same size this would make money The streak is small and the length is about 6 ft. long at present and 6" thick in the center Though it is showing better with better grade of ore than it was when we began work: So it figures better have shipped a small batch of ore the other day as we had it out And at the high price of lead now, I thought the price of lead may drop soon we would have had more ore to ship Though the dead work as to be done first and we have had a lot of it Though as far as we have gone the mine is in shape We have been steady at work since last June and have expended in cash & labor close to $4000 Besides the work in the lower tunnel we have retimbered the Dago Tunnel on the hill over 350 ft. in: Also put in car & track put in. This will be continued as soon as the snow will permit There is a great deal to be done to make the mine a pay proposition Though if we can keep at it I believe we will evenin (sic) out sure. [At last, the money thing, and next back to the lease.] Will look lease & bond papers over when I receive them and if OK will sign same & forward I hope Mr. Phillips will come in & we will get through sure. Yours Truly R. Kilvert.[16]

"Mr. Phillips" had ignored Kilvert for months. He finally wrote him on January 21, 1925, probably incentivized or intimidated by B.P. and his letters conveying copies of Kilvert's reports. Referencing letters from B.P. and Kilvert, Rufus advised Kilvert that some of his crowd in La Junta who advanced the money at the time Messrs. Reynolds [A.J.] and Kerr had tried to open up the mine were still inclined to put in a little more money provided that a lease secured from Mr. Morse would be satisfactory to them. Toward this end, Phillips asked Kilvert to write details of how much had been spent and how much progress had been made. Not the communication Kilvert had hoped to receive, probably wondering how much more was needed beyond what had already been reported, Kilvert ignored Phillips' request.[17]

In fact, he was of two minds when it came to Rufus and his La Junta crowd. On the one hand they had the jack he needed. On the other hand, he was about over their cunning ways. The year 1925 was shaping up to look a lot like 1924, which was not good. Save for the fact that Reynolds' last best chance still sported clues and promised sufficient treasure to at least underwrite another year of burrowing, this promise was a poor substitute for high-grade ore actually in sight, not to mention enough of someone else's money in-hand to properly recover it.

B.P. Morse's proposed new Vermont/Ocean Wave and Reynolds Tunnel lease reached Richard Kilvert on January 24, 1925. It was not Richard Kilvert's first lease—remember he was a mossback. Maybe hard to imagine given his grasp of the King's English, he not only was experienced in mining, he was masterful in the art of financing mining. After much haggling with B.P., his first look at the terms in the January 24th document before him produced mixed emotions, and an immediate rejection of certain clauses. Kilvert's immediate rejection of certain clauses would lead to an out-of-character B.P. compromise.

Kilvert advised B.P. on the same day he received the new lease that "paragraphs 5 and 9 are problems." Paragraph 5 placed restrictions on him regarding formation of a company. He wrote, "this is a small problem." Paragraph 9 specified royalties he would be obliged to pay B.P. You guessed correctly. He wrote, "this is a big problem." [From B.P.'s perspective, the royalties were standard fare for B.P. As it was for A.E., his elephant corral may have been populated by losers as well as darlings, but they all were expensive elephants irrespective of their potential.] Then Kilvert got specific:

> <u>Royalties</u> *I think the royalties scale is too high especially on the low grade ores The scale we had on The Fleece was as follows: On all ore of the net balance of $50.00 or under=10%; Over the value of $50.00 and not exceeding $100.00=15%; $100 and not exceeding $200= 20%; $200 and not exceeding $400=30%; $400 and not exceeding $500=40%; $500 and up = 50% The expense of Smelter treatment and freight from the mine to the Smelter is about $22.50 per ton These high prices raises cain (sic) with the shipper on low grade ores Now we have to figure on shipping low grade ore I hope you will help me on this so we can make it go Mr. Phillips speaks of the Royalties in his letter I received the other day. Any way I am signing Lease papers and believe you will find them all Satisfactory to all concerned Paragraph where it states the working of the mine continuously each month this is right only there ought to be a clause set in there covering natural conditions As you know snow slides & snow get very deep here. I am writing Mr. Phillips to day (sic) and will write you results when I hear from him again [apparently among Richard Kilvert's many saving graces was an ability to forgive if not forget.] The bond paper I suppose Mr. Humphrey over looked as none came. Yours Truly R. Kilvert.*[18]

Rome was not built in a day. Neither were the kinks in B.P.'s new lease ironed out in a day. That would take the better part of three weeks. On February 16, 1925, B.P. sent Kilvert a revised, signed lease. B.P. wrote, "I have changed the royalties a little so as to make it easier for you." He did not change the restrictive language regarding the forming of a new company. Instead, he advised Kilvert that he was concerned the property could end up in the hands of someone he did not know or have confidence in, but that he would work with Kilvert should the occasion arise. As for the "money thing," B.P. wrote:

> *I believe that if you can get Mr. Phillips interested with you there so that you can have enough money to do with, you will make good on this proposition. The little amount of ore you shipped in January ran net $324.52 and*

there was only 13,000 pounds of it, so that it shows there is good ore there
if you can get it out. You have got to get the property in shape so as to mine
economically and I think Mr. Phillips will be glad to go in with you. Let me
know if there is anything I can do. Yours very truly, B.P. Morse.[19]

In addition to the "money thing" was the "market price thing" and the "inflation thing." You would expect Kilvert to be on top of these matters and he was.
He also was on top of ensuring that B.P. and Rufus Phillips understood that he
was. A week passed before he responded to B.P. On February 24th he wrote:
"Your letter and lease paper received many Thanks for making changes in the
Royalties on the low grade ore You know the price on Smelting is three times
higher than used to be Also the freight is much higher Think of a charge of
$15.17 per ton treatment on Lead ore it is too high." [20]

In the same reply Kilvert told B.P. that Phillips had asked for information on
the bond and a purchase price. Kilvert asked B.P. to quote one. He also reported
that he had sent Phillips the settlement sheet from the smelter to show ore values, and that he would resume work as soon as the road up to the mine improved.
Bravely, he would proceed without Phillips if need be, probably meaning he
would work without paying wages or merchants until funds arrived. Happily he
said the smelter gave him $15.00 to $18.00 for lead, but not so happily it was low
on silver content. Apparently suspicious about this, he wrote "when we ship our
next car I shall go with it."[21]

As so often was the case, not much work would occur. On March 5, 1925,
Kilvert updated B.P. on his troubles and apologized to him for not including
Phillips' letter in his earlier mailing. He explained that he had been distracted
by "having Mrs. Kilvert sick and worrying about the snow slide in the canyons."
He reported that investors from Leadville had contacted him but they did not
work out. They wanted three-fourths of the lease for $4,000. This was not the first
investor inquiry, nor would it be the last. He ended with a request to borrow $500
to buy coal. He proposed repaying it with proceeds from the sale of the next ore
shipment. [22]

Surprisingly, probably even to Kilvert, B.P. promptly sent $500. Kilvert
thanked him and as usual also noted that despite expressing interest in partnering, Phillips had taken no action in this regard. In fact, Phillips eventually
informed him that he declined further investment at this time. Kilvert was rec-
onciled to not needing Phillips. He reminded B.P. that he had invested $3,000 in
cash and labor and with a few more ore shipments he would not need La Junta
investors. A month later he was not so sure.

On April 25, 1925, in his normal handwritten style with little attention
to punctuation and spelling on brown paper, Kilvert wrote B.P. that in light of
Phillips decision not to invest, he would "make different arrangements to carrie
(sic) on the work… though money is very tight at present every where (sic) you

go Though I am figuring with a Leadville man now." The "Leadville man", Terry Conners by name, wanted the entire lease. Kilvert was willing to pursue this only if B.P. approved. Kilvert was willing to take a small share to get his money back. He also had another man in mind who was willing to go in with him for $3,000 and no more. Kilvert asked B.P. for advice. He closed with reporting that there had been two more large snow slides in the canyon, one 200 yards long and 40 ft. deep. "We are going to try to get supplies over the slide Monday or Tuesday next if we can possible." [23]

Morse was quick to respond. He did not know Terry Connors and advised Kilvert to get references, especially bank references. As for values, B.P. would sell the property for $175,000, but would give a better price for a cash deal. Kilvert also was quick to respond. In a May 5th reply he was all about money. He needed it "yesterday." His heart-felt appeal from anyone else would have rung hollow, but from Richard Kilvert it rang true. The allure of Reynolds' last best chance infected everyone who turned a hand to prosecute it, but if care was not taken, the infection could turn to gangrene green.

> *When I wrote you the other day I forgot to say that if you help me with the little money to get Coal This money to be returned out of ore shipments with 8% interest which I feel safe in offering as I want to keep the rains (sic) in my own hands if it does take me longer to open up the mine If I give some one controle (sic) they would do the dictating and Ball things up — I don't care if I can eat until I get things in shape which I feel sure of doing.* [24]

On May 13, 1925, in a brief note to Kilvert, Morse reopened an old door and closed two others. He advised Kilvert that he would provide Phillips an option for $150,000, a lot less for cash to settle claims on the Reynolds estate [and a lot less than his earlier price of $300,000]. He did not want to lease to Terry Connors, a stranger. He again suggested Kilvert make a trip to La Junta that would accomplish something. More letters would not. And he could not loan Kilvert money. "I have managed to keep myself broke and my nose right to the grindstone all the time on account of this estate." [25]

Undeterred, somehow Kilvert through sheer determination and faith in purpose limped along without B.P.'s assistance, sub-leases, or investor funding. The allure of treasure thought to be so close at-hand was strong indeed. On June 14th Kilvert reported finding ore in the cross vein running north and south in the lower tunnel that "carries good values." Silent for two months, on August 9th he had enough encouraging news to again rattle B.P.'s cage.

> *Dear Mr. Morse You will think by this time that I am out of the world Not so I am still on the job First the cross cut vein which we found some ore in the showing is good but spotted in values Got some assays running away up*

and some samples not pay Now we get on top of the cave stope and find it is a small streak of brittle Silver and when ever we got a little of that in a sample it would run good So it as been sample right along Though by doing so have found out the small streak which runs had to have all different streaks run separately to find it out. At the furtherest point in the cave stope and up about 40 ft. the caving ground as opened up Showing quite a breast of ore samples from some shows values of $38.00 per ton gross value It shows about 4 ft. to 5 ft. wide.

Though it is very dangerous to get at until the cave has been timbered which will take quite a lot of timbers As there is pieces of rock in the cave that will weigh 20 tons to the piece SO you may think it looks a wild place to go in I went over on top of the cave to get sample from furtherest point it looked not very good so I did not loose any time there Though this cave will have to be timbered up We thought of cleaning this cave out Though had to quit on account of the ground moving on the sides So now I figure to go up on top of it —also drive around it on the tunnel level It will be the cheapest as the ground could not be held with Timbers Now on the west end near the receiver I have found where the vein was lost or left when they worked the mine before They have driven all of 900 ft. of tunnel off the vein —shall open the vein at this point — as it looks good for what I have done strong vein well mineralized will write you as soon as I get it more opened up The cross vein which we found the ore in is covered by a claim called the Sunset It is not patented nor the annual work recorded when I go down to Lake City will look I up —Will write you in

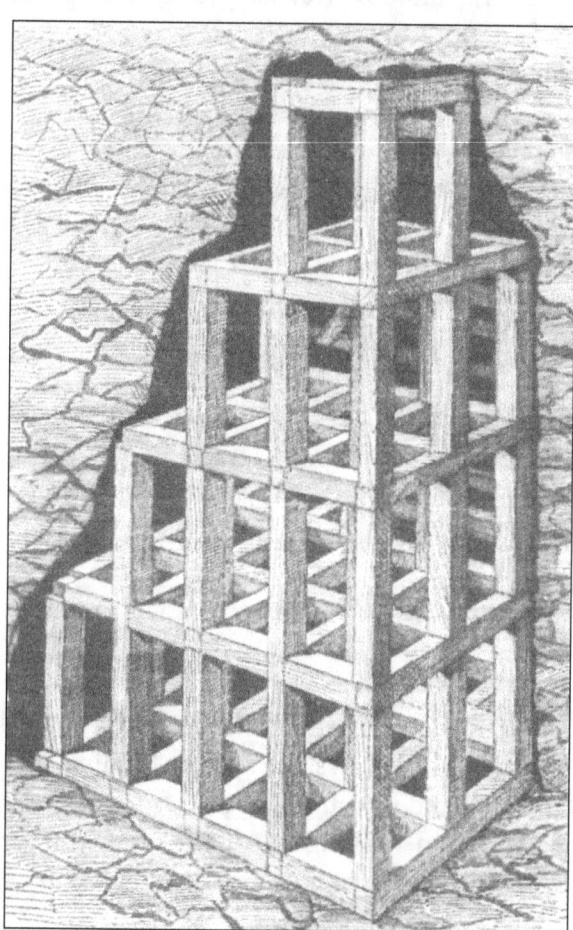

Square Sets. Time-consuming and expensive to construct, when the ground was unstable safe tunneling required them. *(Dan DeQuille, 1877 Comstock Mine)*

a few day again. Yours Truly R. Kilvert. [He also reported Phillips was coming to see him this month and bringing some people with him – have we heard this song before?] [26]

Kilvert's sacrificial diligence paid off. Also helpful was a landlord [meaning B.P. Morse] desperate to settle the debts of his father-in-law's estate, and maybe a pen-pal investor [meaning Rufus Phillips] he knew but did not really trust. So it appeared, landlord Morse was prepared to negotiate on lease terms and investor Phillips was prepared to come to Kilvert's aid. Morse's flexibility was surprising. As for Phillips' renewed interest in funding Kilvert, "show me the jack" was the wisest reaction to his familiar siren's song. On August 17, 1925, Rufus wrote to B.P.:

> *There seems to be a little disposition on the part of our bunch here to do this providing the lease is satisfactory in every way and there is an option to buy. Mr. Kilvert says he is unable to do very much because the air in the mine is so bad that they cannot stay on duty very long. His immediate need is money enough to put in an air line something like we figured on before. It seems that the cost of putting air in with the compressor is practically prohibited because of the high price of coal. I might mention that the Henson Creek Mines Co. has been dissolved [which he attributed to Andrew Reynolds' failure to advance funds to Kilvert in order for him to succeed].*
>
> *I am writing, therefore, more particularly to ask if in case we decide to go ahead with the proposition again, using Mr. Kilvert in working it out, if you will give us another lease similar to the old one, but with the royalties you have agreed with Mr. Kilvert and including also an option to buy. If this can be done I am inclined to think our bunch here will be willing to take another shot at the proposition. [Also, no doubt to everyone's surprise, Rufus states that he wants the lease to "suit Mr. Kilvert and be entirely satisfactory to him in every particular."]* [27]

By the end of August all concerned parties were on board, or so it seemed. B.P. agreed to favorable lease terms and a marketable purchase option. Kilvert said he would give up one-half of his lease share to someone for financing help. Phillips was pleased with B.P.'s lease adjustments and again had asked Kilvert for his estimate of expenses to proceed. On August 29th Phillips advised B.P. that he was taking a trip for 30 days. A decision would have to await his return. In typical Rufus fashion, he wrote that "although that decision may be if the cost is going to be considerable, to let the matter drop." [Alas, Rufus had lapsed back to his old self. Both B.P. Morse and Richard Kilvert probably saw where this was going to end up.] [28]

Two days later Rufus wrote Kilvert. He claimed he did not understand the estimate Kilvert had sent him, in particular regarding the air line. He advised that one of "his bunch" may visit Lake City but he was not sure. Kilvert should go ahead with another investor if he needed to act soon, otherwise he would take up the matter when he returned from his thirty-day vacation. He apologized for the delays. [29]

From Richard Kilvert's perch, the train needed to leave the station. The winter season in Henson Canyon was in sight. On September 2nd he appealed to B.P.:

> *I am enclosing copy of letter I wrote Mr. Phillips giving him the half interest for a very little money I think I made him this low offer on account we need some money so bad; as you know you cant mine without money Now Mr. Phillips thinks it is too much the way he writes and he as gone away for a season so I don't know what to think of him I am also enclosing his letter in answere to my letter of Aug Now on the back of this is sketch showing where vein is cut in Footwall where I first discovered it. It showed a streak of about 4" of soft manganese going in the footwall have by following it 6 ft. The vein is 3 ft. to 4 ft. thick showing a well-defined vein of black crushed up quartz with some yellow copper... iron...specks of lead It is sure the right vein now Now the thing is to get money to open it up—I wish Mr. Phillips had seen his way clear to go a head (sic) with it If he don't we must try some other way. It is sure a fight Hoping all is well. Yours Truly R. Kilvert.* [30]

More letter churning. B.P. remained hopeful [or desperate] and tried to encourage Kilvert. Kilvert had a prospector's heart and was easily encouraged. On September 14th he wrote B.P.:

> *Just a few lines to say what we have been doing Well we have cross cut the Foot wall at a point 1300 ft. in cutting and showing the course of the right vein: But no ore which was disappointing to me. Have carried on work in cave stope and it is looking very promising: The only thing is to over come (sic) is the bad air: I have been knocked out with it now for over 2 weeks... it came near getting me: Though I am now some better. 2000 ft. of air line we are now figuring on: and to work the mine it as (sic) to be put in. Cant (sic) get men to work in the air as (sic) it is: though we run the compressor in day time by morning the air is foul again; and coal is expensive So I am determined to put in the air line by some means or other. I am getting prices on pipe; but they all seeme (sic) to be very high; though I had prices from one outfit in Denver —of $29.50 per hundred ft. for 8" pipe. Knocked down: Crated in bundles: As (sic) to be put together at the mine. Hope to have it on the job soon. Then it is quite a job to make it up and put it in the mine. Though it is the only thing to win out on —Will write you again soon —how we figure out on the pipe Your Truly, R. Kilvert.* [31]

"How we figure out on the pipe" turned out to be shipping another carload of paying ore. As for Rufus Phillips, Kilvert heard from him in California. He was still undecided about "going in with him". Kilvert was pretty much over Rufus and said as much to Morse. On October 3rd in a note to B.P. he wrote that he would go on without Phillips if necessary. In his own brave but humble way he added, "I hope to make a winner." [32]

By December 9, 1925, Kilvert was completely albeit kindly out

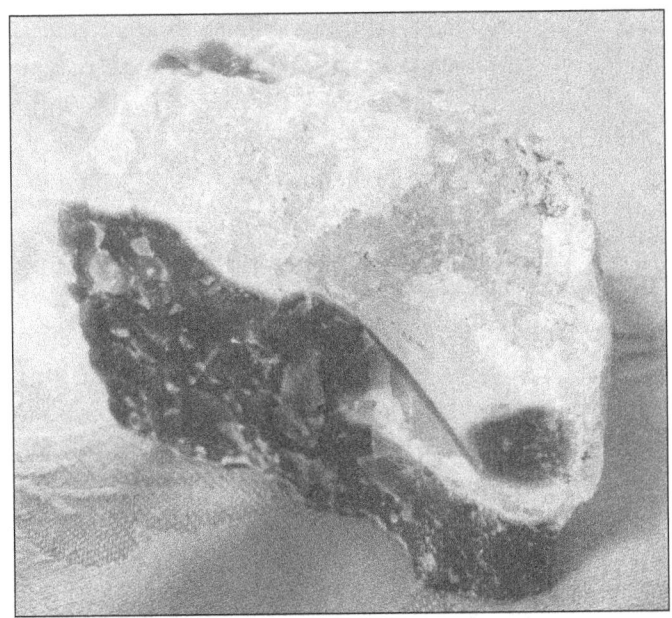

Black Manganese & Quartz. Often containing silver and indicating rich silver-bearing ores were not far afield, brother Kilvert did his mossback class proud by drawing renewed attention to it. In fact he was prepared to gamble his last dollar on the "New" Place. *(Author's Collection)*

of patience with "Mr. Phillips" and advised B.P. of same. He also was out of time regarding the onset of winter and customary down-time for Christmas festivities and family affairs.

Now Mr. Morse I am about through with Mr. Phillips he as played me for the goat long enough. I consider I am through with him for good. Now Mr. Morse I have made other arrangements to go a head with the work. Through Dr. C.A. Davlin—, And two of his friends. I don't know if you remember Dr. Davlin or not he was our mine Doctor on the Gold Links mine when I was there. Mrs. Morse will remember him I am sure He is a nice man—: So I feel easy now I know now we will be able to continue work right away as soon as things is arranged. You say Mr. Phillips did not send you Copy of Mr. Himebaugh Report [Himebaugh was a mining engineer commissioned by Phillips to inspect the mine] – I was lucky enough to get one from Mr. Himebaugh So I am sending same to you for you to look over & take copy of same though please return this copy to me. As I may neede it will write you to morrow concerning several things. [Kilvert ended by saying he was writing Phillips to request return of maps and lease document.] [33]

Phillips in typical Phillips fashion cordially replied. He returned maps and documents, complimented Kilvert on his good work, and left the La Junta door ajar for future investment particularly if Kilvert needed help financing the onsite mill Mr. Himebaugh recommended he construct to process the low-grade ores he should focus on. Phillips could not help seconding Himebaugh's advice. Nor could he help displaying his total lack of self-awareness concerning his two-faced statement of support at the same time he reneged yet again on following through with the jack.

The 1925 drama came to an end with a final flurry of correspondence. B.P. fired the last volley with an encouraging Christmas season word to Kilvert. He did not remember Dr. Davlin but advised Kilvert to go forward with him. "I do not blame you for getting through with Mr. Phillips; he has dragged along terribly and you certainly cannot afford to do this." [34]

Richard Kilvert returned to his place on the 1926 Henson Canyon stage in style. On stationary dated January 3rd with printed letterhead reading *"The Ocean Wave Leasing Co., Lake City, Colorado, R.J. Kilvert, Superintendent,"* he wrote B.P. Morse a lengthy report. He was not yet fully recovered from his close call with death in the foul air of the Ocean Wave crosscut of the Reynolds Tunnel. Lack of oxygen had rendered him unconscious to the extent he was suffering from nerve damage and fatigue. But he had new, honorable partners, Dr. Davlin, and most importantly Ben Poxson and Herman Emperius from Alamosa.

> *I expect you are looking to hear from me before this time. Though not very strong yet it takes me a long time to do a little though I am better some my strength don't gain much [He says 2000 ft. of ventilation pipe is "in", meaning delivered to the site.] We are bussie opening up the old cave stope. Have to raise up and then go over the cave as we go in so doing we get some ore the streak of ore is small and don't make ore fast though this as to be done. So we can get over and get at the other end of cave. As there shows quite a vein of ore which runs about $30.00 it is so mined that that it cant be sorted so will have to ship as low grade ore. Though I look for it getting better as we go up on it.*
>
> *Survey shows we are under the old ore body on the hill [meaning the Ocean Wave] and we are sure right as to the ore body. The ore comes in and out and don't stay; the other day I felt sure we had it. It came in about 12" thick where we were raising in one place in the back of the stope showing some nice ore. The next round of holes it pinched again. Though I feel sure we are on the right track now by keeping after it which we are doing every day In the cave I speak of the is boulders come down – 10 to 15 tons in a piece. We are getting the best of it now I think. Though it is quite expensive Hope to be shipping some ore by the middle of this month if everything goes as it looks now.*
>
> *Now Mr. Morse I would like you to give me the Bond on the property as the Doctor thinks we ought to have a bonded price on the property so as to make it agreeable all round I wish you would send me same. Also I am asking one more thing hoping you will see your way clear to grant it that is extension*

of the Lease for one year You see Mr. Phillips fooled me along and caused me to loose a lot of time. And we will have to loose lot more time on Development before we can expect much returns that means money—Though we will be shipping some from now on we wont be able to make shipments often before the summer Though my friends is going at it with good hope now and I hope you will help me out on these two points Your Truly R. Kilvert. [35]

Two weeks later Kilvert corresponded with B.P. not from the Vermont/ Ocean Wave mine or from his Lake City home, but from the Alamosa Hospital. Handwritten on *"Charles A. Davlin, M.D., Alamosa Hospital"* stationary, he wrote:

I am getting better will be able to go home this weekend Well I have the ventilation pipe in it will be finished by the time I get home then other work will go a head It as taken quite a little money to put it in Though it will make the mine workable now It is quite bad set back to me being in this Hospital. Will write you as soon as I return to Lake City Yours Truly R. Kilvert. [As an afterthought, he wrote on bottom corner: "This letter is short I am weak.*"]* [36]

Even B.P. was touched, but true to his nature he never strayed far from business for long. Four days later he replied c/o the Alamosa Hospital:

Dear Mr. Kilvert: — I am very sorry indeed to hear that you are in the hospital and hope that you will be on your feet in a short time. I note that you have the ventilation pipe and that it will be finished by the time you get home. I certainly hope that this will provide sufficient ventilation so that you can work in the raise and get some ore to ship. With very kind regards, I am Yours very truly B.P. Morse. [37]

Whatever landed Richard Kilvert in the Alamosa Hospital, the after-effects of oxygen depredation or something else, neither he nor B.P. said. True to his nature, he had made sure work on the ventilation pipe continued in his absence, indicating that he was able to hire a crew of some size. He recovered enough to be back in the mine by March. On March 9th B.P. responded to his March 3rd report. "It looks to me as if you should be encouraged. I believe that you will run into a good body of ore there, and, while all that comes more or less in and out, it has produced some wonderful ore." He also informed Kilvert that he favored his requested lease extension and bond as long as he [Kilvert] was in charge. [38]

By the end of March Kilvert was showing signs of complete recovery. On March 31st he reported great progress. For the first time, probably in his entire life, his report was both typed and on leasing company stationary. His spelling, grammar, and punctuation did not reflect the same degree of improvement.

I received your letter of March 9th which should have been answered before this time; Though have been bussie all the time [he crosses out the "ie" and writes in a "y". He says they are working every day and taking ore out every day but the streak is small.] We have the cave catched up and drifting is commenced each way on the vein. When we come to a point where we are satisfied with the ground standing we then shall we commence to up raise as I figure the ore is above us. We are now underneath the old workings on the hill. And our chances ought to be good weather as been bad of late which puts us back with out side work we have four men a work and my self steady every day we have part new floored the bording house and fixed it up and have a good bording house running. [39]

Kilvert continued his informative report. He thanked B.P. for extending his lease and bond. He credited his friends, never referred to as "investors", with advancing $5,000 and willing to put up $5,000 more. He had four men on his payroll. He asked B.P. to put his partners' names on the lease and bond so they can continue "witho`ut him in case something would happen to me man has no lease on his life." B.P. agreed. Kilvert's friends added to the lease were Dr. C.A. Davlin, head physician at the Alamosa hospital; Herman Emperius, Vice President of the American National Bank of Alamosa, and District Court Judge Ben T. Poxson. Poxson also was the nominal leader and chief spokesman of the group. As an after-thought apparently important to Kilvert, he added: "And Mr. Ramsay is working with me in the mine." [James Ramsay, a miner like Kilvert, was mistakenly identified as a member of the "over-the-hill mossback class" by those who did not know him. Fortunately, Kilvert knew better. Sadly within months, friend Ramsay was dead from smallpox.] [40]

On May 6, 1926, T.A. Henahen filed his annual *Colorado Bureau of Mines Inspector's Report* on the Vermont/Ocean Wave Group and Reynolds Tunnel. It

JOHN JAMES RAMSAY

York, Ewart, Kilvert and John James Ramsay were cut out of the same whole-cloth. Born August 20, 1873, in Dublin, Ireland, Ramsay emigrated to Leadville as a boy with mother and father. His father died in Leadville in a mining accident. He moved to Tonopah, Nevada, another booming mining community, with his mother who died there. When he arrived in Lake City is unknown. Unmarried, smallpox killed him on August 20, 1926. His friends buried him in the International Order of Odd Fellows (IOOF) Cemetery. He, too, would have been considered one of Lake City's "mossbacks."

was a good report, free of ambiguities. He reported five men employed at the Ocean Wave. Perhaps for the first time, he also reported on safety conditions, and "insurance" coverage, a new thread in the nation's social fabric that a decade later would be woven into an even greater safety net called "social security."

> *They have compensation insurance. The State Compensation Fund, insurance carrier. There is telephone. Safety and sanitary conditions, in general, are satisfactory. The ore is lead-zinc sulphide in quartz gangue. The vein is from a few inches to 3 feet wide. Values are in silver, lead and zinc. There are 3 levels in the mine, but only the bottom level is worked at this time. This level is opened by a crosscut 1200 ft. long, in to the vein, then drifts on the vein on both sides of the crosscut, for several hundred feet. At a distance of 1000 ft. from the crosscut another vein, called the South vein, is cut. A level and some stopes have been opened on this vein, and one stope is worked at this time.* [41]

Henahen reported that production was about half a ton of ore per day valued at $78.00 per ton, but no ore had been shipped in 1926. He also noted that the surface plant included a steam powerhouse [apparently this term included the boiler], compressor room and blacksmith shop, bunkhouse [probably home to Rowland Ewart's kitchen, but maybe that was in the boardinghouse], boardinghouse, stable, office, and residence. Nothing remains of these buildings. Apparently nothing remained of a mill, or maybe it had never been built, or maybe it had been pilfered.

The inspector noted that "horses are used for underground haulage. Powder is stored in a surface magazine, a stone building." The powder house was impressive and often mentioned over the years. Horses for underground haulage not so much. Cousin Harry and John York had Fred when they first began, but it was not long until their bare bones or no bones budget could not afford a horse. Richard Kilvert's budget did. [42]

Three months later Kilvert and Morse had another opportunity to get a fresh assessment from a Mr. J.D. Fisher, a seasoned and trusted mining engineer. J.D. and B.P. were well-acquainted from a number of A.E. Reynolds ventures. B.P., ever the skeptic and ever-mindful of turning a profit, asked Fisher to size up prospects at the Ocean Wave. J.D. did not mince words, nor did he throw cold water on the treasure hunt. Actually, neither hot nor cold, Fisher's report did not do much to settle matters.

> *My dear Bradish: While I did not so state in my report to you, I will be agreeably surprised if they open up anything worthwhile where they are now doing their work: ore shoots are not usually continuous for 485 feet vertically in that country; I only hope you succeed in getting them to clean out the upper workings as a good look at what the conditions are in the productive part of*

the Ocean Wave vein will be of considerable value to you. Yours very truly,
J.D. Fisher. [43]

Fisher's observations were not music to B.P.'s ears. Far more harmonious were the dated writings of Hollister and Ingham. More in tune with Fisher was current thinking within the U.S. Geological Survey. The vertical 485 ft. Fisher referenced was the distance between the lower Ocean Wave crosscut with the ventilation issues and the Dago Tunnel, fourth level of the old Ocean Wave works. While the current work on the upraise, plus the depth of a Dago Tunnel shaft long abandoned, had reduced the vertical distance considerably, there remained up to several hundred more feet of blasting before the two levels would be connected. Finding a valuable ore body in the process aside, great value would accrue simply by establishing natural ventilation akin to what had been achieved on the Vermont side of the Reynolds Tunnel. All that was needed was the will to do so, and someone else's jack.

Despite his displeasure with Fisher's conclusions, B.P. concurred with his recommendation and instructed Kilvert to execute his plan. He wrote to Fisher:

> *I would like to get this done as I think a great deal as you do that they are leading a blind chase. Howland Bancroft in his book [USGS Bulletin 478] on this district states that the veins of Lake City are roots of veins and the country has been subject to an enormous amount of erosion. He has often told me he doubted if we ever found anything that deep in the Ocean Wave."* *[This advice, of course, ran counter to the driving principle and core belief of A.E. Reynolds that the Vermont/Ocean Wave was his best chance to regain his kingly stature. B.P. had been operating on the same principle and core belief, at least until now.]* [44]

Kilvert was in no mood to argue. He was too weak. On August 17th he wrote B.P., "I have been on the sick list for quite a time and still don't seem to gain any strength. Well I suppose I am too old to gain much strength." He noted that B.P. had seen Fisher's report—Kilvert had not—and hoped that he said everything was in good shape. He said the area Fisher looked at when he was in the mine was improving since he left. "This ore is found in the north and south ven if this ore pitched to the east going up it would throw the apex on the meate auger [adjacent Meat Augur Lode] ground so far it pitches to the west but not much. This is a thing we must not say anything about [approaching trespassing territory]. As long as it keeps its course it is going it is all right." Kilvert also reminded B.P. that he had cleared out the old workings, meaning the Dago Tunnel, a year ago, for 400 ft. but had not finish it. He agreed better values laid nearer the surface—they were working too low where they were but had seen "some specks of gray copper" which was encouraging. He planned on shipping a car of low grade ore soon. His friends, the Alamosa investors, would be there soon to talk about plans. [45]

Two weeks later, on August 30th, 1926, with little warning Richard Kilvert was dead. His wife by way of a Western Union Telegram to a friend announced, "Mr. Kilvert died at nine this morning burial at Ft. Lupton." Otherwise he passed quietly into the night. [46]

Richard Kilvert never traveled far from Lake City and its mines once he settled there. His plans occasionally included taking the Denver and Rio Grande railroad to Sapinero and on to Denver or La Junta to meet with B.P. or Phillips' crowd, but like so many plans, journeys there or anywhere other than the hospital in Alamosa never materialized. His duties in the mines did not permit him being away. At age 66, the need to travel finally arrived. His first train in decades was his last train. Fare was paid as far as Lupton. This train was not bound for glory, but by all accounts Richard Kilvert was.

The last Reynolds' mossback from the last generation that pioneered Henson Canyon, John York and Rowland Ewart, and now Richard Kilvert—visionaries who knew what they were doing and what they were looking for—were gone. Now it was up to Kilvert's *Ocean Wave Leasing Company* friends to carry on without him. Visionary Kilvert had foreseen that day and had negotiated his lease to facilitate such a transition. Like so many others before them, they too had been smittened by the prospect of treasure. Unlike the mossback's before them, they were neither prospectors nor miners although fairly counted among that prairie dog community. Nevertheless, it was their turn to "take hold" of Reynolds' darling elephant and make the Vermont/Ocean Wave a paying mine. Wise use of their jack as long as it could last was back in their hands.

Notes—Chapter Eight: Mossbacks
[1] January 1, 1924, MSS 1220, Box 23, FF1654.
[2] January 9, 1924, MSS 1220, Box 23, FF1655.
[3] January 15, 1924, MSS 1220, Box 23, FF1656.
[4] Ibid.
[5] January 19-23, 1924, MSS 1220, Box 23, FF1657-58.
[6] February 27, 1924, MSS 1220, Box 23, FF 1664.
[7] June 3, 1924, MSS 1220, Box 23, FF1679.
[8] July 5, 1924, MSS 1220, Box 23, FF1683.
[9] July 10, 1924, MSS 1220, Box 23, FF1684.
[10] July 17, 1924, MSS 1220, Box 23, FF1686.
[11] July 21, 1924, MSS 1220, Box 23, FF1686.
[12] July 30, 1924, MSS 1220, Box 23, FF1688.
[13] November 20, 1924, MSS 1220, Box 23, FF1704.
[14] December 5, 1924, MSS 1220, Box 23, FF1706.
[15] January 14, 1925, MSS 1220, Box 23, FF1711.
[16] January 20, 1925, MSS 1220, Box 23, FF1711.
[17] January 21, 1925, MSS 1220, Box 23, FF1712.
[18] January 24, 1925, MSS 1220, Box 23, FF1712.

[19] February 16, 1925, MSS 1220, Box 23, FF1714.

[20] February 24, 1925, MSS 1220, Box 23, FF1716.

[21] Ibid.

[22] March 5, 1925, MSS 1220, Box 24, FF1717.

[23] April 25, 1925, MSS 1220, Box 24, FF1724.

[24] May 5, 1925, MSS 1220, Box 24, FF1726.

[25] May 13, 1925, MSS 1220, Box 24, FF1727.

[26] August 9, 1925, MSS 1220, Box 24, FF1737.

[27] August 17, 1925, MSS 1220, Box 24, FF1738.

[28] August 29, 1925, MSS 1220, Box 24, FF1739.

[29] August 31, 1925, MSS 1220, Box 24, FF1739.

[30] September 2. 1925, MSS 1220, Box 24, FF1740.

[31] September 14, 1925, MSS 1220, Box 24, FF1741.

[32] October 3, 1925, MSS 1220, Box 24, FF1744.

[33] December 9, 1925, MSS 1220, Box 24, FF1755.

[34] December 18, 1925, MSS 1220, Box 24, FF1757.

[35] January 3, 1926, MSS, 1220, Box 24, FF1759.

[36] January 18, 1926, MSS 1220, Box 24, FF1762.

[37] January 22, 1926, MSS 1220, Box 24, FF1763.

[38] Ibid.

[39] March 31, 1926, MSS 1220, Box 24, FF1774.

[40] Ibid.

[41] Henahen, T.A., *Colorado Bureau of Mines Inspection Report, Ocean Wave*, May 6, 1926.

[42] Ibid.

[43] March 31, 1926, MSS 1220, Box 25, FF1792.

[44] August 6, 1926, MSS 1220, Box 25, FF1792.

[45] August 17, 1926, MSS 1220, Box 25, FF1793.

[46] August 30, 1926, MSS 1220, Box 25, FF1794

CHAPTER 9

Shot Out Streak

When you're tired out like a tramp
And hungry as a bear;
And you hike yourself to camp
Unto your simple fare;
That's the time a scout enjoys
His dope, so near the flames,
With his friends, those good old boys
With funny western names.

Gathered 'round the old camp fire,
Back in the Days of Gold,
Good old scouts would never tire
Of stories ten times told.
For those stories played their part
In keeping up good cheer,
And are treasured in the heart
With memories ever dear.

It is not the tales or jokes,
Which were so freely told;
Neither is it songs nor smokes
Which bring back days of old
To our hearts, and keep them near
Where they will sweetly thrill,
'Tis the spirit of good cheer,
Good fellowship, good will.
— W.F.E. Gurley [1] —

Then I looked on all the works that my hands had wrought,

And on the labor that I had labored to do:

And behold, all was vanity and vexation of spirit,

And there was no profit under the sun.

— King Solomon [2] —

Reynolds' mossbacks, those seasoned burrowers with prairie dog natures, were gone. Dead. Called to stand in their place were Alamosa city dwellers, investors—a banker, a doctor, and a county judge—none of whom possessed anything approaching prairie dog traits. Savvy enough to appreciate this shortcoming, they managed to enlist the services of H. E. Fossette to take over where Richard Kilvert and the others had left off. Fossette was not a mossback but he was available. Not so savvy, our Alamosa investors failed to discern the difference between "available" and "advisable." That skill resided with B.P. Morse.

From B.P.'s vantage point, a more-than-simply-absentee owner and lessor, he was concerned. Without knowledgeable and trustworthy supervision, notably Richard Kilvert, he feared that the Alamosa investors were certain to squander their money and lose faith in the mine. The likely outcome of that, B. P. knew from experience, was he would be forced to modify or terminate the lease. Not inclined to wait and watch, B.P. again sought the advice of J.D. Fisher. Friend Fisher was assigned the task of once again evaluating the current treasure prospects and advising him on which of the veins before them would lead to paydirt. B.P. also overruled his own better judgment and reached out to supposed-friend Phillips in an effort to help the Alamosa money-men [and himself] spread their risk. Rufus Phillips and his La Junta partners, as we have seen, not known for dealing in good faith, were at least flush with cash. In America's "roaring twenties" investors with cash abounded, but unfortunately for San Juan mining interests risking it on an abundance of emerging technologies like radio, automobiles, and aircraft was more appealing [and usually more rewarding]. Customary eastern and foreign sources were unfruitful hunting grounds. Alamosa and La Junta, not known as fountains of capital, would have to do. Morse shared his concerns and plans with Phillips in a September 21, 1926 letter:

> *Mr. Kilvert with whom you had correspondence in regard to the Ocean Wave died several weeks ago. A few weeks ago while in Del Norte, I met the parties who have been financing him in his work on the Ocean Wave. These parties are Mr. B. T. Poxson, County Court Judge, Dr. Davlin, well-known physician of Alamosa, and Mr. Emperius who is in the banking business. [Morse suggested to Phillips that he too may want to invest.] I interested myself to the extent of sending my engineer, Mr. Fisher down there to map this situation, especially in relation to ore chute to the Dago Tunnel and to the*

present tunnel level. While down there Mr. Fisher examined the cross vein quite thoroughly and this is not a vein but a fault. In the showing on the south fault, Fisher found ore which was of the exact tenor as found in the Dago tunnel, a sample of which he was able to get in town. It is the same character of gray copper and high grade, and I cannot help but believe that he has in a way solved the problem there of ore chute. I think it is one of the best gambles I have ever seen and a chance for you to recuperate the money previously put in there.[3]

Alas, his zeal for treasure had not abated. The Vermont/Ocean Wave with its Reynolds Tunnel remained the apple of B.P.s eye, the last best chance to make a mine. And J.D. Fisher's September 27, 1926, preliminary report supported what B.P. Morse wanted to believe.

I returned from the Ocean Wave yesterday [September 26] where I made a survey connecting the Dago tunnel, so far as accessible, with the development of the Vermont tunnel level, also, tying in the Lellie No. 5 cross–cut tunnel with the drift on the vein to the west therefrom, covering area where the trespass by the Lellie people is alleged to have been made. [Recall that Kilvert had been concerned about this possibility.]

The ore in the north and south "fault" has lengthened out to about feet (sic), and, while it is not as good on the ends of the lense (sic) as it is in the middle, it is certainly a very encouraging showing considering the depth at which it occurs [could Ingham and Hollister have been correct after all?]. The work done since my last visit shows more pronounced evidence than ever of this lense of ore having been cut off by faulting on its southern extremity; it is quite possible that their problem can be successfully worked out in the long run provided they ~~can be induced~~ *[lined out by Fisher] stay with it through the lean spots which will no doubt develop between where they now are and the horizon at which the downward extension of the Dago Tunnel ore shoot is likely to be encountered.*

The Dago tunnel has been cleared out for a distance of 356 feet which is alleged to be about the beginning of the main ore shoot; it is unfortunate that this work was not carried to the point where there would be no question as to the exact position of this ore shoot as we would then have definite data on which to compute its projection on the Vermont tunnel level, and in the event that they get Mr. Phillips to join them, I would suggest that this be done immediately.[4]

The Judge wrote B.P. on October 5, 1926, advising him that he was waiting for Fisher's full written "examination and survey" before contacting Phillips. He added that he had not heard from the mine in two weeks [not a comforting admission]. His last visit to Lake City was September 10th [also not comforting].

We have been waiting daily for Mr. Fisher's report as we are anxious to learn the approximate location of where the Ocean Wave vein crosses the north and east vein which we are now working on. I wrote Mr. Fisher about a week ago, but have not as yet hear from him. Telephone connections have been out between here and Lake City for about two weeks and as the men at the mine very seldom go down town, they do not seem to get our mail nor do we seem to get much word from them.

We would rather go ahead with our own money then (sic) to make any misleading statements to Mr. Phillips, as you realize that this would be bad business on our part as we are not, in one sense of the word, promoters; and on the other hand, Mr. Morse, I do not feel that this is a promotion scheme as far as we are concerned. However, I believe the prospects of this property really merits any future development work which we do, providing this work is based upon a report of a good mining engineer such as Mr. Fisher.[5]

Perhaps out of politeness, perhaps hedging, the Judge also wrote Phillips on October 5th, and uncharacteristically received a prompt reply. On October 7, 1926, Phillips acknowledged receipt of the Judge's letter, and quite characteristically expressed interest in joining his team.

[I] am free to admit that I am somewhat interested in the proposition you outline regarding a half interest in the Ocean Wave. I was sorry to hear of the death of Mr. Kilvert and also Mr. Ramsay, not having heard of Mr. Ramsay's death until the receipt of your letter.

It occurs to me on second thought that your letter is not quite definite enough for me to submit anything to the bunch here who might be interested in the proposition. About all I can say, therefore, is that it is possible I might get them interested again when you are ready to make your proposition definite setting a time limit in which we can either accept or reject it. Hoping, therefore, to hear from you again at your convenience, I am yours truly....[6]

Whether Phillip's cagey approach raised caution flags with the Judge is unknown but probably was the case. Without a doubt Morse saw them flapping in Phillips' wind. He had seen enough of Phillips over the years to be leery of anything he said. For the time being at least, Fisher's assessment of the Vermont/Ocean Wave was the Judge's primary concern. On the 11th of October, Fisher advised him that he was not ready even to discuss his findings. The Judge's testy response was in the next day's mail.

My dear Mr. Fisher: Your letter of October 11th received today, and I am sorry that you find it impossible to make your trip to Creede this month, as we were very anxious to talk over the Ocean Wave situation with you. I might

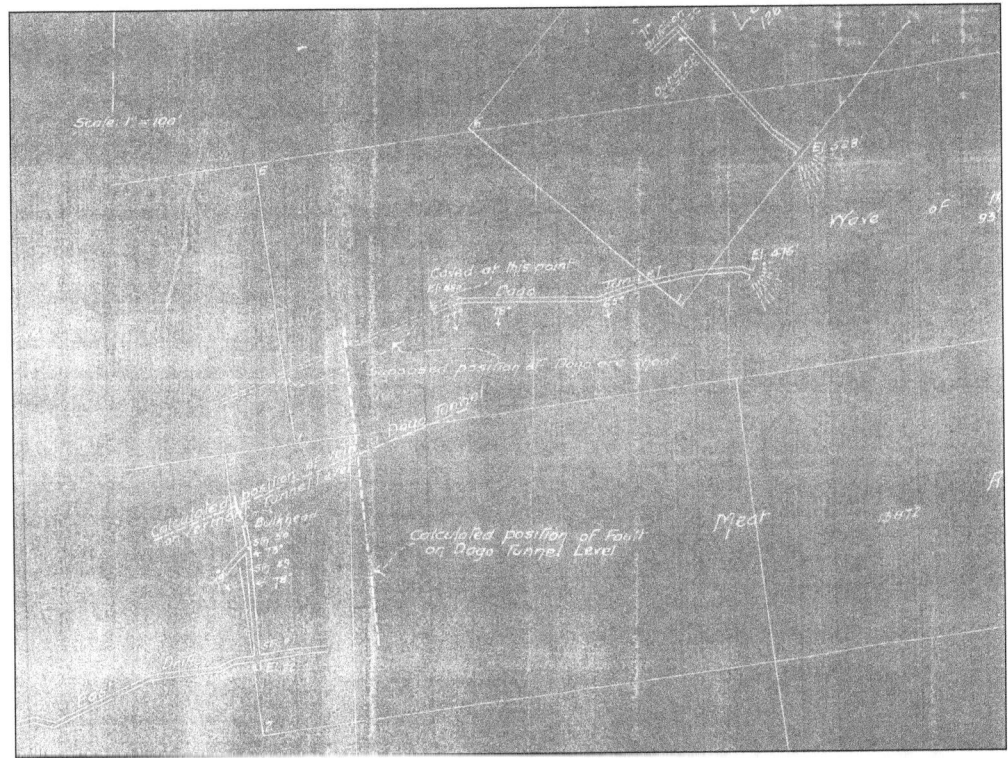

Close Enough? Friend Fisher's detailed October 18, 1926 survey of a half-century of Vermont/Ocean Wave development served two purposes. First, it encouraged those who still kept the faith. Second, it further frustrated those whose faith was nowhere to be found. Notice the proximity of current tunneling to the proven Dago vein. *(Author's Collection)*

> *say that we are up against the gun on this proposition at the present time; in as much as they shot out the ore streak some three or four days after you left there, so as we not being expert mining men or even practical mining men, are somewhat at a loss as just what our next move should be.*[7]

Poxson went on to ask Fisher for advice on development strategy and costs, but interestingly not on the prospects of finding ore. The fundamental question was "should the Alamosa crowd invest more in development or abandon the project altogether." This same question had begged a definitive answer repeatedly over the forty-year history of the mine.

Engineer Fisher's response to the Judge was slow in coming for reasons he openly shared with benefactor Morse. It also was restricted to "engineer-speak," meaning far afield from the "money-thing." Fisher forwarded the Judge's letter to Morse with penciled notes in the margin. He highlighted "shot out streak," and wrote:

> *BPM. This is only a small part of their grief — the map shows that what ore they have taken out <u>doesn't even belong to them</u> — I haven't broken the news to them — it might kill the Banker!! — I think it best not to say anything to them until you & I go over the maps together — I will complete the sections tomorrow — I think they are going to show us something interesting. F. Enclosed is copy of my reply to this letter. F.* [8]

On the same day the Judge wrote Fisher, he also wrote B.P. with a status report on his dealings with both Fisher and Phillips. The Judge said he had not seen Fisher's maps or recommendations but expected them in a few days. Apparently, he continued, the ore streak was shot out and he was at a loss what to do next. He shared that he also had updated Phillips. Neglecting to mention the ore shoot status, but noting they had replaced horse and wagon with a truck to transport ore to the Lake City railhead, he enclosed the letter he had written Phillips and proposed

> *that for a one-half interest in the lease that he and his associates would advance $8,000 an amount equal to our investment, and that all of this money would be used in the actual development of the property. If we go ahead with this proposition, very little of the money that we have invested has been lost, when you take into consideration the ore that we now have in the bin, the pipe line, the coal on hand, the truck, the cleaning of the tunnel and new timbering which we have done.* [9]

Poxson ended his letter to Morse stating that Phillips had his proposal and should decide in the next week or ten days. He asked Morse to write Phillips and encourage him to accept it. Before Judge Poxson heard from Phillips, Fisher wrote him on October 13, 1926:

> *I regret to note that your ore has played out in the N and S fault — I am not at all surprised at this happening, as, when I examine the ore at the time of making the survey, the evidence of faulting was more pronounced than ever on the south end of the lense where it was cut off "slick and clean" by the fault plane.*
>
> *This further strengthens my belief that the small lense you have just exhausted was not "in place" where you found it but was dragged in to the fault from an east and west fissure at the time the faulting took place. There is no doubt that the Dago ore shoot and the ore in the fault had the same source of enrichment as the two ores are physically and chemically identical, and the finding of this character of ore at this depth seems to me to be an excellent indication of finding ore in place as soon as we can get on the right east and west vein.*

I am to begin on the sections of the fault and the Dago tunnel tomorrow, and I feel satisfied that they are going to be quite helpful in correlating the work on the fault with the Dago tunnel ore body. [He inserted that he planned to meet Morse in Denver to go over the maps before briefing the Judge.] In the meantime if you can get any first hand (sic) information that is really reliable on the Dago ore shoot, I wish you would send it along — what I want particularly to know is — how far in from the mouth of the tunnel was the ore found — the length of the ore shoot, and if there was any evidence of a N and S vein or fault in the Dago tunnel.

It is very unfortunate that Mr. Kilvert did not clean out the Dago tunnel as far as the ore shoot — I think that that should be one of the first things done after you get straightened out. [10]

On October 15, 1926, Judge Poxson summarized his situation in a letter to Morse:

Have been very much interested in such information as we have been able to get from Mr. Fisher, and if I have been able to interpret his letters rightly, I believe that he will, when his report is finished, be able to connect up the Ocean Wave vein with the Vermont Tunnel where we have been working; and it may be that the Ocean Wave vein comes into the Vermont Tunnel at the point where the big cave occurred and possibly is responsible for the cave. If his survey should prove this theory, it will be very easy for us to open up the cave stope again and drive a prospect tunnel into the East wall where there appears to be a vein going out. [He ends his letter noting that he has yet to hear from Phillips.] [11]

J.D. Fisher's long awaited report reached the Judge on October 18th. Ironically, it was good news all things considered. Apparently, the observation that they were encroaching on neighboring claims was considered a normal circumstance that could be mitigated in due course, or Fisher's preliminary look was in error and he was too proud to admit it. At the very least, Fisher's report was an excellent description of the legal and geographic circumstances at hand, and a reasonable strategy for continuing the project. The Alamosa leaseholders were encouraged. Two days later Fisher followed up with an encouraging letter. [Fisher's letter also illustrates how overlapping claims can lead to legal issues that can close otherwise productive mines.]

On October 20, 1926, Fisher posted the following letter to Poxson. It included his map covering a portion of the Ocean Wave lease. He was not able to determine if the Dago Tunnel vein extended to the Vermont tunnel, but he considered it a "high grade ore shoot" nevertheless. He wrote:

J. D. FISHER REPORT [12]

Findings Developed by Examination and Survey
Ocean Wave/Vermont Mine
October 18, 1926

(1) That the discovery shafts of the Sunset and Evening Star claims are on the Meat Auger, invalidating these locations.

(2) That the outcrop of the fault fissure, from which the last ore was mined, will lie within the Meat Auger claim.

(3) That the east end line of the Evelyn is too far west to cover the apex of the fault.

(4) That it might be advantageous to locate another claim lying immediately to the west of the Evening Star.

(5) That it is very improbable that the main east drift is on the Ocean Wave vein, based on the dip of the Ocean Wave vein in the Dago tunnel, the main east drift lies too far to the south to correlate it with the Ocean Wave vein.

(6) That the N and S vein on which the last work was done is very probably a fault fissure on the west side of which a "thrust" of 50 feet or more has taken place.

(7) That the ore recently found in, and mined from this fault or fault fissure, was not "in place" but was dragged into the fault from an east and west vein at the time the faulting took place, this would also indicate that the faulting was post mineral and that the east and west veins are the veins in which commercial ore bodies will be found.

(8) Based on the hearsay location of the Dago ore body, the fault will cut this ore body as shown on maps and the greater position of the Dago ore body will be found to the east of the fault, that is between the Vermont tunnel level and the Dago tunnel level.

(9) That there is a possibility of the vein going west from Stn. 50, in the drift on fault, being the faulted western portion of the Ocean Wave vein.

(10) No trespass has been made by the Lellie people on the Wave of the Ocean ground.

(11) That the extension of the west breast of the vein cut in the Lellie No. 5 tunnel might prove profitable, while it dips to the north and away from the Ocean Wave vein, still it must intersect the Ocean Wave on surface and have a NW dipping intersection therewith, downward, from the intersection.

Recommendations:

(1) That a lease be secured forthwith on the Meat Auger and Gimlet claims in order to protect the extraction of any ore that might be developed on the fault.

(2) That the Sunset and Evening Star claim be relocated and a claim taken up to cover the ground south of the Gimlet where the fault would pass through going south.

(3) That the Dago tunnel be cleaned out and the limits of the ore shoot definitely determine as well as the nature of the fault or north and south vein which is said to cut through the ore shoot.

(4) The advisability of attacking this ground through the Lellie lowest tunnel on account of ventilation.

(5) That the ground to the east of the fault on the Vermont tunnel level be prospected wither by driving through the cave or driving a cross-cut around it to pick up the vein going east, after picking up the vein, drift east on it to a point that would be vertically (allowing for dip) below the center of the Dago ore shoot, and, at this point, upraise.

J.D. Fisher

The survey further shows that the vein on which the main east drift has been driven is very unlikely to be the Ocean Wave vein but is a parallel vein lying to the south of the Ocean Wave vein. While the work you have done has been somewhat disappointing in as much as it has failed to develop any ore bodies of commercial importance, still, in view of the fact that the ground in which the Dago ore shoot should be encountered on the Vermont tunnel level has not yet been prospected it is obvious that your objective has not been reached and that the possibilities of your enterprise are still undetermined.

In consideration of the amount of money you have now expended, and, the fact that the real possibilities of the property are still ahead of you, as shown by the survey, I believe you would be doing yourselves an injustice in abandoning this property without prospecting the ground containing the real possibilities. You have now got the mine in excellent physical condition so that all further money expended from this time on will go into actual development.

There is an apparent horizontal displacement on the west side of this fault of from 50 to 75 feet, and, I think without doubt, some vertical displacement can be based. In the outlining of your future development I would suggest that you first of all open up the Dago Tunnel to the point that would demonstrate the exact position and extent of the rich ore shoot and the dip. The determination of these facts would enable you to lay out with reasonable accuracy, the development work from the Vermont tunnel level necessary to get under the Dago ore shoot, which in a general way, will consist of crosscutting around the cave in the north and south drift, in, approximately, the direction shown by the dotted red line shown on accompanying map, until the vein you found in the stope on the east side of the fault is picked up, thence drifting thereon in a easterly direction to a point which would be under the middle of the Dago ore shoot, and at this point upraise.

The fact that the ore found in the fault above station-49 is identical with the ore of the Dago shoot, is, in my opinion quite significant and would lead to the conclusion that in whatever vein it was originally deposited, its source of enrichment and that of the Dago shoot were the same.[13]

Fisher had done his part, and more. Not only had he produced helpful maps and a detailed assessment, he also had consulted with Carl Sigfrid, Morse's Ouray, Colorado attorney, concerning possibly encroaching on a neighboring claim and vice-versa. Sigfrid had not considered this a serious problem, but had advised nothing more be said about it and Fisher dutifully had neglected to include this finding in his report. Only Rufus Phillips had been missing [surprised?] in action. The Judge had noted this state of affairs in an October 28th letter to Fisher. Poxson had provided the La Junta bunch Fisher's map and report, and Phillips had advised Poxson that his group would vote and likely agree to invest, albeit with provisions. They would be in a position to decide in 30-60 days. Definitive decisions seemed imminent, but not so.

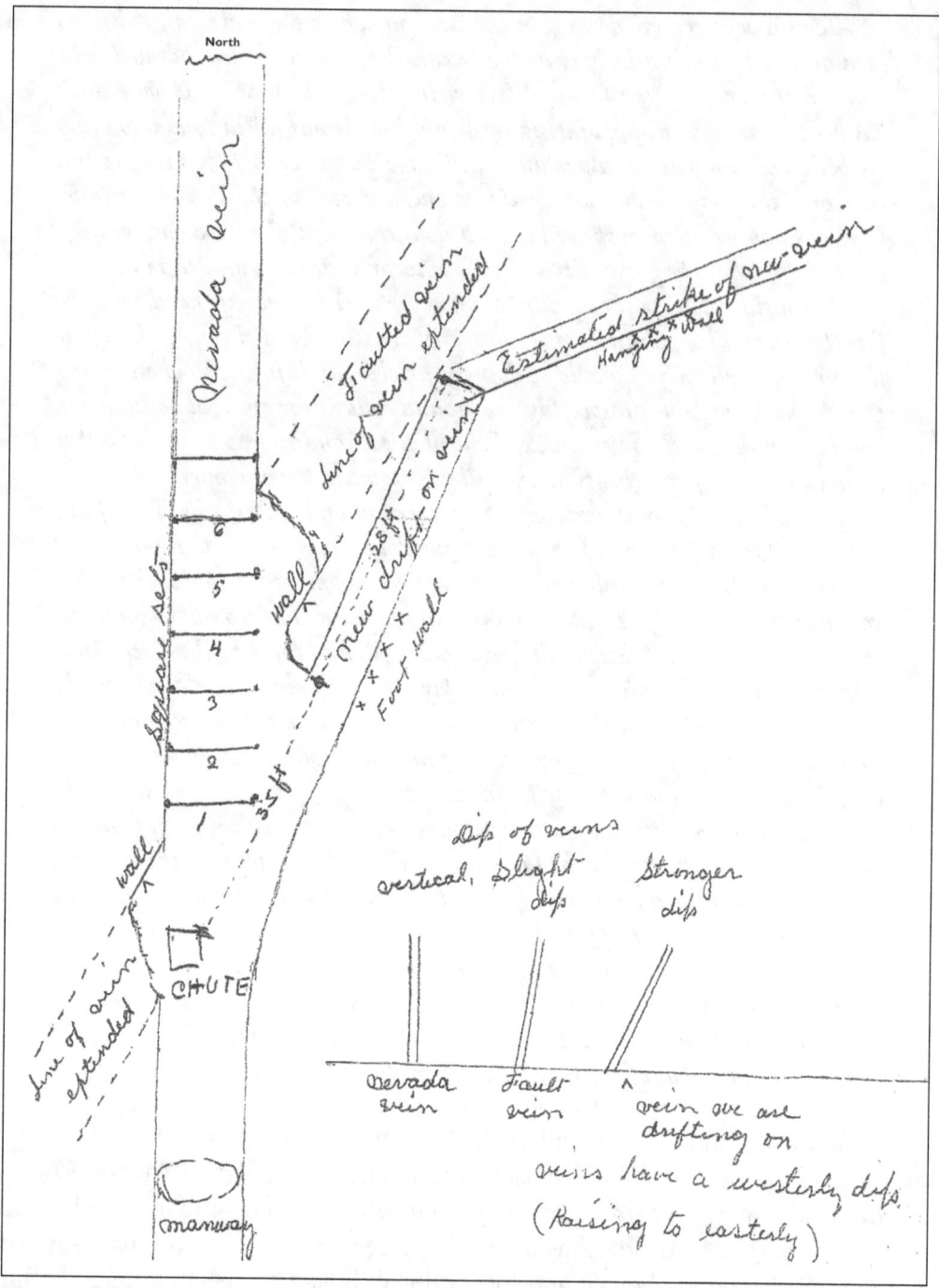

Station 50. Another name for "The New Place," Superintendent Fossette's sketch reveals a great deal of attention was paid to it. It also was unstable ground given the need for at least seven square-sets. Note at least two levels connected by a chute and a manway, and a drift to bypass the square-set zone. All of this testifies to the magnitude of effort that went into this section of the underground workings. *(Author's Collection)*

Poxson was not happy with Phillips' behavior nor response, and surely was concluding that Phillips was not acting in good faith. He said as much in his letter to Fisher.

> *The only thing I don't like is the 30 to 60 day proposition, in as much as our options on the Ramsay and Kilvert interests will expire on December 9th. He seems to be a very peculiar man to deal with, as in one letter he talks favorably and in the other he wishes additional concessions and delays in time.* [14]

The options referred to were with the widows of his former partners. If he thought the only thing he was not going to like was Phillips' schedule for a decision, he was about to learn the rest of the story about the man. Poxson replied to Phillips that he needed a commitment by November 10th. The Judge also appealed to Fisher and Morse to intervene. They did, but to no avail. Within the week, the proposed Poxson-Phillips partnership was dead. Writing to Morse, the Judge explained what Morse could have easily but reluctantly predicted.

> *Our proposed deal with Mr. Phillips has been given up, owing to the fact that they wanted 60 to 90 days within which to think the matter over and by that time we felt that the winter would be so far gone that it would be impossible to get in any supplies until spring, so we have made arrangements to operate the mine ourselves. We have ordered a new machine, also another car of coal, which will give us two cars to start with, also a winter supply of powder, etc. Our plans are to follow the suggestions made by Mr. Fisher and drift east on the Ocean Wave vein to a point approximately under the center of the Dago ore chute and then upraise. In doing this, I do not believe that we can miss the ore providing there is any there, which of course is the chance we are taking.*
>
> *We shall be glad to have you make out the new lease at this time for us for a five-year period and also included the bond for $150,000. With machine work, we are hoping that we will open up something worthwhile within the next three or four months. I am sorry that we could not interest the Phillips crowd, but possibly it is just as well that we didn't, as those that are now associated are very congenial and we have no trouble in deciding matters nor regarding assessments, etc., which makes a great difference in propositions of this kind, as you are no doubt aware.* [15]

Always the gentleman, Ben Poxson was also better advised than he let on. Unappreciated by Landlord Morse, spreading their risks motivated him more than raising additional funds to continue development of the mine. Even if the Judge was strapped for cash, Banker Herman Emperius and Dr. Davlin were not. That aside, by virtue of sitting on the bench, the Judge had much experience determining the character of those before him. He was not comfortable with Rufus Phillips' character.

The Alamosa partners spent the balance of 1926 negotiating a new lease with B.P. and transferring Richard Kilvert's and John Ramsay's interests from their widows to Poxson, Emperius, and Davlin. They purchased new equipment—including a gasoline compressor and new drills—and laid plans to install a mill totaling $15,000 to improve the economics of shipping lower grade ores. Eighteen to twenty tons of ore were ready to ship but snow was already too deep to get it to the Lake City railhead. Likewise, the new compressor was on the Lake City depot loading dock awaiting delivery to the mine when road conditions permitted. Until it arrived, the workforce would have to hand drill. Snow was also preventing supplies from getting to the mine. The Alamosa crowd had no lay-abouts. Noting that the delay in their development work was considerable, they reported that "if the roads do not open up shortly, we intend to use sleds for such supplies as are immediately necessary and try to get along the best way we can until more favorable weather conditions are available." Snow was also blocking efforts to clean out the Dago Tunnel. Unable to get up the mountain to the Ocean Wave portal, they chose to redirect efforts to access it from below, from the Vermont Tunnel.[16]

Taking in stride the customary breaks for Christmas and New Year festivities, on January 3, 1927, Poxson reported to Fisher that work was producing good results at the Ocean Wave/Vermont. "They have been busy for the last two weeks cleaning out and retimbering the cave so that they will be able to get to the point where the vein appears to go East."[17] On January 10, 1927, the Alamosa crowd met with Fisher and reported finding characteristic Dago ore in working the Vermont Tunnel east of the fault:

> They went up in the old stope over the cave at the north end of the fault fissure and started driving east where their man reports he has now a 'perfect foot wall with 10" of quartz showing 'bunches' of high grade ore, similar in character to the Dago ore. As he advances on it, it is taking an east and west course conforming to that of the Dago shoot. I consider these developments quite encouraging, particularly as they are in support of the facts developed by the survey and also of the theory that the north and south vein is a fault fissure.
>
> While it would be an agreeable surprise if they encountered a continuous ore body at the horizon, still it is not without the bounds of a possibility, for the reason that a substantial vertical movement downward on the east side of the fault could have lowered the Dago ore shoot to this horizon. If they find an ore body they will of course drift under it from the tunnel level. They talk of abandoning the steam plant and putting in a portable air unit like you have on the Commodore lease.[18]

A new lease, five years in keeping with Emperius' request, was executed on January 19, 1927. It accompanied good news from the mine that they had "run across a stringer of ore that looked as though it might lead to an ore body." On February 5th Poxson wrote Fisher with more good news.

> *You will notice that he [Superintendent Fossette] started a new drift at the chute, running along side (sic) of the former square-sets for a distance of 35 ft., then he followed a small quartz seam with a westerly dip for 28 ft. to the north-east, where he cut a vein running east with a slight strike to the north, with a south dip, which is explained more fully in his report. This new vein, according to strike and dip, conforms with the Ocean Wave vein, and from a conversation with Mr. Fossette over the phone, he seems to think, from the appearance of the walls etc., that he has the right vein. You will notice from his report what he has to say regarding the vein matter etc.*
>
> *We shall be very glad to have you go over his report and sketch and tell us what you think of the matter. You may also make the extensions on your map if you wish and then return Mr. Fossette's drawing to us. In following the quartz seam for 28 ft., I thought possibly they might have been working on the Lillie Vein which might cross at some point in that vicinity, however Fossette says that the quartz seam seems to disappear on intersection with the new vein. You will notice that the vein they have been following up to this time has had the same dip as the Lillie vein and also a similar strike, however the new vein encountered has the proper strike and dip for the Ocean Wave vein. The only thing that I cannot get through my head, is why the quartz should disappear and lime-spar should take its place at the intersection, but possibly this does not have any significance. [In his own handwriting he reveals somewhat of a self-deprecating spirit: "my head is a little thick anyway."]*
>
> *More grey-copper, lead, zinc etc. were found in the quartz while driving the drift from the chute to the intersection of the new vein. Any suggestions you may be able to give us at this time will be greatly appreciated, as your suggestions and survey in the past have worked out to the* Nth *degree. They are making excellent progress at this time, about two feet per day by hand work [they are only drilling one-foot deep—three-foot deep holes would be typical if they had use of a power drill], shooting twice a day, vein matter breaking excellent, with heavy talc seams on the walls.*
>
> *With kindest regards from us all, I am Sincerely, B. T. Poxson. [In hand writing at bottom of page he writes, "Excuse all mistakes as my Steno is in Denver so it is up to me to try and get by". More deprecation.]* [19]

Fisher's assessment and Superintendent Fossette's first-hand observations were promising. Perhaps his induction into the fraternity of mossbacks was yet possible. He had demonstrated a depth of experience and knowledgeable interpretation of the mines geology that surely encouraged the Judge. At long last, the Vermont/Ocean Wave looked to be a paying mine and Fossette could share in the accolades. Reynolds' last best chance might not be a bust after all. On May 4, 1927, Fisher wrote Morse with a progress report, and a warning. Ventilation problems were in the offing, and the absence of track necessitating mucking dirt with wheelbarrows signaled wrong priorities.

> *The survey just made of the Ocean Wave shows that they are on the same vein that carried the Dago ore shoot above. They have still 75 feet to drive to the east to get under the alleged position of the Dago shoot provided it comes straight down. They are now 105 feet east of the fault and the heading shows a little lead, zinc and chalcopyrite. They have made a great mistake in not driving this east work from the main tunnel level — they went east from the top of the ole (sic) stope 27 feet above the main tunnel level — as soon as the warm weather comes they are going to have trouble with their ventilation I am afraid, furthermore they are now wheeling their dirt in a wheelbarrow over 100 feet.*[20]

Two days later Fisher reported more bad news to the Judge:

> *The heading of the east drift from the raise on May 1st measured 105 feet from the north and south fault. The survey of this work would indicate that you are on the Dago Tunnel vein, the last 45 feet of the drift and the supposed course of the Dago vein check within 1 degree in course and 3 degrees in dip; one could not ask for anything closer than that. The heading shows a little mineralization, copper, lead, and zinc, not however, of the same character of the Dago ore.*
>
> *Without knowing the length of the Dago ore shoot, but assuming that it is 150 feet in length, your drift is just now reaching what would be the western extremity of the ore shoot. There is a decided change in the last few feet of drifting and, in my opinion, the condition for making ore is better in the breast than at any time since you left the fault. I suggested to Faucette that he continue the drift for 75 feet and, while I will be agreeably surprised if you get ore at this level, it is more than likely you will have to raise to get it.*
>
> *I am afraid you are going to have reason to regret not having done this work from the main drift level as outlined in a letter and map to you of Oct. 20th, 1926. While you saved 27 feet of raising by doing what you did, it is going to cost you a lot more than that in bucking bad air and low labor efficiency, particularly if you raise from this level.*[21]

On May 10, 1927, Poxson replied to Fisher on letterhead no longer reading *Judge Poxson, County Court, Alamosa,* but instead *The State of Colorado, Executive Chamber.* If anyone was impressed with the judge's promotion, no one said so. What impressed the boys at the mine and B.P. in Denver was the part about getting on the "lost" vein. Not so impressive, the assay values were subpar.

Glad to know that you feel that we are on the right vein and that at last the long lost "child" has been found. It should be some encouragement at least, to know that we have the right vein. [He informed Fisher that Fossette had sent him a sample of vein material.] I can say that it looked like a "hungry" piece of ore, however I had it assayed with the following results: Gold 0.6 oz.; Silver 1.5 oz.; Lead 0.3 %; zinc 5.7%; total value: $21.09. [22]

Poxson did not jump to any conclusions. Instead, he asked a series of questions about what to expect going forward, for instance should they anticipate entering a mineralized zone? Poxson also explained their thinking concerning ventilation. Their plan was to go back and drive a tunnel at the main tunnel level with machines when they knew where the vein was, then raise up from that level. No doubt Fisher—he had the benefit of hindsight—considered this wasteful, but that was the only option at this juncture.

On May 12, 1927, Fisher answered the Judge's questions. He began his letter by restating his belief that Fossette would have to raise in order to:

get the main body. [His belief was] based on what was demonstrated in the [adjacent] Lellie development. I am agreeably surprised at the gold content of the sample you had assayed. The difference in the ore you have just encountered and that of the Dago ore shoot might be accounted for by the greater depth, or, again, it may be the edge of the ore shoot itself and might change very quickly to an ore characteristic of the Dago ore, but of this, I would not be too sanguine. [He goes on to say that the improved mineralization "augurs well" for "making ore."] [23]

On June 1, 1927, Poxson wrote to Fisher:

Just received a letter from Fossette, in which he states that the vein has widened out to 3 ½ feet, but that the mineral and quartz have both disappeared, which is very [dis]couraging indeed. I guess you were right when you stated that you would be agreeably surprised if we encountered any ore at this level. Maybe if I live to be old enough, I will get something through this hard "old shell" of mine, and hope at the same time that I will profit by experience [more self-deprecation].

Don't know what the attitude of the others will be when they read this letter. From the tone of his letter, I really believe that Fossette is getting discouraged at last, as after a few lines of explanation, he wondered off on to another mining proposition.

Sorry to report that the present outlook is so dark and inasmuch as you mentioned that you would be going over in this district again within a short time and that you intended to drop in at the mine, I will be glad to have your views after another inspection. [24]

In a letter dated June 8, 1927, Poxson again reached out to Fisher for advice. Without stating as much, both men were beginning to experience palpable anxiety.

> *We are making plans for future operations at the Ocean Wave relative to an upraise and I want a little advice from you…I received a letter yesterday from Fossette in which he states that as the weather is warming up considerable that the air is getting bad. He also states that the vein has widened considerable. So much so that they are now following the foot wall and are not able to break to the hanging wall unless they widen the drift considerable. The vein material is approximately the same as explained to you while in Denver, a small three inch seam of Blue Quartz along the foot wall containing very little mineral.*
>
> *Now our intentions are to start up the power plant, providing some arrangement can be made to take care of the air situation from the air line and this is what I want your advice on. No doubt many mines whose air condition is much worse than ours have been operated by solving the air problem and I am wondering if some arrangement cannot be made with our present plant to take care of this situation with very little expense. We feel that we can make much greater headway with a machine and at no more expense than by hand, at the same time saving considerable time in developing the property.*
>
> *Is there not a small blower that could be attached to our present air pipe and be operated from the compressor line, that would start an air circulation sufficient to keep the raise clear for at least 300 feet, by extending the line from time to time? [Poxson adds that he is planning to visit the mine in the next week and wishes Fisher could join him there.]* [25]

Unstated but implied from the Judge's status report, the power plant is not being used to drive pneumatic drills because it is less expensive and nearly as efficient to rely on hand-drilling. This is difficult to believe, but maybe the case. That matter aside, Poxson's ventilation lament must have tempted Fisher to reply, "I told you so," but he resisted the urge and instead dispatched an immediate response. On June 8, 1927, the same day he received Poxson's letter, he wrote:

> *Your favor of the 8th Inst. Regarding the solution of your ventilation problem at the Ocean Wave at hand. I would suggest the following method, altho' I doubt very much if you will find it effective, at all seasons of the year, on a 300 foot raise put up from the drift you are now driving on account of the "trapped" situation which you have.* [26]

Fisher advised against resorting to an air or steam driven fan system. Instead he suggested an electric motor driven by a generator. In effect, he advised wiring the tunnel for electricity, a Virginius/Revenue Tunnel innovation A.E. Reynolds profited from forty years earlier. Fisher suggested contacting Morse Brothers Machinery & Supply in Denver and asking for Mr. Graham. Tell him you are "leasing the Reynolds-Morse Corp. mine." The initial cost for equipment will be high, but it will soon be recovered with less coal consumption and the advantage of an independent ventilation system. Fisher continued:

> *You had better go to the office and get from maps the length of the tun-nel and drift so that Graham can estimate the cost of wiring from the power house to the fan. In view of the amount of friction you have on the east end of your ventilation pipe I would suggest that you set your fan at some convenient point near the east end (say 75% east and 25% west of the entire length of the line.) In successfully getting the best of your air situation, there is one thing that cannot be too strongly impressed upon you and that is to get the joints in your pipe perfectly tight — get several yards of cheap unbleached cotton cloth and a 5 gal. can of asphaltum paint — tear the cotton into strips and wrap the joints carefully, saturating the cotton with the asphaltum paint. On account of the great length and crookedness of your air pipe, it does not take very many small leaks to render your ventilating system ineffective. [Fisher advised that Fossette measure angles where pipe will have to go up raises and have joints fabricated, otherwise they won't be tight enough trying to use straight pipe. He said fan type should be reversible — Graham could advise] so that you can take advantage of the "up-cast" and "down-cast" seasonal periods of natu-ral circulation. [If all this was too expensive, he advised putting] "a series of "boosters" in the air line every 200 feet apart. The problem with this was it would consume all of the compressor capacity and a lot of coal.* [27]

Sound advice for sure from J.D. Fisher, but soundly dismissed by Judge Poxson and his Alamosa partners. Apparently they concluded Fisher's ventilation advice was too expensive or too difficult, at least for the time being. Instead, they abandoned working the lower tunnel level and pursued Fisher's earlier sugges-tions to finish cleaning out the upper-level Dago Tunnel. On July 4, 1927, while on other Lake City business, Fisher visited the mine [probably at the behest of Landlord Morse] and advised B.P. on what he observed:

> *I stopped off at the Ocean Wave: the lessees are now cleaning out the Dago tunnel in search of the ore body that is supposed to be in this tunnel. They had to abandon the lower work on account of the air situation. P.S. The Ocean Wave Taxes were bought by the County Dec. 1926 and sold to Lee Carmen, Lake City, Colo., Jan. 3rd, 1927 — they amount to $98.38.* [28]

Failure to pay property taxes when due was common among Henson Canyon mine owners. So was quick sale of that delinquent property to the highest bidder

REDEMPTION

In response to a Reynolds-Morse Corporation [organized by Bradish and Anna Reynolds Morse to adjudicate the A. E. Reynolds Estate] inquiry, the Hinsdale County Treasurer reported that the following properties had been sold to "L.C. Carman for back taxes for 1925 of $152.92, and for 1926 of $141.62 plus delinquent interest and the cost of redemption total $316.62. Claims affected are the Castle, Burro Cabin, Ocean Wave, Wave of the Ocean, El Norte, and El Sud." [29]

By paying Lee Carmen for the back taxes, interest, and fees that he had paid to the county, and paying him the prescribed interest on his purchase price [investment], the original owners were entitled by law to redeem their property. The new owner had no legal basis to object. B.P. Morse was quick to act. One short month after learning of Carmen's purchase, the Reynolds Estate redeemed the delinquent properties in August 1927 and work quickly continued at the Ocean Wave. [30]

at annual January auctions conducted by cash-strapped county officials. There was no shame or animosity attached to any of the parties in this process. In the case of the Ocean Wave [and associated claims in the Vermont/Ocean Wave Group], it was interesting that the highest and probably only bidder was Lee Carmen. Carmen was one of the early Italian owner/miners that profited greatly from their work there decades earlier, and the reason the Dago Tunnel was so named, in all fairness, for this reason he also could be considered a Reynolds mossback. In all fairness, sentimental leanings were not among the reasons he purchased his old stomping grounds.

The situation had been resolved promptly in keeping with state law. Attention returned to activities at the mine. On July 20, 1927, Fisher wrote to the *Reynolds-Morse Corporation* rather than B.P., reasons unknown. [B.P. had transitioned Reynolds Estate matters into the corporation to better manage [shelter] estate assets.] Fisher was brief:

> *The Ocean Wave lessees have now reached what appears to be the Dago underhand stope; they have cleared out about 20 feet of the caved portion of the drift where it is alleged the Italians shot out the stulls after the lease was taken away from them.* [31]

Despite being incredibly hard workers, Italians were not held in high esteem in Colorado, especially during the early development of the Dago Tunnel and especially after the Italian strike at the nearby Ute/Ulay mine. It was quite plausible that their lease on the Ocean Wave had been "taken away from them," and it was quite plausible that they had retaliated by effectively preventing anyone else from profiting from their work by sabotaging the tunnel. Fisher certainly had thought so, although there does not seem to be any animosity toward Carmen, and there are no known records supporting this view. In any case, Fisher was pleased to see the landlord redeem the property and the lessees reopening the tunnel. His satisfaction was short-lived.

On August 13, 1927, disaster struck again. Oddly on *Ocean Wave Mining & Reduction Co.* rather than *Reynolds–Morse Corp.* stationary, Morse informed Poxson, Davlin, and Emperius that their Ocean Wave lease dated January 1, 1927, was cancelled due to "failure to perform." The letter unceremoniously quoted the conditions specified in the second paragraph of the lease that had been violated.

> *The property is to be worked steadily and continuously from the date of the aforesaid agreement, with at least two persons employed in underground work for at least twenty-five shifts to the man during each calendar month. As you are aware, all work was discontinued on this property July 20th, 1927.* [32]

What prompted this action is unknown. Like A. E. Reynolds, heirs Bradish Morse and Anna Reynolds Morse were continually in need of funds as they sorted out Reynolds Estate debts and assets. Other leases on properties in Creede and elsewhere were generating decent royalties at times [at times quite generous royalties], but perhaps the estate also needed the Vermont/Ocean Wave royalties. Or maybe their darling elephant, their Vermont/Ocean Wave/Reynolds Tunnel treasure hunt, had finally worn them out.

For reasons also unknown, by the return of winter conditions the lease was restored. Apparently the Alamosa investors were not worn out. On December 1, 1927, W. H. Cary, Morse's new Denver office manager, wrote Morse, who was in Old Hickory, Tennessee still working on Reynolds' WWI legacy matters. Cary reported that hand-drilling development work continued in search of the Ocean Wave mineral vein, and that a shortage of funds still prevented the use of power equipment. [Based on Bureau of Mine inspection reports, no ore had shipped in 1927. Both lessor and lessee knew development work was essential. Both also knew that no shipped ore was unacceptable.] Denver Office Manager Cary cautiously continued:

> *Saw Judge Poxson today and he seems to be very much elated over the condition at the Ocean Wave. They have been able to explore the old workings enough to practically verify some of the old tales about the property. While the Dago Tunnel is caved so badly, due to the stoping above that level, no examination could be made of the floor but enough could be seen to ascertain that the ground had all been stoped for a considerable distance along its length. The last lease on these workings covered the ground above the tunnel but a small*

underhand stope was made, which is now practically filled up; they were able, however, to get down in it a little ways and found a high grade streak in the vein that was almost solid gray copper. From what could be seen it appears as though the vein was widening out a little with depth and on the old drift it was about 5 feet wide.

They seem to be positive that the vein is going down strong below the Dago level, and in order to get away from the old workings, and from the water flow [water?] they have run a parallel drift in the hanging wall 5 feet from the old drift and are now in 40 feet. At this point, they are commencing to sink and think they will catch the vein at a depth of 15 feet. Should this be the case, they will follow the vein down and at a practical depth will develop it by drifting both ways.

This now makes a very nice little proposition as they will be able to prove up the ore deposit with very little work. All of their theories show that this vein should or could go to quite a depth and if the values are in the vein where it is encountered, it would appear that they would be quite extensive. Within two or three weeks we should know if the Ocean Wave is going to be a mine. Poxson says there is no doubt of it. Yours, W. H. Cary. [33]

Two days after Poxson's and Cary's chance meeting, Poxson received an informative if discouraging report from the mine which true to his character he nevertheless shared with Cary and Morse. W. C. Martin, a recent recruit working alongside Superintendent Fossette, wrote Poxson in his almost unintelligible style, as if Fossette's style was not vexing enough. Why Martin and not Fossette we do not know. Why Martin used a series of asterisks to introduce paragraphs we do not know, another mystery nearly as profound as the location of the body of high-assay ore teasing them all on. Martin wrote:

*****In making ditch along footwall to divert water at Fossette heading from the underhand and almost opposite where I got the sample from hanging wall that I sent you and which you had assayed ($130.00), I encountered a streak of ore coming out of the footwall and going across the caved drift into the underhand. Underhanders had worked it almost to the end as they did the hanging wall streak. The streak was 3 to 4 inches wide, got a couple of sacks of the grade of inclosed (sic) certificate. Assay of Certificate: Gold = 0.14 oz.; Silver = 232.06 oz.; Lead = 34.3 %. Total Value: $171.71. (This sample contains large quantities of copper.)*

*****The foot and hanging wall streaks are over 4 feet apart, but it looks as if they might get together further in the drift. This is only a guess but our work will reveal the correct situation a little later.*

*****In sinking the shaft I drilled through about five feet down, expecting to go into the underhand, instead drilled through eight inches plus of* *what looks like mighty good ore — distance was 31 inches from shaft. Then, I raised up 2 feet, which would be only about 3 feet below drift level and drilled through again; 29 inches — then proceeding had eight inches of ore similar to what came out of first hole. Both holes let a stream of water through about the size of a lead pencil and no great pressure.*

*****I thought in about two more cuts out of bottom of shaft or say four feet, I can be right on top of our ore streak, then "see it", but the drillings sure look good.

*****It is rather puzzling to find they have not underhanded deeper where we drilled thru but we have got to accept what we find and let the "single-jack" reveal the true situation.

*****We are getting away from some of the mythical phase of the matter and as progress is made we are getting a lot of encouragement — at least I feel that way.

*****It will take perhaps a week or ten days to get into the ore streak.[34]

Morse, of course, had heard optimistic reports from his lessees too often to count, and too often to be optimistic himself. Nevertheless, he was hopeful that they would locate "paying ore" given the amount spent on the property. In a December 6th reply to his Denver office manager, Morse expressed hope that they finish development work by spring so they could start shipping ore. He expected a small vein of high-grade ore, not a wide vein of medium or low grade ore. [35]

The New Year found B.P. Morse in a dark mood. He and his prized mining engineer, J. D. Fisher, had had a falling out. Troubles began when Morse modified his employment arrangement by putting Fisher on per diem instead of a retainer. As usual, B.P. was short on jack. As usual, Fisher was easily offended. Matters worsened when Morse questioned one of Fisher's invoices and thus his integrity. The final straw was Morse advising Fisher that he was overpaid. Clearly, frustrations had blossomed into frayed nerves.[36]

Then came disappointing news from the Ocean Wave. On February 15, 1928, Anna Reynolds Morse at home in Denver reported to Bradish in Old Hickory Judge Poxson's most recent findings:

Judge Poxson says that on account of severe cold weather and the large flow of water in the Ocean Wave, very little development work is being done and nothing on the ore body. They still think they have a good showing, both streaks making about 14 inches of high grade, but it will be spring before they can do anything on it. They are doing some work in the mine every day and getting things in shape as well as they can under the conditions.[37]

"Delays until spring" was bad news enough, but a "large flow of water" spelled big trouble and thus big expenses ahead. On May 8, 1928, W.H. Cary reported still more trouble:

Poxson called, said that things were not looking very good at the Ocean Wave; they sunk a winze 40 feet below the tunnel level and drifted on the vein about 75 feet but there was no vein to speak of. The larger vein they caught on the tunnel seemed to be a bulge in the main vein and it would look as though the vein was pinching out with depth. They are still working and have lost but ten days since September.[38]

On May 21, 1928, two weeks later, a no doubt exasperated Morse replied:

Sorry to hear that the Ocean Wave is not looking very good, as I hoped that the 40 feet winze would show something worthwhile. It would certainly appear that they could get something at 40 feet unless the Dago's bottomed the thing before they quit.[39]

Those pesky Italians again. First Morse and now Poxson were beginning to lose faith. Mine inspector Henshaw's annual 1928 June report (Appendix A) was not helpful. Henshaw also explained Martin's relationship with Fossette and the Judge. He also has provided us with a handy summary of the status of the Reynolds' estate treasure hunt.

On July 2nd Poxson appealed to Cary for help. Apparently replying to an inquiry from Morse, Poxson wrote that he was having Mr. Fisher come to Creede for some work and wondered if Mr. Morse would be willing to have him go to Lake City also "to look over the Ocean Wave property." In addition, maybe breaking the news for the first time, Poxson informed Cary that the "Alamosa crowd" had partnered with W. C. Martin and organized the *W.C. Martin & Company*. Apparently, Martin was experienced and even wealthy. Apparently another mossback, Brother Fossette, had had enough. Poxson wrote:

We have worked steady since obtaining the new lease, and I believe the proposition is at a point where Mr. Fisher will be able to determine whether or not future work will be justifiable. If Mr. Morse can see fit to send Mr. Fisher to Lake City, I will be glad to personally take him from Creede over, so there will be no expense for transportation; and if this is agreeable, I will be glad to have you get in touch with Mr. Fisher before he leaves Colorado Springs. Very truly yours, B. T. Poxson.[40]

Cary promptly advised Poxson that Fisher no longer worked for the Reynolds family. The Judge had to have known this, but tried to shed some expenses anyway. It did not matter. Poxson was in contact with Fisher on other matters, including interest in investing in Creede properties, and kept him informed of developments at the Ocean Wave as well. For his part, it would be true to Fisher's nature that he would have seen no need to advise Poxson of his problems with B.P., or any visits to Lake City. On August 17, 1928, Cary reported to Morse:

Poxson says they are following a 3-inch streak of ore in the Ocean Wave which assays 39 oz. silver and 41% lead. This is not opening up and they are quite discouraged. They will know by September 1st whether or not they shall continue with the lease.[41]

Interests were converging. Despite the tease of rich ore just ahead, and another partner and a new lease, Poxson and his Alamosa crowd appeared ready to throw in their hand. Besides, opportunities in Creede looked more promising. Morse was not surprised. He had seen his own hand play out this way before, just as more than once his father-in-law's hand had played out before him. The Reynolds legacy's last best chance to make a mine out of the Vermont/ Ocean Wave was taking another turn for the worse. On October 5, 1928. Martin reported from the mine that he had broken into the vein but could tell nothing about it yet. Expressing rare skepticism, Cary's sarcasm was surprising. "It seems to me that they are always just breaking into a vein."[42]

On December 12, 1928, more Ocean Wave news arrived at Morse's Denver office in the form of a check from the *American Smelting & Refining Company* in Leadville. The Ocean Wave lessees finally shipped ore netting $342.80. Morse's 15% royalty netted him $51.42. The news was good in terms of shipping ore that had some value. The news was pathetic in terms of the meager quantity of ore and its marginal return relative to invested time and money. The lessees agreed. Their share netted out at $292.42, hardly a dent in a month's much less a year's worth of labor costs alone.[43]

At whose initiative is not known, but the Martin and associates lease was cancelled effective January 1, 1929. If any work had been conducted through the end of the year, it was minimal. No additional ore was shipped. On June 22, 1929, Cary reported to Morse on Ocean Wave matters for the first time in six months. Most likely a great deal of churning had transpired during that period of time— landlord and tenants just could not help themselves—but no known records prior to Cary's June report have survived.

As the matter came up before while you were here [Denver office], and as I knew you were in accord with it, have arranged to give Jim Flood a 5 year lease on the Ocean Wave property under practically the same terms and conditions as the one held by Poxson and Martin. I believe Flood has secured the necessary money for this project, together with the lineup of other properties, and he will be in a position to commence work shortly. Have arranged with Poxson that the Martin lease will be cancelled without any trouble and Flood has guaranteed to give Martin a sub-lease on the block of ground he wants. As it is necessary for Flood to close up some other business before this lease is known, have not yet made out the formal lease but will do so upon demand, and you will probably be here [he was in Old Hickory, Tennessee] by that time. We must get something out of the Ocean Wave if possible, and we could never look for much the way Martin is puttering around. Flood is going to put his mill at Capital City, a mile [actually three miles] from the Ocean Wave. [44]

Martin and Poxson gracefully relinquished their lease. Martin retained the right by virtue of a sublease to continue work in the Dago Tunnel. Jim Flood, it turned out no stranger to Henson Canyon opportunities, was expected to shovel more funds into the properties including building a mill in Capital City. And the Reynolds heirs' faith in A.E. Reynolds' last best chance to recover the estates' investment and redeem A.E.'s reputation had new life. What could possibly go wrong?

The hunt for treasure was back on, first for the jack, then for the ore. Discussions among Landlord Morse, the La Junta bunch, and the Alamosa crowd also was back on. Of particular significance at this stage of Morse's quest was the character of the Alamosa crowd, chief among them Judge Poxson. Of course J. D. Fisher's assessment was important, even motivating—Morse was eager to earn lease fees—but he had learned the hard way that the integrity of his investors and lessors was far more important than engineering reports.

Of special importance in this regard is Judge Ben (B.T.) Poxson. Judge Poxson exuded honesty and exceptionalism born of a life of overcoming adversities. Confident in his own judgment regarding seizing opportunities when they were presented to him, he welcomed additional investors but wanted to be as truthful as possible about mine prospects and risks. He was not your run-of-the-mill mine speculator, nor was he a mossback although in his later years he could be credited with many of their attributes. Indeed, Ben T. Poxson exemplified yet another class of extraordinary young Americans daring enough to invest in a Henson Canyon treasure hunt.

Ben followed the maxim to "go west young man"—and both he and Colorado were the better for it. He rose out of obscure poverty to stand with the rich and famous, notably as an aide to Colorado's governors. Over six decades he held political appointments from four Republican and three Democratic governors while running his mining and other ventures. Born June 12, 1893, on the family farm near Jackson, Michigan, young Poxson moved from there to Alamosa in 1914 to teach school. He eventually became school principal. His career in public service began when William "Billy" Adams, Colorado's "cowboy governor" from Alamosa, asked him to fill a short-term vacancy as Alamosa postmaster. After two years as postmaster, Ben moved to Denver to become Gov. Adams' secretary. That association opened many doors, including doing the actual work of the governor for nine months when Adams was ill. In addition to being "assistant governor," he served as head of the Colorado Industrial School for Boys in Golden, president of the Colorado Mining Association, chairman of the Colorado Home for Dependent Children, and for twenty-six years as chairman of the Colorado Racing Commission. His election to Alamosa County Judge in the mid-1920s coincided with partnering with A.E. Reynolds' heirs Brad Morse and Anna Reynolds.

Investing heavily in the Vermont/Ocean Wave project until management issues—notably the death of Richard Kilvert, his diligent mine superintendent—and operating costs exceeded his risk tolerance, he nevertheless became even more a part of other Reynolds' family ventures in Creede, Gunnison County, and Summitville, Summitville mines produced more than $11 million in gold. In Creede he owned and operated the Emperius Mill which processed an estimated $32 million in gold, silver and other minerals. The best he could point to regarding his investment in the Vermont/Ocean Wave was it endeared him for life to the Reynolds' family, a mutually beneficial relationship to be sure. His contribution: he played a pivotal role—bringing to bear honest grit as much as abundant jack—in the finest westering tradition. [45]

Farm labor early in life was not all Ben experienced. He also was introduced to science and industry. One of Ben's grandfathers was a blacksmith, the other was a druggist. Schooling through the eighth grade was available within walking distance of the farm, but in order to attend high school Ben boarded in Albion, Michigan. He paid his own way by working as a waiter, eventually as a chef, and later caring for a doctor's horses in exchange for a small wage and living quarters above the stables.

Ben not only graduated from high school in Albion, he also graduated from the small college [now Eastern Michigan University] there with a degree in

---

BEN T. POXSON

In October 1988 the *Chronicles Publishing Company* printed "a compilation of casual conversations taped with Ben Poxson" which provides rare first-hand insight into why his character was so characteristic of America's "manifest destiny." Among his recollections, he starts with his own immigrant roots: "one side" of his family came from England. His father and nine of ten sons emigrated to southern Michigan and took up farming. The oldest son remained in England to inherit the family title of "Earl". The other side of Ben's family was from Ireland. "Unfortunately, they got mixed up on the wrong side of Bloody Mary's escapade and were ostracized to the Isle of Man for one hundred years. Then they came back into England again but they settled in Wales." No doubt listening to this conversation around the family dinner table made a lifelong impression on young Ben. Work hard. Stay on the right side of the law.[46]

Business Administration. He accepted a teaching appointment in Boine City, Michigan, for one year, considered moving to Marion, Ohio the next year, but instead chose moving to Alamosa, Colorado to set up a "commercial department" and be principal of the Alamosa high school. Before Ben could turn down with a clear conscience the Marion appointment, he felt it necessary to travel there and discuss the matter directly. He explained to the Superintendent of the Marion school system, a Mr. Warren G. Harding, the opportunity presented him in Alamosa. Superintendent Harding counseled him that Alamosa was the choice he should make. Comforted, he made his way to Alamosa. Not long after, Superintendent Harding made his way to Washington, D.C., no longer a superintendent but 29th President of the United States. Ben would experience many more divine appointments that would help perfect his character and enhance his prospects. President Harding was but the first, Colorado's "cowboy governor" Billy Adams would not be the last.

Ben married his childhood sweetheart. They would have one son and spend nearly fifty years together in Colorado. He and his new bride traveled by train to Alamosa by way of Denver. The newlyweds had all of $10.20 to their names, but Ben had a secure job and found the local landlords and merchants friendly and trusting. Surely another divine appointment, they rented the upstairs of a banker's home. Ben explains.

> *This banker was cashier of the bank whose vice-president, Mr. Emperius, was later to become my partner.....Emperius was also mayor of Alamosa when I arrived. I also named our mining company in Creede after him. He passed away when we were in partnership at which time I incorporated the company and gave the corporation his name. It's still in existence: Emperius Mining Company—the operating company at Creede.*[47]

Further insight into Ben Poxson's frontier character comes by way of his early years in Alamosa. He volunteered to be a deputy sheriff. In 1918 Governor Adams, who was a cattleman from Alamosa and had befriended Ben, was instrumental in getting him his appointment as the Alamosa postmaster. This job paid $3,000 a year, a thousand dollars more than high school principal, so Ben gave up public education and went into public service. While he had many outside interests that made him a very wealthy man, including a Ford Motor Company dealership and numerous mining interests, he continued in public office in one capacity or another until very late in his life. After his two year term as postmaster expired, he ran for and was elected County Judge. He served as County Judge until Governor Adams persuaded him to move to Denver to be his secretary.

Ben T. Poxson, called Judge Poxson even after he left the Court, or B.T. Poxson among business acquaintances, also was gifted in his ability to make lifelong friends. His work ethic, honesty, and genuine love of people were infectious.

When it came to the Reynolds' Vermont/Ocean Wave project, these characteristics were in great demand. Future life-long business partner Herman Emperius certainly thought so. Introduced to Ben shortly after arriving in Alamosa, he became a mentor and soon business partner of Ben's. He was wealthy and willing to loan Ben his share of their ventures.

Likewise, Dr. Davlin recognized Ben's character when he volunteered to learn how to operate the Alamosa hospital's newly acquired x-ray equipment. In part as a consequence of this, he appointed Ben a hospital director. Imagine two things. First, medical diagnostic equipment taken for granted today was revolutionary and intimidating then. In addition to everything else he was responsible for, for nine years Ben also performed all of Alamosa's x-rays. Second, the good doctor's judgment of character that would serve the people of Alamosa well, also revealed attributes of Ben Poxson that endeared him to those around him and helps explain why he and those he associated with usually prospered. Anna Reynolds among the best of all.

Anna's father had amassed kingly assets that now were weighed down by kingly debts. Anna and husband Brad's journey out of this mess to lucrative partnerships with Ben Poxson's Alamosa crowd soon involved George Garrey, an accomplished mining engineer you will meet soon. Anna and Brad brought the elephants to the party. Ben, Herman, and Dr. Davlin brought the jack. George Garrey would bring the mining expertise. Anna's singular duty would be salvaging as much as possible the remaining Reynolds family reputation. In doing so, she first would remain fixated on the mining industry and her father's elephant corral. Knowing nothing about elephants, she also wisely would turn to associates her father and her husband trusted who in addition to earthly attributes brought heavenly integrity. As noted, integrity was rare but one of Judge Poxson's strongest suites.

Anna soon learned that Richard Kilvert's management of the Vermont/Ocean Wave, underwritten by Judge Poxson's bunch of Alamosa investors, was a high-water mark in the three decades-long hunt for the Vermont/Ocean Wave motherlode. She also was quick to appreciate that Judge Poxson and his Alamosa crowd were people she could count on to help underwrite the development of her father's dormant elephant corral into a circus of investor opportunities. Should she throw more of her own "good money after bad?" Or was "the bad" really not so bad after all? Bravely, Anna was willing to do what she could to find out. Doing what she could included learning to value the advice of George Garrey.

With legal and leasing help from Judge Poxson and Carl Sigfrid still residing in Ouray, within a handful of years most of the Reynolds elephants were sold or earning their keep. Leases for Creede and Summitville ventures were most productive. The May Day, Revenue Tunnel, and Gold Cup remained promising. The Vermont/Ocean Wave and Reynolds Tunnel were not overlooked, but in all cases what would begin as promising leases or purchase agreements would never make it to the altar.

DIVINE APPOINTMENTS

The Judge and his Alamosa partners, Dr. Davlin and Herman Emperius, were interested in mining but uncertain how to go about getting involved. This problem was solved when Richard Kilvert, a Henson Canyon mossback in need of financial backing, also was in need of medical attention. After nearly dying from oxygen deprivation while working his Vermont/Ocean Wave lease, he made his way to Dr. Davlin's Alamosa hospital. Davlin was the Gold Links Mine doctor when he worked there years earlier.

As divine appointments go, Kilvert casually explained his finance situation in Henson Canyon to Dr. Davlin, who appeared to take little notice during his treatment of Kilvert. Sometime later in discussions with Emperius and Poxson, Davlin recounted Kilvert's tale. Emperius spotted an opportunity immediately. Poxson replied, "That's the place we ought to start [meaning investing in mining]. What kind of fellow is this man?" Without hesitation, Davlin answered, "Well, he's a nice old fellow. There's one thing about him, he's honest." Hearing this, both Emperius and Poxson responded, "Okay, let's do it!" [48]

The Judge soon found that Richard Kilvert was not only honest, he was hard-working, just like the Judge. Poxson also had more than a fair share of his own divine appointments.

> I worked many years from seven o'clock in the morning until as late as eleven o'clock at night. Several times I've handled three or four jobs at one time. While other people were out playing or having a good time, I was still working. The first person to have a truly great impact on my life was Governor Adams, but from a financial standpoint, my partner, Mr. Emperius, was like a father to me. I think the whole thing was that I had the ambition to take charge of something or take on something. It seems like everything that I started in was halfway a failure when I took an interest in it, and by good hard work, situations worked out very successfully. [49]

Ben sized up the Vermont/Ocean Wave through the same lens. His work ethic as well as his heart is demonstrated by his efforts to improve conditions at the State Industrial School in Golden, Colorado. In 1933 Governor Adams asked him to visit the Industrial School to see if he had any solutions for the troubles they were having. At that time this was the only alternative for even the youngest of offenders to the State Penitentiary in Canon City. Poxson ended up staying until 1936 and in later years summarized his approach by saying he just treated the inmates fairly and respected them as individuals. When asked not long before his death what he thought was the key to his success, he replied,

> I have never looked at life as a problem. Life is a pleasure, an opportunity, a gift. When you stop and think about it, there really are no hardships in life. It's just the way you look at things. Problems are just a part of the order of the day. Looked at from the right side, they don't become problems anymore. [50]

When Judge Poxson and his Alamosa partners came to the aid of R.J. Kilvert, he came with this very attitude. Kilvert believed there was merit in A.E. Reynolds' vision of a paying Vermont/Ocean Wave mine. Ben Poxson believed there was merit in R.J. Kilvert's ability to make it so. Despite the problems he was encountering, all Kilvert lacked was someone else's jack. Two years later Richard was dead and the Judge was forced to render a different verdict. The death of his trusted Superintendent spelled the end of the Judge's commitment to the Reynolds family's Vermont/Ocean Wave treasure hunt but it prepared the way for another divine appointment.

If any lasting benefit was going to come of the Judge's Vermont/Ocean Wave experience, it was going to come through Creede. Yes, he was disillusioned over Henson Canyon and Lake City, never mind prospects there, but the Creede mining district was another matter. So would be his relationship with Anna Reynolds Morse and George Garrey.

Where and when George, Anna, and Judge Poxson actually met face-to-face is unknown. Poxson's divine appointment with Creede prospects is not. In the midst of the Judge calling it quits in Henson Canyon and moving equipment he salvaged from the Vermont/Ocean Wave to Alamosa, a chance encounter during an overnight stay in Creede would change not only his plans, but his disposition, and his station in life. During the course of the evening, he met the lessee of the Commodore Mine and learned that it was another one of Reynolds' elephants. Quickly persuaded that that prospect looked favorable, and not attributing his problems with the Vermont/Ocean Wave to its owners, he agreed to a Commodore sub-lease. Thus began his very profitable association with the Creede Mining District, and as far as we can tell, it also was the beginning of his very profitable relationship with George Garrey, Anna's trusted Commodore Mining Company chief engineer and soon husband.

Getting to know Garrey in this role, Poxson would enter into a joint venture with him in Gunnison County to develop the Fairview-Cleopatra Mines in Chicago Park. Despite plummeting silver prices dooming this project [by the summer of 1933, the effects of the Great Depression brought silver prices to a historic low of $0.30 per ounce and forced the temporary shutdown of just about every silver mine in America], Poxson and Garrey bonded. A year later the two would find success together investing in a gold mine in Summitville as well as in additional Reynolds' properties in Creede.

Creede and Summitville paydays underwritten by Poxson and his Alamosa pals, directed by Anna with the advice and consent of George, tended to erase memories of Vermont/Ocean Wave disappointments. By a strange twist of events, an unantici-pated dividend of Reynolds' last best chance had found its way to the Judge. Ben Poxson, satisfied with the integrity of the Reynolds heirs and impressed with George Garrey's engineering advice, agreed to join in many speculative ventures that would be kinder to the Judge than Henson Canyon had promised to be. The critical dif-ference, of course, when everything else was said and done, was the inescapable reality that the ability to operate profitably and pay dividends required dependable rail service.

Mining engineer George Garrey was born in Reedville, Wisconsin in 1875. He grew up in Aurora, Illinois. His father was a physician. He graduated from the University of Chicago in 1898, taught high school for two years in Aurora, and returned to college to earn his Master of Arts degree in geology. In 1904 he graduated from the Michigan College of Mines with an "Engineer of Mines" degree, joining a growing new class of professionals with formal education rather than knowledge acquired on the job.

WALL STREET CRASH OF 1929 [51]

The *Wall Street Crash of 1929*, also simply known as *the Crash of '29* and *Black Thursday*, was the most devastating stock-market disaster in American history. The crash marked the beginning of widespread and long-lasting consequences for the country in general and San Juans mining in particular. Though economists and historians disagree on exactly what role the crash played in the ensuing nationwide collapse of the economy, many regard it as the catalyst of the Great Depression. Some historians, however, believe that it was actually a symptom of the Great Depression rather than its cause. The crash was also the starting point of important financial reforms and trading regulations, subjects for another day.

At the time of the crash, New York City had grown into the world's major financial capital and metropolis. The New York Stock Exchange (NYSE) was the largest stock market in the world. The roaring twenties were a time of prosperity and excess in the city, and, despite warnings of dangerous levels of speculation, many believed that there was no limit to what the market could sustain. Highly leveraged trading with higher and higher prices was nothing to be concerned about. In the cautionary words of Irving Fisher, a highly regarded economist of that day, "stock prices have reached what looks like a permanently high plateau." But what did that mean, really? The "permanently high plateau" part of his assessment bounced off of deaf ears. The euphoria and financial gains of the nation's great bull market were shattered on October 24, 1929, when share prices on the NYSE collapsed. Why on that particular date is still a controversial topic. Nothing in particular happened on that day to explain the collective collapse of investor confidence in the American way of life.

A weekend lull did not help. Stock prices continued to fall, at an unprecedented rate, for a full month. After the crash the Dow Jones Industrial Average (DJIA) recovered early in 1930, then plummeted again, only reaching a low point two years later, in 1932! It was lower at its July 8, 1932 nadir than it had been since the 1800s. The market did not return to pre-1929 levels until late 1954.

Pulsebeat of the Nation. The Wall Street crash of 1929 signaled the start of a nationwide depression lasting through the next decade. Banks failed, taking the deposits of their clients with them. The crowd in front of New York's American Union Bank were about to learn the sad news. Bad news in Lake City and Henson Canyon in the form of unemployment and high prices for everything except silver. *(National Archives)*

George was clearly well-prepared for success. He had worked for the fledgling U.S. Geological survey two years before signing on with the *American Smelting and Refining Company*, a Guggenheim affiliate, where he was in charge of offices in El Paso and Mexico City. In 1908, he joined a consulting company. Three years later he returned to Guggenheim as chief geologist. In 1914, he moved to Philadelphia and opened his own consulting engineer and geologist office. From there he moved to the *Tonopah-Belmont Development Company's* exploration department where he was responsible for the firm's mines throughout the western United States and British Columbia. In 1923 he returned to independent consulting. In 1927 he worked for the *Reynolds-Morse Corporation*. In 1938 he would marry the boss.

Notes — Chapter Nine: Shot-Out Streak
[1]   Gurley, W.F.E., "The Spirit In It," *Lake City Silver World*, August 3, 1922. Once again, Gurley's penchant for poetry captures the spirit of San Juans westering and the "American Experience."

[2] Ecclesiastes 2:11, KJV.

[3] September 21, 1926, MSS 1220, Box 25, FF1796.

[4] September 27, 1926, MSS 1220, Box 25, FF1798.

[5] October 5, 1926, MSS 1220, Box 25, FF1799.

[6] October 7, 1926, MSS 1220, Box 25, FF1799.

[7] October 12, 1926, MSS 1220, Box 25, FF1800.

[8] Ibid.

[9] Ibid.

[10] October 13, 1926, MSS 1220, Box 25, FF1800.

[11] October 15, 1926, MSS 1220, Box 25, FF1800.

[12] October 18, 1926, MSS 1220, Box 59, FF36.

[13] October 20, 1926, MSS 1220, Box 25, FF1801

[14] Ibid.

[15] November 12, 1926, MSS 1220, Box 25, FF1804-05.

[16] December 4, 1926, MSS 1220, Box 25, FF1807.

[17] January 3, 1927, MSS 1220, Box 25, FF1811.

[18] January 10, 1927, MSS 1220, Box 25, FF1812.

[19] February 5, 1927, MSS 1220, Box 25, FF1816.

[20] May 4, 1927, MSS 1220, Box 25, FF1826

[21] May 6, 1927, MSS 1220, Box 25, FF1826.

[22] May 10, 1927, MSS 1220, Box 25, FF1827.

[23] May 12, 1927, MSS 1220, Box 25, FF1827.

[24] June 1, 1927, MSS 1220, Box 25, FF1830.

[25] June 8, 1927, MSS 1220, Box 25, FF1831.

[26] Ibid.

[27] Ibid.

[28] July 4, 1927, MSS 1220, Box 25, FF1834.

[29] July 11, 1927, MSS 1220 Box 25, FF1835

[30] Ibid.

[31] July 20, 1927, MSS 1220 Box 25, FF1835.

[32] September 9, 1927, MSS 1220, Box 39, *Reynolds-Morse Corp. Ledger*, pg.165.

[33] December 1, 1927, MSS 1220, Box 25, FF1850.

[34] December 3, 1927, MSS 1220, Box 25, FF1850.

[35] December 6, 1927, MSS 1220, Box 25, FF1850.

[36] January 11, 1928, MSS 1220, Box 26, FF1854.

[37] February 15, 1928, MSS 1220, Box 39, *Reynolds-Morse Corp. Ledger*, pgs. 253-54.

[38] May 8, 1928, MSS1220, Box 26, FF1870.

[39] May 21, 1928, MSS 1220, Box 26, FF1872.

[40] July 2, 1928, MSS 1220, Box 26, FF1878.

[41] August 17, 1928, MSS 1220, Box 26, FF1882.

[42] October 5, 1928, MSS 1220, Box 26, FF1886.

[43] December 12, 1928, MSS 1220, Box 26, FF1894.

[44] June 22, 1929, MSS 1220, Box 26, FF1915.

[45] Patty, Mike, "Ben T. Poxson, Longtime Political Figure Dies at 97," *Rocky Mountain News*, August 1, 1990.

[46] Poxson, B. T., *Reminiscence*, pgs. 5, 17, 41, 55.

[47] Ibid., pg. 5.

[48] Ibid., pg. 17.

[49] Ibid., pgs. 41, 51.

[50] Ibid., pg. 55.

[51] *Wikipedia*, "Wall Street Crash of 1929."

CHAPTER 10

1933

The Gold Seeker's Song [1]

Take up the oxen boys, and harness up the mules;
Pack away provisions and bring along the tools;
The pick and the shovel, and a pan that won't leak;
And we'll start for the gold mines. Hurrah for the Peak!

Then farewell to sweethearts, and farewell to wives,
And farewell to children, the joy of our lives;
We're bound for the far west, the yellow dust to seek,
And as we march along we'll shout, Hurrah for Pike's Peak!

Then crack your whips, my jolly boys, we'll leave our homes behind,
And many lovely scenes that we'll often call to mind,
But we'll keep a merry heart, and we'll steer for Cherry creek;
For we're bound to hunt the yellow dust — Hurrah for Pike's Peak.

We'll cross the bold Missouri, and we'll steer for the west,
And we'll take the road we think is the shortest and the best;
We'll travel, o'er the plains, where the wind is blowing bleak,
And the sandy wastes shall echo with — Hurrah for Pike's Peak.

We'll sit around the campfire when all our work is done,
And sing our songs, and crack our jokes, and have our share of fun;
And when we're tired of jokes and songs, our blankets we will seek,
To dream of friends, and home, and gold. Hurrah for Pike's Peak.

Then ho! For the mountains, where the yellow dust is found,
Where the grizzly bear, and buffalo, and antelope abound;
We'll gather up the dust along the golden creek,
And make our "pile", and start for home. Hurrah for Pike's Peak.

As treasure hunts go, ferreting out Vermont/Ocean Wave silver had not gone well. Every fresh clue unearthed fresh new challenges with fresh new costs. Every fresh cost had to be underwritten by someone else's jack. The vicious circle had been unending—instead of treasure, someone else's jack unearthed fresh new clues. As disheartening as all of that was, the events of 1933 made matters worse. In fact, they upset the natural order of things everywhere and forever.

THE REST OF THE STORY [2]

Anna Reynolds Morse Garrey's parents, A.E. Reynolds and Dora Earll, married in Columbus, Wisconsin, on April 25, 1883. They resided for a time in Lake City but relocated to Denver after their only child, Anna Earll Reynolds, was born in Columbus on January 26, 1884. Anna was one of the first graduates of the Misses Masters School (Dobbs Ferry, New York) to gain entrance to a four-year college. That she did so was due largely to A.E. Reynolds' criticism that the Dobbs Ferry institution was not preparing his daughter for the challenge of higher education. Stung by Reynolds' remarks, the faculty was determined to prove him wrong. Anna and classmate Daisy Lewis, after graduation in 1903, were admitted to Smith College. They completed the course of instruction as members of the class of 1907.

Anna married Bradish P. Morse in 1913. He was a successful businessman, a partner in *Morse Brothers Machinery and Supply Company of Denver*, a firm that specialized in recycling the machinery and equipment of inactive mines, mills, railroads, and industrial plants. After his father-in-law's death in 1921, Bradish administered the Reynolds estate through the *Reynolds-Morse Corporation*. After Bradish's death in 1931, Anna took his place. Family friends Carl Sigfrid and George Garrey advised on legal matters, geology and investments. Anna and George, married on December 10, 1938, successfully retired estate debts through sale, forfeiture and leasing of mining properties. They emerged from the Great Depression and World War II well-endowed and able to support numerous Denver social and cultural organizations. George, at age 82, died July 23, 1957. Anna's journey through life, as is so often the case, is sweetly summarized in her obituary. [Also as is so often the case, we learn more about her famous father.]

> *Anna Earll Garrey, 98, died peacefully in the Gunnison Public Hospital Thursday, August 19, 1982, after a brief illness. The deceased had been vacationing at her summer home in Gold Creek in Gunnison County, accompanied by her daughter, Mrs. Eudora Moore, when she was suddenly taken ill. Mrs. Garrey, a life-long resident of Denver, had been making her home with her daughter, Mrs. Moore, in Pasadena, for the past several months.*

So much had changed over the half-century since America's gold-seekers, mass emigrations really, rushed west to Colorado's Rockies and beyond. In the San Juans the goldbug was joined by the silver bug and prospects like the Vermont and Ocean Wave developed into promising mines that called to another generation to try their hand. American exceptionalism showed new signs of pioneer grit. Survivors of America's Civil War in need of restoration and new opportunities

Although never actually a resident of Lake City, Anna Garrey had a pioneer heritage here and held large property interests in the county for a number of years. Her parents were Albert Eugene Reynolds (1840-1921) and his wife, Eudora (Earll) Reynolds (1852-1916), who resided briefly in Lake City following their marriage in 1883. A.E. Reynolds was associated with the general merchandise business in Lake City in the early 1880's, purchasing the firm of Hartman & Co. in 1882 and the Smith & Bacon store in 1883. The Reynolds business occupied a portion of the Hough Bank Block on Silver Street, in the room currently occupied by the Black Crooke Theatre.

Reynolds used the profits from his mercantile interests to invest heavily in the then developing mining industry of the San Juans, selling his Lake City business in 1885 to concentrate exclusively on mining matters. In the years to follow he was to become one of Colorado's most successful mining entrepreneurs, and at the time of his death, in 1921, was in possession of more mining property in Colorado than any other individual. Reynolds was associated with such celebrated mines as the Virginius of Ouray, the Commodore in Mineral County, the Durant at Aspen and the Gold Cup and Gold Links mines in Gunnison County.

In Hinsdale County, A.E. Reynolds owned several of the premier properties, owning there the Frank Hough mine on Engineer mountain, the Ocean Wave, and Belle of the West. He also had substantial interests in the Golconda, Golden Fleece, Palmetto, and Vermont mines.

Anna Earll Reynolds, the only child of A.E. and Eudora Reynolds, was born at the home of her maternal grandmother in Wisconsin on January 26, 1884. She later moved with her family to Denver and lived there for the majority of her life. Anna was first married to Bradish P. Morse, Denver manufacturer, in 1913 [actually 1914?]. Mr. Morse died in 1931 and in 1938 she was married to noted geologist and engineer George H. Garrey. Mr. Garrey predeceased his wife in 1958 [actually 1957?].

In the year after her father's death Mrs. Garrey took an active interest in the management of the Reynolds' estate. She was called on to inspect the various mine holdings and, in the dark days of the Depression, was forced to decide what properties would be let go for taxes and which would be retained.

Mrs. Garrey is survived by three children from her first marriage [Ann, Reynolds, and Eudora]

took a deep breath and answered that call. Born into the nation's recovery and industrial revolution, another product of America's euphoric "manifest destiny," A.E. Reynolds also had answered that call.

Between A.E. Reynolds' 1899 decision to exploit the lower workings of the Vermont and Ocean Wave mines through an ambitious haulage tunnel, and daughter Anna's transition a short thirty years later from Denver socialite to heiress-in-charge of the family's immense but troubled mining empire, not only had so much changed, so much could never be the same. A world war [another was coming] accompanied by a worldwide pandemic, a fickle global silver market, a revolution in Russia that would cast a dark shadow over the rest of civilization for the rest of the century, and a crippling national depression that witnessed the death of her husband had dealt Anna and the entire San Juans mining community a weak hand. So what was to come of a treasure hunt like her's?

By all reliable accounts, *Silver World* "boosterism" accounts for sure, Vermont/ Ocean Wave high-assay silver-bearing ore was far from depleted. Also far from depleted was the urge to find it. Short of that, there was plenty of low-grade ore that was treasure enough as long as there was a railroad that could get it to market, and a market with silver prices that made doing so worth the trip. Oh, there also was that matter of someone else's jack. Adequate operating cash was one of every mossback's greatest challenges. Once the responsibility of the owner, that too had changed forever. Now lease-holders had to pay for the privilege. Of all the Vermont/Ocean Wave lessees, Mossback Kilvert and his Alamosa partners had looked like a harbinger of good times ahead. So did W.C. Martin, Jim Flood, and B.N. Ramsey—the family would count on them. The family didn't count on the loss of the D&RG rail service.

So what else could go wrong? Well, economical rail transportation could be terminated, that's what could go wrong. Inflation could result in mining costs that exceeded silver market prices, skilled labor could flee to new boom towns and new industries, investors could flee mining projects in favor of emerging technologies, that could go wrong. In the case of Lake City and Henson Canyon mines, by 1933 all of these matters had gone wrong. The first indication serious trouble was near had come on July 26, 1929 when the Denver & Rio Grande (D&RG) railroad suspended service between Lake City and Sapinero due to lack of business. Every mine in Henson Canyon, few though they be, already struggling to meet payrolls, suspended work. Entrepreneurs, Jim Flood included, suspended investments. Public outrage and railroad regulatory agencies would force the D&RG to resume service in early December, but the damage to investor and community confidence was irreversible. The October 29th crash of the red-hot New York Stock Exchange, and the erosion of silver prices to 46.5 cents/ oz. by January 1, 1930, were the next gut-punches. They destroyed what little stomach remained for undertaking risky Henson Canyon mining ventures. Faced with a loss of mining opportunities, local merchants lost customers and the Lake

City community lost skilled workers. In 1920, the total population of Hinsdale County was 538 men, women and children. In 1930, 449 souls remained.

Still, occasional work continued at the Vermont/Ocean Wave. Unfound treasure in a mine laced with clues could not be ignored—a series of State Mine Inspector reports testified to that [3]—especially by desperate men struggling to just get by. W.C. Martin had had a better idea. He found time and funds to recover marketable ore from the mine dump—this practice was not contemplated in his lease or sublease—enough to justify shipping a carload to the Leadville smelter. On January 23, 1930, he informed the *Ocean Wave Mining & Reduction Co.* that they would soon receive royalties from Leadville. Why is not clear, but he also shared his assessment of conditions at the mine, particularly the area covered by his sublease with Jim Flood, and what should be done about them. Apparently this was his way of compensating the landlord for breaking his lease and saying goodbye. Still, his assessment was valuable.

> *Dear Sirs: In looking over the work done on the Ocean Wave Property I regard the effort to explore the ground under the Dago Tunnel level as of the greatest importance. The work was completed and a careful examination made of the ground so long inaccessible. You have been advised of the conditions this work showed and I dare say they were disappointing to you. To me disappointment does not adaquatly (sic) express it.*
>
> *Then on the strength of a surface showing I started a tunnel above the Dago and drifted toward the Lillie workings, following a vein which would ultimately lead into Lillie workings. Here again the results were disappointing, as the showing of ore was not as good as on the surface. I have been in every hole on this and adjacent properties I could get into, many of them most unsafe, with the hope I could pick up some tangled thread that might lead to something worthwhile doing some work whereby the property would make production. Unfortunately I found no such place. There are of course some development programs which might yield results but they are beyond my means.*
>
> *In view of what I have stated it seems the best thing I can do in justice to myself and to you is to relinquish my lease. This I shall do if you will let me know who to turn such stuff as is here over to. The cabins are in good shape and I made a list of what I found here when I come. The same is here now. Kindly let me know your wishes in the matter. thanking you for your consideration, I remain, Yours, W. C. Martin.*[4]

In fact, Martin was not aware that Flood's lease had never been executed, or that his own lease had already been terminated effective January 1st. Martin's lease did not really matter at this point. The unexecuted Jim Flood lease also was in jeopardy. Flood had second thoughts about investing in mines with rail service on shaky ground and what was shaping up to be a prolonged economic downturn. By April, B.P. Morse also was having second thoughts about continuing to be a landlord. He confided in Office Manager Cary that he was ready to sell his father-in-law's favorite elephant, at bargain-basement prices if need be. In response to his Ouray attorney, Carl Sigfrid, steps were initiated to redeem the Vermont/Ocean Wave properties again seized by the county for failure to pay taxes. On April 25, 1930, back taxes, interest, fees and penalties were paid to the Hinsdale County Treasurer. Morse instructed Cary to take the following actions:

> *I would send Sigfrid a check for the Ocean Wave expenses so that we can get this cleaned up with him. I think that we had better hold the redemption certificate as security for these advances so that we can get it back if the mine ever produces anything or we sell it. My opinion of the Ocean Wave is that if there is any possibility of making a sale on it, even for a small amount, we should do it. I doubt whether there is anything there or not, and if we could get five or ten thousand dollars out of it I think we ought to let it go.*[5]

B.P. Morse, A.E. Reynolds' son-in-law and Executor of the Reynolds Estate, was worn out. Reynolds' last best chance to make a mine had played a major role in a losing battle to save the heirs from financial ruin. But no sooner had B.P. confessed defeat than B.N. Ramsey—not to be confused with long-deceased John James Ramsey—threw him a lifeline. On April 26, 1930, just one day after he ran up the white flag, Ramsey requested a thirty-six month lease. Ramsey was well aware of Reynolds' legacy, and his proposition took Martin's approach to another level. He wanted to mill all the ore he could find on the mine dump [27,000 cu. yds. by some estimates] and open up "new mill ore if there was any to be opened in the property [meaning underground]." Ramsey continued.

> *I have about one hundred and fifty tons (sic) of mill ore from the Vermont Group here at my mill [yet to be built in Lake City] and will soon have my mill running. I have my mill fit out with crusher rolls, ball mill, Wilfley tables and floatation machine and can save the ore close everything at the Ocean Wave is wide open and there will not be any thing (sic) left there if some one (sic) don't look after it.*[6]

Ramsey's proposition amounted to sorting mine waste to retrieve higher-grade ore on the one hand, and thwarting the threat of vandalism on the other hand. Scavenging mine waste was not only Martin's idea, it was as old as mining itself, and increasingly common as the effects of the nationwide depression took its toll on employment opportunities. Not to leave any stone unturned, Ramsey threw in the threat of the railroad ceasing service altogether and making everyone's mines uneconomical if large quantities of ore were not shipped soon. Better for him to mill and ship the ore for a percentage. As for vandalism, he would board up the powerhouse and secure the "pipe dies, steam gauge machine drills, and a lot of other small things."[7]

Once again, nothing came of this matter. In fact, nothing came of the Jim Flood lease negotiated but never signed despite W.H. Cary remaining hopeful as late as May 1930. Bradish Morse, for all practical purposes a Tennessee resident now, was beyond disappointment. On May 3rd Cary shared the bad news.

> *Dear Mr. Morse: As Flood seems to be the logical one to take hold of the Ocean Wave, have taken the matter of lease up with him several times and am trying to bring him to a show down as to what he will do. He is in Lake City now and when he returns we should know definitely whether or not he is going ahead with the proposition. Had a letter from Ramsey wanting a lease, he had one on the Vermont, but Ramsey is no good and about all he wants to do is to haul the Ocean Wave dump ore down to Lake City and treat it in a small mill he is putting up.*[8]

On November 21, 1930, in a letter rather formally addressed to "Mr. Sigfrid," not "Carl," his deceased father-in-law's trusted Ouray attorney, Morse provided a rare glimpse into the impact of the depression on his efforts to settle Reynolds Estate matters. It also revealed his state of mind regarding finding a suitable home for his darling Vermont/Ocean Wave and Reynolds Tunnel elephant.

> *Dear Mr. Sigfrid: On account of mining conditions being at such a low ebb I thought it a little better business on my part to stay down here [Old Hickory] this winter rather than try to do anything with the properties, as it is a forgone conclusion that about the only property we have is the Summitville to do anything on that has sufficient gold to be interesting with the possible exception of the Gold Links.*
>
> *Mrs. Morse has been down here for the past three weeks and will probably stay until we return sometime in December so as to be home for Christmas. We have had quite a time down here with bank failures. Our bank, The American having bought out the Caldwell bank to prevent a "run" being made on them, as they were envolved (sic) more or less in young Caldwell's failure in the investment business. Two of the smaller banks, one large bank in Kentucky and one in Arkansas closed, in which he was envolved (sic), and it is quite a situation as people here are not as accustomed to bank failures as they are in Denver. It has slowed up local business terribly as they do not know where the thing will end*[9]

Throughout 1931, Bradish Morse was preoccupied with Reynolds estate affairs in Tennessee. He also was preoccupied with his health. As far as he was concerned, Colorado silver mining was dead, and so were viable leasing propositions. According to his former and favorite mining engineer, J.D. Fisher, the worldwide market for silver also was dead, or nearly so. Gold to the extent it could be located was back in the catbird seat in the San Juans. Probably in need of work himself, Fisher reached out to B.P. with a market assessment he had prepared for anyone who would listen. In Morse's case he explained his absence over the past year and in so doing provided a clear explanation for why the price of silver was not going to return to historically high levels hovering around $1.00 per oz. He also was looking for information on Colorado silver prices, and for a consulting engagement.

> *Dear Bradish: I have been quietly working, both here and abroad, for almost a year on the silver situation for a group of interested people. It is needless to say that the universal recognition of silver as a trade medium meets with much resistance from many strong and important quarters. One of the less important arguments is that advanced by those who are apprehensive over an overproduction of the metal, even on a 40 to 1 ratio [relative to gold], or 50 cents per ounce. It is amazing to find how many people believe that pure silver is produced in Mexico and Peru by steam shovel methods!! In meeting this argument, I have used the arbitrary figure of 65 cents as the production cost per ounce of silver, not where it is a by-product in base metal production, but where it is the chief metal mined, based on an average content of 27 oz. of silver per ton of ore mined. This figure is considerable higher than that arrived at from a large amount of production cost data, where, however, base metals have, more or less, been a by-product, and vice versa.*
>
> *A comprehensive survey of world sources of silver reveals the fact of how few strictly silver miners there are compared to multi-metal mines. In view of your Creede interests [meaning the Commodore] it is possible that you are in a position to furnish accurate accurate [repeated in original typed letter] silver production costs. If you care to furnish them, they will be appreciated. The silver situation is one of the most interesting subjects I have ever tackled, particularly from international aspect. I will ask you to read the enclosed article and give me your reaction to it. Perhaps it may be an idle wish to hope for the universal recognition of silver as an international medium of any "fixed" gold-silver ratio, much less on anything like 20 to 1, nevertheless there are many straws in the wind blowing in the right direction, both here and abroad, and, who knows what the ultimate outcome may be.*
>
> *No lasting good can come to the silver mining industry through the purchase by our Government of a specific amount of silver at an arbitrality (sic) fixed price. As I see it, the inevitable and ultimate result of such an action on the silver producer would be similar to that of the wheat farmer arising out of the Relief Board's purchase of wheat at an arbitrary price, namely, the worst kind of a boomerang.*[10]

Bradish Morse's health worsened throughout 1931. January rumors of his imminent death were exaggerated but plausible given his attacks of pleurisy, congested lungs, and bouts of pneumonia. Reports of his death on December 28, 1931, were accurate. His obituary, "Native of Ware is Dead in Colorado," read:

Denver, Col., Dec 28 (AP) — Bradish P. Morse, 60, Denver clubman and treasurer of the Morse Brothers' Machinery & Supply Co., died in his home, yesterday, from heart disease, aggravated by a serve cold. Mr. Morse recently spent several months in Nashville, Tenn. on business, and while returning to Denver with his son, Reynolds, to spend the holidays with his family, caught the cold which resulted fatally (sic). Mr. Morse was born in Ware, Mass. After studying at Amherst College, he entered the newspaper business. Friends here said he became publisher of a weekly paper at Palmer, Mass. A fire that destroyed his plant ended his newspaper career and he joined his brothers, Calvin and Willard Morse, in Denver, in 1893.[11]

Interesting, is it not, that what consumed B.P.'s attention and energy for the better part of his adult life was not even mentioned in *The Rocky Mountain News*. Nor was his surviving wife Anna, nor the Reynolds mining legacy. While A.E. reigned as a mining king, owning thousands of properties, he had acquired and had lost fortunes. As executor of A.E.'s estate, son-in-law Morse had earned millions and had expended millions leasing the most promising elephants and retiring the most pressing debts. Why was that not noteworthy? Maybe the editor ran short of column inches. In any event it did not matter. Widow Anna knew the rest of his story and she knew that she would have to live it for him. She also knew that her father's best chance and now her best chance to redeem fame and fortune still waited patiently in the family's elephant corral. Unlike her father and husband, she was not sure which were the best elephants to cut out of the herd. Bucking the headwinds of the worst depression in the nation's history, Anna braved the 1930s knowing full well her destiny was being shaped by circumstances far beyond her control. The fate of the D&RG Lake City Branch would make that painfully obvious all too soon.

Critically important from the first track laid between Denver and Durango, even more critical for Henson Canyon mines was the last track laid between Sapinero and Lake City. When it came to rail service, remote Lake City's fortunes were no better nor worse than the fortunes of the remote Henson Canyon mines. And as we have seen time and again, the fortunes of Henson Canyon mines were highly dependent on economical rail service. There was no escaping that joyful reality when service commenced in1889. There was no escaping that harsh reality when service was terminated in 1933.

Contrast August 1889 with May 1933. Memories of that arrival heralded for months by the chants of the gandy-dancers, prayed for and schemed over for a decade beforehand, the first scheduled Lake City passenger train with two freight cars piloted by P.J. Ready at the throttle, had not faded. The Second District, Third Division, Lake City Branch of the D&RG originating at Sapinero was open for business. Thirty-six difficult miles separated Sapinero and Lake City. Locomotive and cars crossed ten bridges averaging twelve miles per hour. Finally, the gap was closed—better late than never. The 1880 county population of 1,487 had dropped to 862 in 1890, but with the aid of the D&RG came revival. The population nearly doubled to 1,609 by 1900. Marginal mines increased production and profits. The Vermont and the Ocean Wave revived, too. Sadly the D&RG did not. When the mines again began stumbling in the early 1900s, so did the town's favorite uncle.

Thirty-three profitless years later, the Denver and Rio Grande would call it quits, and the Lake Fork community would harbor no illusions about the dreadful consequences of this decision. The mournful lyrics of *Ghost Train* dramatized all that needed to be said. What was left of the local community had called upon local and state politicians and regulators to save the Lake City Branch Line and were dogged by failure. It was not as if no one really cared or tried.

Resolved to leave Lake City to its own devices in 1929, D&RG management had nevertheless succumbed to pressure from partisans and politicians and kept the trains running a while longer. Under the watchful eye of the state Public Utility Commission (PUC), the D&RG succeeded in scaling back service and hopefully their losses. Shorter trains ran less frequently. Maintenance was deferred. But instead of austerity producing a paying proposition, a legacy of derailments and washouts were its rewards. In 1921 epic flooding damaged the depot, swept away several smaller buildings, torn up the right-of-way, and upended four miles of track north of town. Severe floods returned in 1929, again destroying much of the track-bed. The final blows to solvency were less direct but just as decisive. By 1931, heavy-duty trucks able to travel long distances on paved highways were gradually reducing the traffic on rails, traffic already being reduced by the nationwide depression. Fewer travelers and freight shipments showed no signs of improving any time soon. As Christmas 1931 approached, D&RG management's idea of an ideal present was gifting the Lake City Branch to anyone willing to operate it. With taxes running over $20,000 a year against estimated revenues of $8,400 a year, even the dullest observer could master the math. One sarcastic journalist wrote this about the D&RG's delusional largesse:

> *If you haven't enough trouble of your own, here is a chance to get an operating railroad free of charge. The (D&RG Railroad) has notified the State Public Utilities Commission that it will give its thirty-nine mile branch between Sapinero and Lake City to anyone who will agree to operate it and pay the taxes, or if you do not care to take on that much responsibility the railroad will lease you the branch for $480 a year and throw in the free use of a locomotive and coach.*

In the bustling '90s the Lake City branch was one of the thriving feeders of the Rio Grande system. Hundreds of travelers were going in and out of the booming mining camp and hundreds of tons of rich ore were being transported to the smelters but 1932 finds the branch such a burden that it is willing to give it away to stop the expenses of taxes and operation. [12]

Imagine. There were no takers. Next, the D&RG petitioned the Public Utility Commission [PUC] to close the depot and received permission to do so. Having succeeded in poking its nose into the PUC tent, within months the D&RG requested permission to close the line completely. Expecting that request would also be granted, Mike Burke had other ideas. Who was he? A risk-taking entrepreneur, of course, cut out of the same whole-cloth as A.E. Reynolds. He owned the Ute-Ulay. He needed economical rail service more than anyone, town and county included, and was not ready to walk away from his investment. The local community, what was left of it, wisely came alongside.

Burke was another one of those adolescent San Juan pilgrims that had cast aside their eastern heritage for western adventure. Not exactly a mossback, he was an ordinary man capable of extraordinary accomplishments. Born in Massillon, Ohio, on August 31, 1867, to Patrick and Elizabeth Burke, he likely was a typical hotheaded Irishman from childhood. His father was a prominent figure in the coal mining industry in Ohio, not a profession for the timid. Young Mike attended school through the sixth grade, then at age twelve he bolted, probably from his hotheaded Irish father most likely just like him. Wise beyond his years, he accumulated considerable wealth through mining interests in Cripple Creek before discovering Henson Canyon. He soon laid down a lot of his chips there.

Burke bought the Ute/Ulay in 1925 for $35,000. Much like A.E. Reynolds with the Vermont/Ocean Wave, he knew a bargain with a huge upside when he saw it. Like Reynolds, he discovered needed renovations would cost him dearly, $265,000 over the next ten years. Unlike A.E., he was well-financed. He installed modern mining equipment, built a new 100-ton flotation mill, constructed a 60-ft. high dam on Henson Creek [how he obtained permits to do that one can only imagine], with a hydroelectric plant [a Reynolds dream, but also a regulatory miracle]. Apparently he saw no need to spread his costs by making his mill available to other Henson Creek operations, nor is there any indications Vermont/Ocean Wave lessors tried. [13] Regardless, Burke's investment would result in the Ute/Ulay becoming the biggest producer [by some accounts $14 million over the life of the mine] of paydirt in Hinsdale County. Unfortunately, with every year of production the quality of the ore failed to keep up with increasing costs, making the importance of economical rail service greater and greater.

Of course, Burke's bottom-line was important to the D&RG, too. A high volume of ore shipped by rail kept both the D&RG and Mike Burke solvent. Sadly, this marriage in heaven would not last. Metal values declined, inflation

Same Silver Vein - Same Promise. Burke's "big buy" proved to be the most profitable mine in Henson Canyon. The Vermont/Ocean Wave, 3.5 miles west on the same silver-rich vein, was close behind. *(Harvey DuChene, U.S. Dept. of the Interior)*

rates rose, other people's jack found more promising places to land. The onset of the nationwide effects of the depression ended confidence in the economy at large and what remained of Lake City's good times in the process. Ute/Ulay fortunes, in turn, served as a clear gauge of the attractiveness [meaning return on investment] of Henson Canyon mines overall. The Vermont/Ocean Wave Group, once one of the top four producers in Hinsdale County, was no exception. If the Ute/Ulay could not make a go of it with all the technology and milling available onsite, what chance did smaller and more impoverished Henson Canyon mines have?

All concerned parties—Mike Burke, the D&RG, Lake City Fathers—made do with hard times until the D&RG could hemorrhage cash no longer. General business activity needed to support the railroad had been steadily declining for decades. A hard-to-argue-with barometer of this was the number of city residents. In 1910 there were 405. In 1920 residents numbered 317. In 1930 there were 259. Sales figures of ores from county-wide mines also were hard to dispute. Total revenue from mine production in 1929 was a paltry $11,506. Two years later it was $327. [Imagine, $327. Today a teenager with a paper route could make more than that.] In 1931, the D&RG proposed replacing rail service with bus and truck service provided by its subsidiary, the *Rio Grande Motor Way*. Rail service would be provided only on an as-needed basis. Not seeing the silver lining in this approach, the Public Utilities Commission rejected it.[14]

Failing to sell or even give the railroad away to another operator, the D&RG simply abandoned it. The PUC hesitated to act—entrepreneur Burke did not. He had assured the D&RG and the PUC that he alone would supply enough ore to keep the Lake City Branch solvent. Having heard that promise before, the D&RG countered that keeping the railroad safe maintenance-wise much less solvent would require an investment of $250,000. After two weeks of hearings, the Interstate Commerce Commission concluded that the Lake Fork region had

furnished little traffic to the branch for at least 5.5 years and has been at a low ebb for a much longer period.... It may be that production could be increased when the demand for metals improves, but there is no assurance of production on a scale sufficient to support the cost of operating the line or to warrant the expenditure necessary for rehabilitation.... [15]

Confounded by such countervailing arguments, the state PUC had punted to the Federal Interstate Commerce Commission (ICC). Apparently better staffed to understand the problem, or more insulated from local politics, the ICC approved the abandonment of the Lake City Branch. When the last steam whistle blew on May 25, 1933, it surely sounded more like a funeral dirge. Already humbled by its shuttered railroad depot, the Queen of the San Juans in happier times had nothing to be happy about now.

Neither was Mike Burke happy, but being the entrepreneur he was, nor was he discouraged. He needed rail service to survive. He needed the Lake City Branch, or something akin to it. True, there were more and better heavy-duty trucks being manufactured, but railcars had greater capacity and reliable rail service was more economical. "Getting his Irish up," Burke concluded he needed rail service but he did not need the D&RG. For some time he had considered organizing his own railroad company if necessary. Now it was necessary. Out of compassion or maliciousness, you decide, the D&RG delayed ripping up the track and advanced the sale date of the right-of-way. Any buyer who could pony-up $16,000 could have it. Burke could. He committed to advancing $1,000, and paying the $15,000 balance over three years. He agreed to pay the 1933 taxes of $20,000, maintain the track and bridges, and make no stops along the route. [Why "no stops along the route" was never explained.] Burke's railroad company, the *San Christobal Railroad*, was in business, except for one minor matter. It possessed no rolling stock, most importantly a locomotive. Of course, entrepreneur Burke had a plan. He would retrofit his precious Pierce-Arrow, the last word when it came to American industry's contribution to automotive power and prestige. The D&RG had pioneered the idea [the D&RG Southern would operate one], he could retrofit a roadster, too.

Mike Burke's six cylinder 1928 Pierce-Arrow, built by South Bend, Indiana Studebaker Corporation, was up to the task. [The Studebaker family, you will recall, designed and built hardy replacements for the typical farm wagon that became popular with gold-seekers rushing across the Great Plains, and the U.S. Army in need of heavy freighters capable of keeping up with the demands of frontier outposts across the West.] Sold as a sedan touring car, it was powerful and sturdy enough to navigate what passed for cross-country roads, sturdy enough to be converted into fire engines serviceable for decades to come.

The virtues of the Pierce-Arrow had not been lost on Burke. Also not lost on Burke was the importance of getting his Lake City ore to Pueblo and beyond by rail. Turning to the *McFarland-Eggers Denver* machine shop, his once elegant touring car was converted into a version of the Rio Grande Southern Railroad's

---

1933

Worldwide events that unfolded in 1933 marked a turning point in the trajectory of global affairs that also marked a turning point in the economic wellbeing of the San Juans and especially Henson Canyon mines. The viability of the Vermont and Ocean Wave mines, always handicapped by their remote locations and predominantly low-grade ores, were subject to failure even when metal prices were not depressed and transportation costs were not high. 1933 was exceptional in these matters and more. Three years after it began, 1933 marked the height of America's and thus the world's Great Depression and offered no hope of improvement. In Henson Canyon's case, this meant that the cost of production would exceed the value of silver. In the case of the Vermont/Ocean Wave, this meant that capital available for speculative investments was scarce to nonexistent.

Little wonder that the Reynolds heirs faced strong headwinds in their attempts to continue the hunt for Vermont/Ocean Wave treasure. Bare-bones development funds—their own jack or someone else's—failed to cover wages. Experienced miners—mossbacks by another name—willing to work for a share of future profits in lieu of wages were dead or off to better prospects in new boomtowns. Sadly, events near and far throughout 1933 were not harbingers of better days to come.

• The banking system had collapsed nationwide. 25% of the national labor force was unemployed. Prices and productivity was a third of what they had been before the October 1929 Wall Street stock market crash. Factories and farms were lost to foreclosures, mines and mills were abandoned, hungry and homeless people roamed the streets and country. Conditions across the prairie states were worsened by unrelenting drought-induced dust storms. Newly elected Franklin D.

Pierce-Arrow Prestige. The Pierce-Arrow was considered a luxury vehicle. It also was exceptionally powerful and often adapted to serve industrial and commercial needs. Rail-auto service was well within its capabilities. *(Wikimedia Commons)*

Roosevelt introduced America to unprecedented socialist reforms and expansion of the Federal Government. His first hundred days in office [New Deal] helped alleviate the suffering, but it would require rearming and fighting World War II to put the nation's economy back on its feet.

• World War II was all but assured with German President Paul von Hindenburg's appointment of Nazi Party leader Adolf Hitler as Chancellor, the most powerful office in their land. Hitler in a secret speech to his military leaders outlined his vision of a rearmed Germany and *Lebensraum* [meaning expanding "living space"] in eastern Europe [at the expense of Austria, Czechoslovakia, and Poland]. Hitler soon became dictator of Germany and opened Dachau, the first Nazi concentration camp.

• President Roosevelt declared a national emergency and made it illegal for U.S. citizens to own monetary gold or bullion. The U.S. abandoned the gold standard in favor of "fiat" [paper] currency. The price of silver cratered.

• The Chicago *Century of Progress* World's Fair introduced an astounding array of inventions that would revolutionize global communications, commerce, and the daily lives of everyday Americans. The downside: who could afford to purchase them? Less obvious, who would be inclined to invest in speculative mines given an opportunity to purchase or invest in eye-popping technologies and labor-saving consumer products no matter how speculative they might be?

• Leo Szilard envisioned the nuclear chain reaction which led to the development of the world's first atomic bomb, the nuclear age to come, and the prospect of total global destruction.

• Germany withdrew from the League of Nations and the World Disarmament Conference. Albert Einstein flees Nazi Germany and settles in the United States.

• On the 25th of May the last D&RG train pulled out of Lake City, marking the end of the Lake City Branch and signaling the end of Lake City's mining era.

"Galloping Goose." It's little but powerful eighty horsepower six-cylinder gasoline engine with a four-speed manual transmission could pull what amounted
to a bus-sized gondola car brimming with ore. But his plans came to nought as
well. The same global economic forces that stifled Henson Canyon mining, that
plagued the Vermont/Ocean Wave, and that ground down the D&RG Railroad
also cooked Mike Burke's goose. Entrepreneurial railroads with austere operating
budgets could turn up their toes, too. Accounts varied, but certain was the fact
that not even the economic advantages of a Pierce-Arrow could compensate for
the low values of Henson Canyon ores including ores from his own Ute/Ulay.[16]

Alas, Entrepreneur Burke's rail-auto could not overcome the troubled times
in which he operated. Depression-era austerity cooked his goose. So too his Ute/
Ulay. So too the other Henson Canyon mines. So too Anna Reynolds Morse
Garrey's efforts to find a prairie-dog mossback and someone else's jack devoted
to breathing new life into her father's darling Vermont/Ocean Wave elephant.

The card deck of life had been stacked against them all. With the benefit of
hindsight, probably not even another John York or Richard Kilvert with more of
faithful Ben Poxson's cash could have changed Vermont/Ocean Wave fortunes
given the world around them. That world argued that what little cash there was
available including Ben's would be better served invested in motor vehicles or the
endless flood of handy inventions shamelessly promoted everywhere one chose
to look. Hard rock mines were out of favor. What the miners that remained in
Hinsdale County after the end of rail service could look forward to was what
they could salvage from the ore dumps. That did not require someone else's jack.
That did not even require title to the claim. The rest of the community lived off
of the county government and the school system. The Reynolds Estate lived off
of more productive elephants remaining in Reynolds' elephant corral, more accessible elephants that could calve higher assay ores with less need of new money,
and more lucrative emerging technologies beckoning to them from near and far.

San Cristobal Railroad's
"Galloping Goose." Short-lived,
sold to the D&RG railroad in
1939, and dismantled for parts,
it probably looked a lot like
"Goose No. 2" photographed
in Durango, Colorado in 1940
and currently on display at the
Colorado Railroad Museum,
Denver, Colorado. (Russell Lee,
U.S. Farm Security Administration)

In a larger sense, fortress San Juans had fended off unwanted assaults for centuries, but could not deny the changes that the events of 1933 had set in motion. Coping with the benefits and the bereavements of it all would require a decade of austerity and years of reconstruction from a second world war. Lake City, once Queen of the San Juans, would not be spared. Nor could Henson Canyon mines and Reynolds' last best chance buck the tide. Like most everyone else, Anna and George would learn how to hunker down until new opportunities presented themselves. So would the treasure-hunters that came behind.

Notes — Chapter Ten: 1933

1 *Hannibal Messenger*, "The Gold Seeker's Song," Anon, April 28, 1859.
2 *Lake City Silver World*, September 3, 1982; Scamehorn, Lee, *Albert Eugene Reynolds, Colorado's Mining King*, pgs. 26-29, 225-26.
3 See Appendix A for State Mine Inspector reports.
4 January 23, 1930, MSS 1220, Box 27, FF1931.
5 April 25, 1930, MSS 1220, Box 27, FF1941.
6 April 26, 1930, MSS 1220, Box 27, FF1941.
7 Ibid.
8 May 3, 1930, MSS 1220, Box 27, FF1942.
9 November 21, 1930, MSS 1220, Box 27, FF1954.
10 May 3, 1931, MSS 1220, Box 27, FF1942. Silver values had been declining since the Civil War. They recovered for several years following WWI. The average value in 1922 was $0.82 per ounce, declining gradually to $0.53 per ounce in 1929. In 1933, at the height of the Great Depression, the average price per ounce was $0.30.
11 January 6, 1932, MSS 1220, Box 27, FF1989.
12 Smith, P. David, *The Story of Lake City*, pg. 267.
13 Vandenbusche, Duane and Walter R. Borneman, *Colorado Rail Annual No. 14*, pg. 94. [There are any number of reasons Vermont/Ocean Wave operators did not consider the Ute/Ulay mill a viable means to reduce transportation costs. Mike Burke may have wanted too much for the service. Mill technology may not have been suitable for Vermont/Ocean Wave ores. Mike Burke may not have wanted to deal with customers likely to accuse him of cheating them out of their proper share of "mill returns."]
14 Ibid., pg. 92.
15 Ibid., pg. 95.
16 Ibid., pgs. 97-98. Smith, pgs. 268-69.

EPILOGUE

Bones

Of all the many trails that spanned the plains in bygone day,
The Oregon, the Overland, the Platte, the Santa Fe,
And Arkansaw will have a place in romance, song, and lore;
A place which time cannot efface; outstanding more and more.

The argonauts, who were in quest of homesteads, health, and gold,
Trekked o'er these trails unto the west, in border days of old.
Their guarded, covered-wagon trains, by mules and oxen drawn,
Were piloted across the plains by men of nerve and brawn.

These trails were once the only means of travel to the coast;
They witnessed many thrilling scenes, for in that motley host
They served were desperadoes, thugs, grog-mixers, gamblers, vamps,
Whose vicious ways and whiskey jugs debauched the mining camps.

Wolves, buffaloes, and antelope, the prairie dog, and hen;
The Mormon brake, the snubbing-rope, trails, coaches, shot-gun men;
The Conestogas, Schuttlers, Bains; the freighter's six mule team;
Pack-saddles, yokes, and hobble chains, have vanished like a dream.

The vigilantes, wild west life, the scout, the pioneer,
The prairie fire, the scalping knife, stampede, and camp-fire's cheer,
Are now but memories of the past. What of those men so brave?
The plow turns up their bones, oft-cast into an unmarked grave.[1]

The Reynolds family hunt for Vermont/Ocean Wave treasure lasted nearly half a century, energized by their abiding belief that the treasure would materialize in the form of a motherlode worthy of their sacrifices. Family patriarch Albert Eugene Reynolds launched the hunt in 1899. Daughter Anna and husband Bradish inherited the adventure in 1921. Of course not knowing it at the time, 1933 signaled the beginning of the end to any thought of reviving Henson

Canyon mining or their prospects for success. When attracting someone else's jack was necessary, their reputation for honest dealing had always yielded an abundance of subscribers including mossbacks willing to forego daily wages in exchange for a share of hoped-for profits. Speculators signed on to leases and subleases that took the place of stock certificates and baseless annual reports. By 1933 Henson Canyon mossbacks, subscribers, and speculators willing to stomach ever-increasing risks were all dead, or so it seemed.

True believers in Vermont/Ocean Wave treasure also were dead, or so that seemed. Daughter Anna was not dead, but neither was she a true believer. She was a shrewd mining heiress with an eye for other opportunities. She would oversee the retirement of her father's debts, the divestiture of what remained of his elephant corral—relinquishing the Vermont/Ocean Wave and any other properties to the county if necessary—then her duty would be done.

Not even far richer and more accessible mines like the Ute/Ulay, owned by a far more aggressive and determined Mike Burke with far deeper pockets than Alamosa's Ben Poxson crowd, could overcome the economic headwinds gusting out of 1933. Not even Burke's San Christobal Railroad with its nimble Galloping Goose could succeed where the pioneering D&RG had failed.

Lake City's High Bridge. This photo capturing the final stages of construction could just as well be capturing the beginning of bridge dismantlement. Repurposing the lumber of this iconic link to the rest of the world did not repurpose Lake City's economic fortunes. Like the ancient trails leading to the upper Lake Fork valley and the San Juans, its footers and the wooden ties and iron rails it carried would scarcely leave a trace behind. *(Courtesy of P. David Smith)*

GHOST TRAIN [3]

They rooted up the Lake Fork Line,
Its rails were torn away,
From Lake City all the way
Downgrade to the bridge.
But settlers say the train still runs
When food supplies get low,
And storms sweep the mountaintops
With cold, wind-driven snow.
They see it passing Kellogg's Spur,
It slows at Barnum Store,
Through the Gate it passes,
Lights gleaming as before.

The ghost cars roll on phantom tracks,
Stock cars with grass-fed cows,
And double-deckers full of sheep,
Seed grain, farm tools and plows.
There's Sears and Roebuck's parcel post,
New things from Monkey Ward,
San Luis Valley sacks of flour,
Salt meat, dry beans and lard.
The *Silver World* full of news,
The mail from far and near,
All of the things that matter most
Along the rough frontier.

Now rabbit-brush lifts its golden plumes,
Where once pine crossties lay.
The sage and grass grows freshly green
On earth-scarred right-of-way.
Yet when the raging blizzards come,
And snow drifts hard and deep
Against the solid cabin walls
Where settlers rest in sleep;
Then haunting sounds awaken them
Above the Storm's mad roar.
The ghostly whistle rides the wind,
A train that runs no more.

Lake City's Last D&RG Train. Sad day indeed, those who came out to honor its passing knew they were witnessing the end of an age. They knew their lives would never be the same. *(Courtesy of the Lake City* Silver World.)

Burke sold the goose to the *Rio Grande Southern Railroad.* The right-of-way was left to erode away. The rails were salvaged by the *Denver Metal and Machinery Company* and sold to mining companies and the Navy to be repurposed into WWII warships. The spectacular High Bridge was dismantled by Gunnison County and used in the Gunnison Community Church, Gunnison's Ruland Junior High School, and rural Gunnison County bridges. The northern end of the right-of-way was flooded permanently by the Blue Mesa Reservoir filling with the Gunnison River backing up behind its newest dam. [2] Bulk transportation of Henson Canyon low-grade ores was over. Investments in Henson Canyon mines was over. The Vermont/Ocean Wave treasure hunt was over. The only visible remnants of those hopeful days were splintered ties half-buried side by side, dry bones of dead men of a different kind.

In 1946, in customary fashion a nation grateful the world's second great war was over, returned to its routine pre-war chores. In December, for the Hinsdale County Treasurer that included auctioning off the year's current portfolio of delinquent tax properties. The lowest acceptable bid for each parcel was the amount of back-taxes owed plus interest and penalties. When the Vermont/Ocean Wave Group's turn came, no value was assigned to the impressive Reynolds Tunnel, to the thousands of feet of underground workings, to the silver ore laying on the mine dump waiting for prices high enough to make trucking it to a mill worthwhile. No value was assigned to its certain silver treasure still locked securely in its mountain veins.

Nor was a word uttered nor memory stirred for the courageous souls that had breached fortress San Juans, that had prospected and mined Henson Canyon, pathfinders that had laid down *their* bones along *their* cherished dream trails. By 1946 no one cared about treasure hunts or the adventurers that had pursued them. There were no Vermont/Ocean Wave kindred spirits left to care, no moss-back prospectors and miners with wisdom to share, no visionaries with jack to spare. The last of that generation had long ago taken their leave, their final claim a 1933 window seat aboard Lake City's last D&RG train.

Notes – Epilogue: Bones

[1] Gurley, W.F.E., "Historic Times," *Gunnison News-Champion*, July 29, 1939.

[2] Vandenbusche, Duane and Walter R. Borneman, "The D&RG Lake City Branch and a Galloping Goose," pg. 106, *Colorado Rail Annual No. 14*, Golden, CO.

[3] Burke, Marril Lee, *Ghosts of the Lake Fork Region*, pgs.184-85. Marril Lee, not Mike, notes that he has "taken liberties with this poem originally written by Howard Haynes of LaJara, Colorado. In its original form it appeared in the *Colorado Rail Annual No. 14*

APPENDIX A

State Mine Inspector Reports

There was not a more objective assessment of a mine's condition and even potential worth than a Colorado state mine inspector's report. As investor dollars and skilled labor became harder and harder to attract to mining projects, the Vermont/Ocean Wave depended more and more on the inspector's annual visit to keep Reynolds' vision alive.

Bureau of Mines Report [1]
T. A. Henshaw
Ocean Wave
June 2, 1927

H. E. Fossette, Lake City, is Superintendent. Three men are employed. Insurance is provided. Safety and sanitation is good. The vein is a fissure of all widths. The property is developed by a crosscut driven to the north 1180 ft. from the portal. At that point, a vein was intersected and they drifted to the east 1400 ft. from the crosscut, where another vein was intersected. They have driven on this Ocean Wave vein to the SE 125 ft. where a stope was taken out. They are now running a drift off from the back of the stope and have drifted 100 ft. where they expect to intersect another vein in the next few feet. The ore is a sulphide and the values are in gold, silver, lead and zinc. Very little ore is being taken out at present. This property has produced a great deal of money from time to time. [Onsite equipment listed by Henshaw included a Norwalk 16 x 16 compressor, a Mine & Smelter Supply Company *75 hp. tubular boiler, three large air receivers, and several Denver 1" hollow-steel rock drills]*

There are lots of buildings. Everything about the place is kept clean. The walls are solid. There is timber standing on the property for mine use. All openings are protected. Powder is carried in small quantities. No carbide is carried in the mine in bulk. At present, all mining is done by hand. [Notably absent is any mention of the stone powder house, or any explanation why all drilling is done by hand despite the presence of a boiler [albeit no mention of a compressor] being available.]

Bureau of Mines Report [2]
T. A. Henshaw
Ocean Wave
(June 16, 1928)

[T.A. Henshaw reported that he "reached by auto to the foot of the hill; thence by walking.] Two men are employed and insured. There is a telephone on site. The mine is now operated under lease to W.C. Martin & Company. *The superintendent is W. C. Martin. This property is developed by shafts, winzes, crosscuts, drifts driven on the different veins, stopes and upraises. At present, all work is being done in the Dago Tunnel which is located near the top of the mountain. This tunnel has been driven 750 ft. to the west from its portal. At a point 400 ft. west of the portal, a winze has been sunk to a depth of 20 ft., a drift has been driven to the west 75 ft. from the bottom of this winze.*

The ore is an oxide and sulphide, and the values are gold, silver, lead, copper and a little zinc. The mine is, and has been a producer.

One small building is used for all purposes. No fire protection. No mill. Everything about the place is kept clean. The winze is kept in good repair. A windless is used for hoisting material. Car and tracks are kept in first class repair. Walls are solid as they can be…powder is carried in 50 lb. lots… no electricity. All mining is done by hand. One streak is small and very rich. State Mine Inspector.

Notes – Appendix A:

1 Henshaw, T.A., Colorado Bureau of Mines, *Ocean Wave Report,* June 2, 1927.
2 Ibid., June 16, 1928,

APPENDIX B

Glossary of Mining Terms

[*A Dictionary of Mining, Mineral, and Related Terms*, (Amended), U.S. Department of the Interior, Bureau of Mines, U.S. GPO, Washington, D.C., 1968.]

A

Accumulator. A cylindrical tank containing water, steam or air located between a boiler or compressor and a drilling machine to keep constant pressure on the device and absorb shocks.

Accretion Vein. A vein formed by the repeated filling of a channel way and its reopening by the development of fractures in the general zone undergoing mineralization.

Adit. A horizontal or nearly horizontal passage driven from the surface for the working or dewatering of a mine. If driven through the mountain to the surface on the opposite side it is a tunnel. Also called a *drift*. In Colorado statutes it includes a cut either open or undercover.

Adit End. The furthermost end or part of an adit from its beginning, or the very place where the miners are working underground towards the mine.

Adit Level. Mine workings on a level with an adit.

Arial Tramway. A system for the transportation of material, as ore or rock, in buckets suspended from pulleys or grooved wheels that run on a cable, usually stationary. A moving or traction rope is attached to the buckets and may be operated by either gravity or other power.

Agate. A kind of silica consisting mainly of chalcedony in variegated bands or other patterns commonly occupying vugs in volcanic and other rocks.

Air Adit. An adit driven for the purpose of ventilating a mine.

Air Drill. A small diamond drill driven by either a rotary or a reciprocating-piston air-powered motor used in underground workings.

Air Receiver. A vessel into which compressed air is discharged to be stored until required.

Alteration. Change in the mineralogical composition of a rock typically brought about by the action of hydrothermal solutions.

Angle of Dip. The angle at which strata or mineral deposits are inclined to the horizontal plane.

Appropriation. In mining law, the posting of notice at or near the point where the ledge is exposed; next the recording of the notice; next the marking of the boundaries.

Arrastra. A circular rock-lined pit in which broken ore is pulverized by stones attached to horizontal poles fastened in a central pillar and dragged around the pit.

Ascension Theory. The theory of infiltration by ascension in solution from below. It considers that ore-bearing solutions rise from the heated depths of the earth and deposit their minerals at diminished temperatures and pressures.

Assessment Work. The annual work upon an unpatented mining claim on the public domain necessary under U.S. law for the maintenance of the possessory title thereto. The prospector has a year from the following July 1, at noon, to do $100 of work to protect his claim. Five years of assessment work entitles one to patent the claim, meaning acquiring full ownership.

Auxillary Ventilation. A method of supplementing the main ventilating current in a mine by using a small fan to draw air from the main current and force it through canvas or galvanized iron pipe to some particular place, such as the ends of drifts, crosscuts, raises or other workings driven to develop the mine. If the pipeline is long, it may be necessary to place a second fan at some intermediate point in the pipeline. Jets of compressed air may be used in ventilating pipes to force air short distances.

Axial-flow Compressor. One in which air is compressed in a series of stages as it flows axially through a decreasing tubular area.

Axial-flow Fan. A modern type of mine fan in which the mine air enters along the axis parallel to the shaft and continues in this direction outward to the atmosphere.

B

Back. The roof or upper part in any underground mining cavity. The ore body between a level and the surface, or between two levels. That part of a lode which is nearest the surface in relation to any portion of the workings of the mine; thus the back of the level or stope is that part of the unstopped lode which is above.

Bad Air. Air vitiated by powder fumes, noxious gases, or insufficient ventilation.

Bad Ground. Rock formations in which mine openings cannot be safely maintained unless heavily timbered or supported in some manner.

Basement Rock. A name commonly applied to metamorphic or igneous rocks underlying the sedimentary sequence.

Base Bullion. Crude lead containing recoverable silver, with or without gold.

Base Ore. Ore in which gold is associated with sulfides, as contrasted to free-milling ores in which the sulfides have been removed by leaching.

Base Metal. Miner's term for copper, zinc, and lead.

Bench Cut. In vertical shaft sinking, blasting of drill holes so as to keep one end of a rectangular opening deep (leading) thus facilitating drainage and removal of blasted rock.

Black Copper Ore. An earthy, black, massive or scaley form of copper oxide.

Black Ore. Partly decomposed pyrite containing copper.

Blasting Gelatin. A high explosive consisting of nitroglycerin and nitrocotton. It is a strong explosive, rubberlike, elastic, unaffected by water.

Blue Talc. Cyanite.

Bond and Lease. An agreement between a mine owner and leasor which gives the latter the option of buying the mine before the lease expires.

Breast. The face of a working.

Breccia. A fragmental rock the components of which are angular, and therefore it is distinguished from a conglomerate in that its components are not water-worn. There are friction or fault breccias, talus breccias, and eruptive breccias. Any rock formation essentially composed of uncemented or loosely consolidate, small angular-shaped fragments.

Broken Ground. A shattered rock formation or a formation crisscrossed with numerous, closely spaced, uncemented joints and cracks.

Bug Hole. A small cavity in a rock, usually lined with crystals. Synonym for vug.

Bulkhead. A tight partition of wood, rock, and mud or concrete in mines for protection against gas, fire, and water.

C

Calcium. Silvery-white, soft, metallic element. Always combined in nature especially as a carbonate (e.g. limestone), a sulfate, or a phosphate; in practically all natural waters.

Calcium Carbonate. Chalk. White powder or colorless crystals. One of the most stable, common and widely dispersed of materials.

Cap. A plank or timber placed on top of a prop, stull, or post. A flat piece of wood inserted between the top of the prop and the roof.

Carbonates. Ores containing a considerable proportion of lead carbonate, often rich in silver.

Carbon Monoxide. Four parts of carbon monoxide in 10,000 parts of air is about the limit a man can stand for one hour. This gas is formed during mine fires and after explosions.

Carbon Monoxide Asphyxia. Underground workers who survive the initial effects of a mine fire or explosion are usually affected in some degree by carbon monoxide asphyxia. Carbon monoxide causes asphyxia because it combines with the hemoglobin of the blood much more readily than oxygen does, and the hemoglobin therefore carry less and less oxygen from the lungs to the body. Treatment is induced deep breathing of pure oxygen.

Cave. To allow the roof to fall without any retarding supports. Collapse of an unstable bank.

Caved Stopes. Two types: 1. Ore is broken by caving induced by undercutting a block of ore. 2. Ore itself is removed by excavating a series of horizontal or inclined slices while the overlying capping is allowed to cave and fill the space occupied previously by the ore.

Caving. A stoping method in which the ore is broken by induced caving. In metal mining, caving implies the dropping of the overburden as part of the system of mining.

Chimney. An ore chute. A steep and very narrow cleft or gully in the face of a cliff or mountain. A pipe-like more or less vertical natural vent or opening in the earth. An ore body which is roughly circular or elliptical in horizontal cross section but may have great vertical extent. Any extended and continuous rich streak of ore in a vein.

Collar. In a mine shaft, the first wood frame of the shaft intended to keep the top of a shaft from falling in.

Color. The shade or tint of the soil or rock that indicates ore. A particle of metallic gold found in a prospector's pan after a sample of soil or crushed rock has been panned out. Prospectors say dirt gave so many colors to the panful.

Concentrate. In mining, to separate ore or metal from its containing rock or earth. Always proceeds by steps or stages. The ore must be crushed before the mineral can be separated and certain preliminary steps such as sizing and classifying must precede the final operations.

Concentrator. A plant where ore is separated into values and rejects (tails). A device such as a flotation cell, jig, electromagnet, shaking table. A worker who tends concentrating tables, vanners, and other types of equipment used to separate valuable minerals from waste material.

Cornish Pump. A single-acting engine in which the power for pumping operations was transmitted through the action of a cumbersome beam. These pumps began to be introduced early in the 19th century and held the field for practically 100 years.

Country Rock. The rock traversed by or adjacent to an ore deposit. The valueless rock surrounding a lode.

Cousin Jack. A Cornish miner, usually far from home.

Cribbing. The construction of cribs or timbers laid at right angles to each other.

Cross Course. A vein or lode which intersects the main productive veins or lodes. Sometimes known as cross vein or cross lode.

Crosscut. A small passageway driven at right angles to the main entry to connect it with a parallel entry or air course. A tunnel driven at an angle to the dip of the strata to connect different seams or workings, .a passage directed across an ore body to test its width and value or from a shaft to reach the ore body.

Cyanide Process. A process for the extraction of gold from finely crushed ores, concentrates, and tailings by means of cyanide of potassium or sodium used in dilute solutions. The gold is dissolved by the solution and subsequently deposited upon metallic zinc or by other means.

D

Dead Work. Work that is not directly productive such as removal of rock, debris, or other material.

Dike. Dyke. A discordant tabular body of igneous rock that was injected into a fissure when molten that cuts across the structure of the adjacent country rock and usually has a high angle of dip.

Dip. The angle at which a bed, stratum or vein is inclined from the horizontal. The angle of a slope, vein, rock stratum or borehole as measured from the horizontal plane downward; .the direction of the vein or lode as it goes downward into the earth.

Discovery. There must be discovery of a mineral before a location certificate and title can be granted. Discovery cuts serve this purpose.

Dressing a Mine. A method of fraud carried out by seller by systematically mining out all the low-grad or barren spots in the vein, leaving only the high-grade areas exposed.

Drift. A horizontal passage underground. A drift follows the vein as distinguished from a crosscut which intersects it, or a level or gallery, which may do either. A passage driven through country rock to intersect a seam or vein.

Dynamite. An industrial explosive which is detonated by blasting caps. The principal explosive ingredient is nitroglycerin or specially sensitized ammonium nitrate. Frequently called giant powder.

E

Enrichment. The action of natural agencies which increases the metallic content of an ore. Secondary sulfide enrichment refers to the formation of new sulfide minerals which contain a larger percentage of the metals.

Enrichment Secondary. Silver, copper and other lodes decompose at the surface, and the sulfides become converted into oxysalts which are carried deeper into the lode by descending waters. In the zone immediately between the weathered outcrop and the unaltered sulfides, that is, in the zone of secondary enrichment, chemical action takes place between the descending waters bearing oxysalts and the unaltered sulfides, resulting in the formation of a new series of minerals whose members are often very rich in the valuable metal of the lode. As a result of this chemical concentration workable ore bodies may result from rather low-grade ores.

F

Face. The surface being drilled to advance a tunnel or drift.

Fault. A fracture or a fracture zone along which there has been displacement of the two sides relative to one another parallel to the fracture. The displacement may be a few inches or many miles. The amount of displacement of the parts may range from a few inches to thousands of feet.

Firedamp. A combustible gas that is formed in mines by decomposition of coal or other carbonaceous matter, and that consist chiefly of methane; also the explosive mixture formed by this gas with air. Firedamp explosions have been the cause of the worst coal mining disasters in history.

Fissure Vein. A cleft or crack in the rock material of the earth's crust, filled with mineral matter different from the walls and precipitated therein from aqueous solution, or introduced by sublimation or pneumatolysis.

Flour Gold. The finest size gold dust, much of which will float on water.

Flowstone. A coating on the floor or on the wall of a cave consisting of a sheet of calcium carbonate deposited by slowing flowing water.

Footwall. The wall or rock under a vein. It is called the floor in bedded deposits. Opposite wall from hanging wall. The wall rock underlying the lode. That part of the country rock which lies below the ore deposit.

Four-place Set. Squared timber frame used in underground driving to give all around support to weak ground. A cap is support by two posts on a sill-piece or sill.

G

Gallery. A horizontal or nearly horizontal underground passage. A level or drift.

Gin Pole. The center pole of a tripod. A pole used to support hoisting tackle. Any one of the three poles of a hoisting gin.

Glance. Miner's term for galena.

Gouge. A layer of soft material along the wall of a vein favoring the miner by enabling him after gouging it out with a pick to attack the solid vein from the side. The clay or clayey material in a fault zone. Parting layer of soft material between the true lode and the enclosing host rock.

Grade. The classification of an ore according to the desired or worthless material in it or according to value, for example, a gold ore that contains 1 ounce gold per ton would be a high-grade ore, while one containing 4 cents per ton would be a low-grade ore.

Gray Copper. Tennantite or tetrahedrite, a harbinger of high-grade silver ore.

Grizzly. Steel bars used to sort or separate the rock ore as it falls into ore chutes.

H

Hade. The inclination of a mineral vein or fault from the vertical.

Hand Jig. Manually operated moving-screen jig used to treat small batches of ore. The jig box is fixed to a rocking beam and moved up and down in a tank of water.

Hang Fire. In blasting, failure of a charge to explode when expected. Always dangerous to deal with.

Hanging Wall. The rock on the upper side of an inclined mineral vein or deposit. Also called the roof.

Hard Rock. Loosely used to distinguish igneous and metamorphic from sedimentary rock.

Headframe. The steel or timber frame at the top of a shaft which carries the sheave or pulley for the hoisting rope and serves various other purposes.

Hercules Powder. Weak form of dynamite.

Horne Silver. Cerussite. High-grade ore.

Horse. Waste inclusions within ore deposits. A mass of country rock lying within a vein.

Horse Tramming. Horse pulling trams underground.

I

Igneous. Formed by solidification from a molten state. Rocks of one of the two great classes (metamorphic being the other class) into which all rocks are divided and contrasted with sedimentary. Rocks of this class have also been called plutonic rocks and are often divided into plutonic and volcanic rocks for convenience, but there is no sharp boundary between the two.

Igneous Ore. Ore formed by cooling and solidifying from the molten state.

Igneous Rock. Rock formed by the solidification of molten material that originated within the earth.

Incline Shaft. A shaft sunk at an inclination from the vertical usually following the dip of a lode. It cannot use cages, but a skip or carriage traveling on rails. Also called turned vertical shaft or underlay shaft.

Indicator Plant. A plant that indicates by its presence the occurrence of an element in the soil or vein material upon which it grows. For example, astragalus as a selenium indicator which it needs to sustain life.

Infiltration. The filling of a vein with a mineral deposited from an aqueous solution.

Intrusive Vein. When the injected mass has arisen along an open fissure, and solidified there as a wall-like intrusion, it is called a dike. When its path has been less regularly defined and penetrates the surrounding rocks in a wavy threadlike fashion, this irregular protrusion is called a vein.

J – K – L

Joggling Table. An inclined board which moves with a sudden and quick motion used in washing ore.

Knapping. As in flint-knapper, the act of breaking stone to produce a cutting edge or eliminate unwanted waste rock.

Ladder Sollar. A platform at the bottom of each ladder in a series.

Lead. (pronounced leed) Commonly used as a synonym for ledge or lode. Blind lead: a lead or vein that does not outcrop or show at the surface.

Leaser. A Western colloquialism meaning lessee.

Ledge. A projecting outcrop or vein, commonly of quartz, that is supposed to be mineralized. Any narrow zone of mineralized rock. A horizontal layer, therefore a vein or lode is not a ledge.

Ledger Wall. Same as footwall.

Level. A main underground passage driven along a level course to afford access to stopes or workings and to provide ventilation and haulage-ways. Mines are usually worked from shafts through horizontal passages or drifts called levels. These are commonly spaced at regular intervals in depth and are either numbered from the surface (but not always) in regular order or designated by their actual elevation below the top of a shaft.

Lifter. A shot-hole drilled near the floor when tunneling and fired subsequently to the cut and relief holes.

Lode. Strictly a fissure in the country rock filled with mineral, usually applied to metalliferous lodes. As used by miners the term simply means a formation by which the miner can be led or guided. It is an alteration of the verb lead.

Lode Claim. In the U.S. the maximum length along the lode or vein is 1,500 feet and the maximum width is 600 feet. A tract of land with defined surface boundaries including all lodes, veins, and ledges throughout their entire depth, the top or apex of which lies inside of vertical planes extended downward through the surface boundary lines, although such veins in their downward course may extend outside of the vertical side planes of the surface location.

M

Magazine. A storage place for explosives. A building specially constructed and located for the storage of explosives.

Markings. Same as staking by means of stakes, posts, piles of stone, glazing trees, cutting away undergrowth, posting a notice, placing such notice in a tin can attached to a stake or tree.

Mesothermal Deposit. A mineral deposit formed at moderate temperatures and pressures in and along fissures by deposition at intermediate depths chiefly from hydro-thermal fluids derived from consolidating intruding rocks.. believed to have formed mostly between 175 degrees and 300 degrees C at depths of 4,000 to 12,000 feet. Many valuable metalliferous deposits of western North America are of this type.

Mill Run. A given quantity of ore tested for its quality by actual milling.

Mineral Right. The ownership of the minerals under a given surface with the right to enter thereon, mine, and remove them. It may be separated from the surface ownership, but if not so separated by distinct conveyance, the latter includes it.

Mouth. The end of a shaft, adit, drift, entry, or tunnel emerging at the surface.

Muck. Rock or ore broken in process of mining requiring removal in order to continue tunneling.

N

Native Gold. Gold as it occurs naturally. Rarely pure, usually alloyed with silver and sometimes containing appreciable amounts of copper, palladium or bismuth.

Native Metals. Metals such as copper, gold, silver and those of the platinum group that occur in the elemental or metallic state.

Non-nitroglycerin Explosives. Contain TNT instead of nitroglycerin to sensitize ammonium nitrate, and a little aluminum powder may also be added to increase their power and sensitiveness. Usually contain 15 to 18 percent TNT and 82 to 85 percent ammonium nitrate. They are reasonably free of noxious fumes. Main use is in primary blasting in quarries and opencast mining.

O

Open-Stope Method. Stoping in which no regular artificial method of support is employed, although occasional props or cribs may be used to hold local patches of insecure ground. The walls and roof are self-supporting. The stoping of ore in this manner is usually confined to relatively small ore bodies since regardless of the firmness of the ground there is a limit to the length of unsupported span which will stand without breaking. See overhand stoping.

Ore. A natural mineral compound of the elements of which one at least is a metal.

Ore Block. A section of a vein bounded above and below by upper and lower drifts and on one or both ends by winzes or raises and ready for stoping.

Ore Body. Generally a solid and fairly continuous mass of ore which may include low-grade ore and waste as well as pay ore but is individualized by form or character from adjoining country rock.

Ore Shoot. Concentration of primary ore along certain parts of a rock opening. A large and usually rich aggregation of mineral in a vein. it is a more or less vertical zone or chimney of rich vein matter extending from wall to wall, and has a definite width laterally.

Overhand Cut-and-Fill. Two level drives are first connected, the lower and upper one by a raise, from the bottom of which mining is begun. The work proceeds upwards, filling the mine-out room, but in the filling, chutes are left through which the broken ore falls. Stoping in the different cuts always proceeds upwards.. Also called back stoping.

Overhand Stoping. In this method which is also widely used in highly inclined deposits, the ore is blasted from a series of ascending stepped benches. The working of a block of ore from a lower level to a level above. Stull timbering may be required.

P

Peacock Ore. Bornite. High-grade copper ore.

Pelton Wheel. An impulse water turbine with buckets bolted to its periphery which are struck by a high velocity of water. This turbine is most efficient under a head of from 900 to 1,000 feet or more.

Placer. A place where gold is obtained by washing; an alluvial or glacial deposit, as of sand or gravel, containing particles of gold or other valuable mineral.

Placer Mining. The extraction of heavy mineral from a placer deposit by concentration In running water. It includes ground sluicing, panning, shoveling gravel into a sluice, scraping by power scraper and excavation by dragline. Maximum area is 20 acres and claim must be posted and filed the same as a lode.

Plutonic Rocks. Igneous rocks formed deep within the earth under the influence of high heat and pressure, hypogene rocks; distinguished from eruptive rocks formed at the surface.

Pocket. A localized enrichment; a crevice in the bedrock containing gold. A rich deposit of mineral, but not a vein.

Polar Explosives. Explosives containing an antifreeze ingredient and distinguished by the prefix polar. Polar and nonpolar explosives of equal grade possess similar characteristics. Explosives which contain nitroglycerin tend to freeze when stored at low temperatures for lengthy periods.

Pop Shot. A shot fired for trimming purposes.

Porphyry. A term first given to an altered variety of porphrite on account of its purple color, and afterwards extended by common association to all rocks containing conspicuous phenocrysts in a fine-grained or aphanitic groundmass.

Portal. Any entrance to a mine. The rock face at which tunnel driving is started. The surface entrance to a drift, tunnel, adit or entry.

Productive Work. Labor that results directly in the extraction of paying ore.

Propylitic. Applied to any kind of a vein, meaning that the ore solution which has furnished the vein filling has also effected a decomposition or alteration of the wall rock as well, so that the walls of the vein consist of clay, talc, etc.

Prospect. A mineral property the value of which has not been proved by exploration.

Purple Copper. Bornite. A variety of peacock copper ore.

Pyramid Cut. In shaft sinking, a pattern of shot-holes drilled so that the middle holes converge and outline a pyramid-shaped volume of rock. These holes are fired first and thus create a free face or relieving cut .The pyramid cut is mainly employed in raises and for shaft sinking.

Pyrite, Fool's Gold, Iron Pyrite. Iron disulfide, often with small amounts of copper, arsenic, nickel, cobalt, gold, selenium. Brass-yellow or brown tarnished mineral with greenish or brownish-black streak.

Q

Quartz. A crystallized silicon dioxide. Any hard, gold or silver ore, as distinguished from gravel or earth.

Quitclaim. A release of a claim. Specifically a legal instrument by which some right or interest by one person is released to another.

R

Raise. A vertical or inclined opening driven upward from a level to connect with the level above or to explore the ground for a limited distance above one level. After two levels are connected, the connection may be a winze or a raise depending upon which level is taken as the point of reference.

Red Copper. Cuprite, a copper oxide.

Red Cross Extra. Trademark for a high-density general-purpose ammonia dynamite of 20 to 60 percent strength. Used for quarrying, stripping, and general construction work.

Red Crown. A nongelatinous permissible explosive used in mines.

Relief Hole. A borehole that is loaded and fired for the purpose of relieving or removing part of the burden of the charge to be fired in the main blast. Holes drilled closely along a line which are not loaded and which serve to weaken the rock so that it will break along that line.

Replacement Vein. A vein in which certain minerals have passed into solution and have been carried away, while other minerals from the solution have been deposited in the place of those removed.

Rock Drill. A machine for boring relatively short holes in rock for blasting purposes. Compressed air is the usual motive power, but steam, electricity, and electricity in combination with compressed air are also used. Waugh is a stoping drill sometimes called a stopper.

Roof. The ceiling of any underground excavation.

Royalty. A lease by which the owner or lessor grants to the lessee the privilege of mining and operating the land in consideration of the payment of a certain stipulated royalty on the mineral produced.

Ruby Silver. Dark ruby silver is pyrargyrite and light ruby silver is proustite.

Run. A direction in which a vein or ore lies. An inclined passage between levels in a mine.

S

Saline. A salt spring or well, a salt-works.

Salt. To enrich as a mine artificially, usually with fraudulent intent by secretly placing valuable mineral in some of the working places.

Scree. Loose rock collected on the slopes beneath steep mountain sides. Talus. Scree is a more inclusive term that includes loose material lying on slopes without cliffs.

Secondary Mineral Deposits. Primary mineral deposits are eventually subjected to alterations through weathering both chemical and mechanical and give rise to secondary deposits which are divided into three groups: sedimentary rocks, secondarily enriched ore deposits, and residual or detrital ore deposits.

Sedimentary Rocks. Rocks formed by the accumulation of sediment in water or from air. The sediment may consist of rock fragments or particles of various sizes of the remains or products of animals or plants; of the product of chemical action or of evaporation (salt, gypsum); or of mixtures of these materials. Some sedimentary deposits (tuffs) are composed of fragments blown from volcanoes and deposited on land or in water. A characteristic feature of sedimentary deposits is a layered structure known as bedding or stratification. Sedimentary beds as deposited lie flat or nearly flat.

Set. A timber frame for supporting the sides of an excavation, shaft, or tunnel.

Shaft. Often applied to approximately vertical excavations of limited area for hoisting and lowering men and material or ventilation. Often utilizes hoists as opposed to ladders.

Shoot of Ore. A body of ore with relatively small horizontal dimensions and steep inclination in a lode, in contradistinction to a course of ore which is flatter.

Silver. Occurs massive or assumes aborescent or filiform shapes. Native silver often has variable admixture of other metals such as gold, copper or sometimes platinum.

Slimes. Extremely fine sands, slow to settle in quiet water.

Square-Set. A set of timbers composed of a cap, girt, and post. These members meet so as to form a solid 90 degree angle. They are so framed at the intersection as to form a compression joint, and join with three other similar sets. The posts are 6 or 7 feet high while the caps and girts are 4 to 6 feet long. Sills are laid in trenches cut in the floor of the stope if the stope is to be caught up from the level below. Posts are the upright members and the caps and girts are the horizontal members.

Star Drill. A hand tool with a star-shaped point used for drilling in stone or masonry.

Station. The excavation adjoining the shaft at each of the different levels where men and material are removed or delivered.

Stope. An excavation from which ore has been excavated in a series of steps. Frequently used incorrectly as a synonym for room which is a wide working place in a flat mine. The outlines of the ore body determine the outlines of the stope. As a rule stoping is started on each side of a raise-winze connection.

Stull. A timber prop set between the walls of a stope. A timber extending from footwall to hanging wall. Stulls may be placed at irregular intervals to support local patches of insecure ground in which case the stopes are virtually open stopes.

Sump. See winze.

T

Tailings. The parts of any incoherent or fluid material separated as refuse. The sand, gravel and cobbles which pass through the sluices in hydraulic mining now called mining debris. In mining, the residue after most of the valuable ore has been extracted. Distinct from mine waste which is country rock removed to access vein material.

Tailings Pile. The area below or next to a portal where waste rock is dumped.

Talc. A natural hydrous magnesium silicate usually occurring as a natural alteration of magnesium silicate rocks or in metamorphosed dolomites. Color is white, apple green, gray; luster, pearly or greasy; high resistance to acids, alkalies, and heat.

Talus. Same as scree.

Toe. The base of a bank, bench, or slope.

Tramming. The practice of pushing tubs, mine cars, or trams by hand.

Tunnel. A long, narrow subterranean passageway. Horizontal passage that is open to the atmosphere at both ends. A synonym for adit and drift.

U

Underhand Work. Picking or drilling downward.

Underhand Stoping. Mining ore from an upper level to a lower, underhand. Mining downward. The stope may start below the floor of a level and be extended by successive horizontal slices.

Underthrust. A low-angle reverse fault resulting from the sliding of the footwall beneath a relatively passive hanging wall.

Upcast. The opening through which the return air ascends and is removed from the mine. An upward current of air passing through a shaft or the like.

V

Values. The quantity of gold in a cubic year or ton of placer gravel expressed in sterling or dollars. Usually expressed as an assay grade.

Vanner. A machine for dressing ore. An ore separator. The name is given to various patented devices in which the peculiar motions of the shovel in the miner's hands in the operation of making a van are more or less successfully imitated. See Frue vanner. A wide, traveling, shaking rubber belt for the concentration of ores.

Vein. A zone or belt of mineralized rock lying within boundaries clearly separating it from neighboring rock. The term lode is commonly used synonymously for vein. A mineral deposit usually steeply inclined. a vein is typically long, deep, and relatively narrow. A comparatively thin sheet of igneous rock injected into a crevice in rock. When this intrusion is large it is called a dike.

Vein Dike. The product of solidification of the so-called ore magma.

Velocity. The speed at which the detonating wave of an explosive passes through a column of explosives. Expressed in feet per second. A high velocity explosive renders a shattering effect, whereas a low velocity explosive has a pushing or heaving effect.

Ventilation Ducts. Two kinds available: flexible ducts generally consist of flexible tubes made from fabrics coated with rubber or polyvinyl chloride. Flexible ducting is suited for use in temporary installations. It has a higher resistance and a greater tendency to leak than rigid ducting. Rigid ducts are made of steel in lengths suitable for underground transport, often 9 feet and up to 24 inches in diameter. This type duct does not have to be accurately aligned and is therefore used in the smaller sizes particularly in crooked headings. For main tunnels where leakage must be minimized, flanged joints are used with a suitable gasket.

Vug. A small cavity in a rock, usually lined with a crystalline mineral incrustation.

Sometimes written voog, vough, vug, vugh, vogle, and incorrectly called bug, bug hole, vug hole. A mining term for an unfilled cavity in a vein, generally with a mineral lining of different composition from that of the immediately surrounding ore.

W

Wall. The overhanging side of a lode is known as the hanging wall and the lower lying side as the footwall.

Way Shaft. A winze.

Wedge Rock. Refers to low-grade ore at the Comstock lode. When a car was placed in the cage to be hoisted it was specially tagged in the case of good ore. If it was waste no tag was used. It became the custom to throw a wooden wedge on top of the car of very low-grade ore, hence the term wedge rock.

White Damp. Carbon monoxide, a gas that may be present in the afterdamp of a gas or coal-dust explosion, also one of the constituents of the gases produced by blasting.

White Lead. Cerussite. Also called Horne silver.

Wilfley Table. Long-established and widely used form of shaking table. Plane rectangle is mounted horizontally and can be sloped about its long axis. It is covered with linoleum (occasionally rubber) and has longitudinal riffles dying at discharge end to a smooth cleaning area, triangular in upper corner. At discharge end the sands have separated into bands, the heaviest and smallest uppermost, the largest and lightest lowest.

Windlass. A device for hoisting, limited to small-scale development work. A drum set horizontally on rough bearings above pit or shaft and provided with handles at each end for manual rotation.

Winze. A vertical or inclined opening connecting two levels in a mine, differing from a raise only in construction. A winze is sunk underhand and a raise is put up overhand. It is usually sunk in the ore body. When sunk downward from a higher level it may be called a sump.

Workings. Any underground development, usually restricted in meaning to the breasts.

X - Y - Z

X-Frame Brace. A reinforcement of a square set in which two diagonal pieces of timber cross to form an X.

Yellow-Boy. Deposit from the acid waters of a mine or partial neutralization. Ferrous anhydride and other impurities including fine clay carried down with it.

Yellow Copper. Chalcopyrite.

Y-Track. Used in place of a turntable for reversing direction of rail cars and locomotives.

Zinc. A lustrous, bluish-white metal. Sphalerite is principal ore.

Zone of Cementation. That shell of the earth's crust living immediately below the zone of weathering within which loose sediments are cemented by the addition of such minerals as calcite introduced by percolating meteoric waters.

Zone of Enrichment. Interval below the oxidized zone in which a metal (usually copper) has been carried down in solution from the oxidized zone and redeposited as sulfide.

Zone of Saturation. An area which contains capillary or supercapillary voids or both that are full of water that will move under ordinary hydrostatic pressure. The zone between the water table and the lower limit of saturation, sometimes know as the zone of meteoric water. Mine workings in this belt of ground are liable to encounter large volumes of water.

Zone of Secondary Enrichment. The zone in which descending surface waters re-deposit their metallic content derived from the oxidized zone, with the formation in the upper part of this zone of native metals, oxides and carbonates, and in the lower part of secondary sulfide minerals.

Zone of Weathering. Down to the level at which ground water stands, the rocks are full of fractures and are exposed to atmospheric agencies such as moisture, carbon dioxide, oxygen, etc. Here the rocks tend to decay, to be converted into carbonates and hydroxides and to form soils.

Zones of Lode. A lode may be divided into three main zones: (1) the unaltered ore at depth; (2) the gossan or altered surface portion of the lode, containing native metals, oxides, and oxysalts, the result of weathering of the ore; and (3) the zone of secondary enrichment which occurs between the first two zones in which interaction between waters from the gossan and the unaltered ore has resulted in the production of new materials often of considerable economic value.

Bibliography

Bagley, Will, *Overland West*, Vol. I, Univ. of Oklahoma Press, Norman, OK, 2010.

Bagley, Will, *With Golden Visions Bright Before Them*, Vol. II, Univ. of Oklahoma Press, Norman, OK, 2012.

Baker, Steven G., *Juan Rivera's Colorado, 1765: The First Spaniards Among the Ute and Paiute Indians on the Trails to Teguayo*, Western Reflections Publishing Company, Lake City, CO, 2015.

Barry, John M., *The Great Influenza*, Penguin Books, New York, NY, 2005.

Barry, Louise, Ed., "Albert D. Richardson's Letters on the Pike's Peak Gold Region" written to the Editor of the Lawrence *Republican*, pgs. 4-57, *The Kansas Historical Quarterly* (Vol. 12, No. 1), February 1943. [https:www.kshs.org/p/albert-d-richardson-s-letters-on-the-pike-s-peak-gold-region/12926]

Black, Carla F., "Corkscrew Gulch Turntable," pgs. 61-68, *Railroad Model Craftsman*, March 1989.

Brittner, Lynn, "The People of the Horse," *TRUEWEST, History of the American Frontier*, July 10, 2012.

Brown, Robert L., *An Empire of Silver*, Caxton Printers, Ltd. Caldwell, Idaho, 1968.

Burke, Marril Lee, *Ghosts of the Lake Fork Region*, Western Reflections Publishing Company, Lake City, Colorado, 2009.

Carey, Alex, "Memories, Scenes and Humorous High Lights of Lake City," handwritten notes, unpublished, courtesy of the Lake City *Silver World*.

"Central City – Black Hawk Historic District," pg. 2, *Colorado Encyclopedia*, https://coloradoencyclopedia.org/article/central-city, December 14, 2019.

Chamberlin, Rollin T., "Memorial to William Frank Eugene Gurley," *Proceedings Volume of the Geological Society of America, Annual Report for 1943*, April 1944.

Curry, Thomas Sherrod III, "San Juan Scenery the Result of Successive Eruptions, Erosion," *Silver Thread Scenic & Historic Byway*, Summer, 2007.

Darley, George M., *Pioneering in the San Juan*, Fleming H. Revell Company, 1899.

Decker, Sarah Platt, ed., *Pioneers of the San Juan Country (Vol. I-III)*, Sarah Platt Decker Chapter, D.A.R., Durango, Colorado, The Out West Printing and Stationary Company, Colorado Springs, Colorado, 1942.

"Denver, Colorado and the 1918-1919 Influenza Epidemic," *The American Influenza Epidemic of 1918: A Digital Encyclopedia*, University of Michigan Center for the History of Medicine and Michigan Publishing, University of Michigan Library. [https//www.influenzaarchive.org/cities/city-denver.html#.]

Ellis, Richard N., "The Spanish," *The Western San Juan Mountains*, Rob Blair, ed., University Press of Colorado, Niwot, Colorado, 1996.

England, Jim and Sam Bock, "By Rail and River," pgs.19-29, *The Colorado Magazine*, Summer/Fall 2024.

Everhart, William C., ed., *The Mining Frontier*, U.S. Department of the Interior, National Park Service, Region Four, San Francisco, 1959.

Franklin, George Cory, "Major M.V.B. Wasson," *Pioneers of the San Juan Country (Vol. II)*, Sarah Platt Decker Chapter, D.A.R., Durango, Colorado, The Out West Printing and Stationary Company, Colorado Springs, Colorado, 1942.

Gibbons, Rev. J. J., *In the San Juan,1898 Sketches*, Calumet Book & Engraving Co., Chicago 1898 [St. Patrick's Parish reprint, Telluride, 1972].

Greeley, Horace, *An Overland Journey from New York to San Francisco in the Summer of 1859*, pgs.98-106, Alfred A. Knopf, NY, 1964.

Hafen, LeRoy R. and James H. Baker, eds., *History of Colorado (Vol. III)*, Linderman Company., Inc. Denver, CO, 1927.

Hafen, LeRoy R., ed., *Colorado Gold Rush,1858-1859*, Southwest Historical Series (Vol. X), Porcupine Press, Philadelphia, PA, 1974.

Hall, Frank, *History of the State of Colorado (Vol. II and IV)*, Western Reflections Publishing Company, Lake City, CO, reprint of The Blakely Printing Company, Chicago, IL,1895.

Heath, Herman T., "Remembering the First Armistice at the End of 'The War to End All Wars,'" written during Operation Desert Storm, January 16-February 28, 1991, courtesy of Grant Houston, Lake City *Silver World*, July 22, 2024.

History Colorado Library, Reynolds Collection (MSS 1220), Denver, CO.

Hollister, Ovando. James, *The Mines of Colorado*, Promontory Press, NY, 1974. [Original: Samuel Bowles & Company, Springfield, MA,1867.]

Ingham, G. Thomas, *Digging Gold Among the Rockies*, Western Reflections Publishing Company, Lake City, CO, 2008.

Irving, John Duer & Howland Bancroft, *Geology and Ore Deposits Near Lake City, Colorado*, USGS Bulletin 478, GPO Washington, D.C. 1911.

Kendall, George Wilkins, *Texan Santa Fe Expedition*, Harper & Bros., NY, 1844. ["Prairie Dogs," Wikipedia.]

Lake City *Phonograph*, Lake City, CO (numerous citations).

Lake City *Silver World*, Lake City, CO (numerous citations).

Lake City *Times*, Lake City, Co (numerous citations).

Morse, Milo and Fay Bielser, *A Brief History of Mining in Hinsdale County*, B&B Printers, Gunnison, CO 2000.

Nossaman, Allen, *Many More Mountains*, Vol. 1, Sundance Books, Durango, Colorado, 2006

Paul, Rodman W., *The Far West and the Great Plains in Transition 1859-1900*, Harper & Row, NY, 1988.

Paul, Rodman W., *Mining Frontiers of the Far West 1848-1880*, Holt, Rinehart and Winston, NY, 1963.

Poxson, Ben, "A Reminiscence," *History Colorado Library*, Denver, CO. [original: Chronicles Publishing Company, October 1988.]

Reed, Stephen B., "One Hundred Years of Price Change: The Consumer Price Index and the American Inflation Experience," *Monthly Labor Review*, U.S. Bureau of Labor Statistics, April 2014. [https://doi.org/10.21916/mlr.2014.14]

Scamehorne, Lee, *Albert Eugene Reynolds*, Colorado's Mining King, University of Oklahoma Press, Norman, OK, 1995.

Service, Robert, *The Best of Robert Service*, Perigee Books, N.Y., 1953.

Smith, Duane A., *San Juan Gold: A Mining Engineer's Adventures, 1879-1881*, Western Reflections Publishing Company, Montrose, CO, 2002.

Smith, Duane A., *Song of the Hammer and Drill*, University Press of Colorado Press, Boulder, CO, 2000.

Smith, Duane A., *The Trail of Gold and Silver*, University Press of Colorado, Boulder, CO, 2009.

Smith, P. David, *Mountains of Silver*, Western Reflections Publishing Company, Montrose, CO, 2004.

Smith, P. David, *The Story of Lake City*, Western Reflections Publishing Company, Lake City, CO, 2016.

Sprague, Marshall, *The Great Gates*, Little, Brown & Company (Canada) Limited, 1964

Steamboat Pilot, "Elephant Corral Has Helped Make History," July 3, 1941.

Steele, Joe M, *Guide to Lake City Geology*, B&B Printers, Gunnison, CO, 2002.

Strahorn, Robert Edmund, *Gunnison and San Juan*, Western Reflections Publishing Company, Lake City, CO, 2012.

"The Gold Seeker's Song," *Hannibal Messenger*, April 28, 1859.

Twitty, Eric, *Basins of Silver*, Western Reflections Publishing Company, Lake City, CO, 2008.

Twitty, Eric, "Hinsdale County Study, Ocean Wave Mine, Site 5HN1082," [on file in Hinsdale County office]

Twitty, Eric, *Riches to Rust*, Western Reflections Publishing Company, Montrose, CO, 2002.

Vandenbusche, Duane and Walter R. Borneman, "The D&RG Lake City Branch and a Galloping Goose," *Colorado Rail Annual No. 14*, Golden, CO.

Wikipedia, multiple dates and titles.

Wright, Carolyn and Clarence, *Tiny Hinsdale of the Silvery San Juan*, Big Mountain Press, 1964.

Index